Can You Hear Me Now?

CAN YOU HEAR ME NOW?

Join the Conversation to Make
Public Education a Better Choice

SUZANNE RUPP DeMALLIE

HOUNDSTOOTH

PRESS

CAN YOU HEAR ME NOW?

Join the Conversation to Make Public Education a Better Choice

ISBN   978-1-5445-1796-4 *Hardcover*

978-1-5445-1795-7 *Paperback*

978-1-5445-1794-0 *Ebook*

To Craig

Thank you for your love, patience, tolerance, encouragement, and support of all my dreams. I really couldn't have done any of this without your help. You are the co-author of my life's journey.

and

In memory of Gigi

My grandmother, my biggest fan and an avid reader. You always said that I had a gift for writing and should author a book. Thank you for indulging all of my "talents." Every child needs a grandmother like you!

CONTENTS

"YOU'RE THE EXPERT"

March 2018

I hung up the phone and felt like I was going to vomit. I was completely overcome with feelings of weakness and exhaustion. This was one of the most difficult phone calls I had ever had as a teacher, and not for the usual reasons. I just told a mother that her son would *not* be retained in fourth grade next year. Here's the thing—she was disappointed. Finally, she broke her silence and said, "If that's what you think is best. You're the expert."

Thank God she couldn't see my face, but was she able to sense the reluctance in my voice? If only I could have summoned the courage to respond honestly. I didn't think it was best; in fact, I had argued the matter with the assistant principal just an hour earlier. But I was powerless, once again. A teacher without a voice in deciding what was best for her student.

Her son, a ten-year-old boy in my fourth-grade math class, had tested on a mid-first-grade level. A large majority of his class was well below grade level, but he was by far at the bottom. He could not complete any grade-level work independently, even with frequent one-to-one support. In December, I handed him eighteen, one-inch colored tiles and asked him to tell me how many were in the pile. I sat less than two feet across from him and watched his face as he painstakingly tried to count each one. I saw his nervousness and embarrassment. He answered incorrectly—twice. Even after six weeks of using a research-based intervention, he scored a 20 percent on a short, first-grade-level assessment; just basic questions on two-digit numbers.

That afternoon we had a follow-up Student Support Team meeting to go over the results of the intervention. I recommended that he repeat fourth grade out of concern for the severity of his skill gaps, the decline in his self-esteem, and the lack of progress with the intervention. I had communicated with his mother throughout the school year—honestly sharing all of my concerns. His mother agreed with my comments, observations, and even my recommendation for next year's placement. But the assistant principal conducting the meeting disagreed, and she had the ultimate decision. It was the reason for her decision that made me ill. "Too many other fourth-graders with even lower abilities would be moving on to fifth grade. He needed to move with them."

How could our educational system fail to support the individual needs of its students? How can we say that the US is "raising the bar" with more rigorous standards if we push students through the system who aren't meeting those standards? How can we lie to the parents by letting them think that their child is successfully achieving grade-level expectations when, in fact, they are not? How can we let these children down by not adequately preparing them to meet the challenges of the real world? What long-term impact does a failed education system have on society?

That was the breaking point for me. Just like the mother, I was disappointed—but not just with the decision. I was disappointed in the system that enabled the problem and failed to provide a solution. Someone needed to speak up for these children. Someone needed to be honest with the parents. The question was: Do I have the strength and courage to raise my voice and challenge our educational system? Will anyone listen? Will anyone hear what I have to say?

Teachers, how many times have you felt powerless in your classroom? How many times have you sat through trainings and staff meetings being told that you have to use a curriculum that you know is not the most effective for your students; that you must adhere to pacing guidelines that aren't realistic given the academic needs of your class; that you have to relinquish too many instructional days for standardized testing just to yield results that you already know; that you can't remove a student from class who is repeatedly distracting and disrupting the learning environment for all of the other students in the room; and that you can't give a child the help they really need and deserve because there are too few supports for too many struggling students?

Parents, do you ever wonder which educational opportunities and advantages your child is missing out on in public school? Perhaps as you hear about your neighbor's child who attends private school—where the class size is half of your child's, where they have opportunities for in-class and out-of-school experiences nonexistent in the public system and access to the greatest, most advanced technologies? Do you think that a private school would offer services and accommodations that would better support your child's individualized needs *without* the need for an IEP document?

Do you ever wonder if your child might be happier in school or less anxious if they could attend a private school where they don't have to observe other students cursing at their teachers or engaging in brutal physical fights? Do you even know what's really going on in your child's school? Why your child won't use the school bathroom? Why your child avoids eating in the cafeteria? Do you secretly choose not to know, or prefer to just assume the school is just as good as it was for you thirty years ago or the same as it was for your oldest child seven years ago? Do you wish that your income allowed you the choice to send your child to a private school?

Why don't we speak up? What stops us from voicing our concerns to someone other than the teacher in the classroom next door or a friend at back-to-school night? Do you feel like, what's the point? How will my one voice be heard? How will I make any difference in a large public system that seems doomed for failure? Do you worry that you'll be seen as a troublemaker or jeopardize your job as a teacher?

It's okay. You're not alone. I know you're not because I've had all of these same concerns—as a mom whose three children have only attended public schools, and as a teacher in the twenty-fifth largest school district in the country. I have even more fears today as I write this book—knowing that I will be exposing the realities of our educational bureaucracy and questioning the status quo. I've seen the system and dealt with it from many sides, and I have felt that helplessness and hopelessness that you are feeling. But this book *can* make a difference—not magically and not by giving you some false sense of reality. There's nothing sugarcoated here. This is pure honesty—raw and real—with no political agenda. In fact, we cannot rely on politicians, who spend more time campaigning than sitting in a classroom and spout the same rhetoric in each election that they are really going to make a difference. It's up to us, the adults who care for the children affected by poor educational decisions, to initiate change.

Keep reading! This book will give you the facts and the history on the policies and practices that are contributing to some of the problems. I will share my opinions based on my experience. I will pose some questions that we should all be asking, and you will read the stories of real students who rely on public education for a better future. Some of this will be disturbing, and some will be sad, but it will all be honest. And just when you finish educating yourself on the realities of the system, I will lead you to a pathway that I have personally walked, beginning in 2005, which improved many classrooms across the nation. Change wasn't easy, and it wasn't quick. But *it can be done*, and I'm ready to initiate change again—on a larger scale—with your help.

This book is the beginning of a conversation that I invite you to join. Together, we can make a difference so that every child has a "better choice" in our public education system. We will be heard!

THE "WHY" BEHIND
THE "HOW"

I'm not your typical teacher. First of all, I haven't always been a teacher. I graduated from Gettysburg College in 1989 with a degree in business and a concentration in accounting, obtained my CPA license in 1991, and worked for USF&G (a large insurance company) for almost ten years, earning a position as the director of financial reporting. I dreamed of being a math teacher since high school, but for various reasons, I chose a different path in college and then felt my dream was probably just that...a dream, not destined to be a reality.

Even my reason for wanting to be a math teacher wasn't typical. Unlike most math teachers who likely have always found math to be particularly easy for them, I did not. I had intense anxiety related to math after struggling with it in middle school. In seventh grade, I was placed in an accelerated math group and found myself lost in search of meaning behind the algorithms used to solve the equations. Without that meaning, nothing made sense to me, and my math grades started falling in direct proportion to my level of understanding. Everything, especially my self-confidence, came cascading down. The lower my grades, the more anxious I became in class, and the more anxious I became, the more withdrawn I felt. It was as if I was no longer a part of the class. I just watched it from a distance and hoped that my teacher had forgotten I was there.

For likely many reasons, this all turned around in high school, and math became my favorite subject. The anxiety remained with me, but I managed it with the help of my teachers, and I used that fear as fuel in my quest to be successful. I realized the need to self-advocate was part of the learning process and never again allowed myself to fall down that deep hole of helplessness. My experience is exactly why I wanted to become a math teacher. Math is an intimidating subject for many people. I wanted to make a difference for the students who struggled with it and those who loved it by placing emphasis on understanding the "why" behind the "how." I wanted to embolden those who lacked confidence in their abilities by giving them opportunities to discover and use their strengths. Math is much more than just numbers. It's problem-solving, which has all kinds of real-life applications.

My dream to be a math teacher wouldn't be revisited until 2009, when I was about forty-two years old, and again, not in a typical way. By that time, I was married to Craig and had three young children. I had spent the past four and a half years trying to improve education on a national level (we'll talk more about that later) and decided that I wanted to start making a difference in education on an individual level, working directly with the students.

In May 2011, I finished a graduate program at Goucher College, including a student teaching internship in Baltimore City. In a little less than two years, I had earned an elementary teaching certificate, a highly qualified certification in middle school mathematics, a master's degree, and had completed a long-term substitute assignment for my mentor teacher who had left on maternity leave at the start of spring break. It wasn't easy, and on many occasions, I questioned if it was worth sacrificing time with my family, but I innocently thought it would be all downhill from there on out.

Due to a poor economy and limited teaching opportunities, I began my teaching career as a long-term math substitute for a nearby middle school that was part of the Baltimore County Public School (BCPS) system. It was a school that I had attended myself as a student, and one where all three of my own children would eventually attend. In fact, my oldest daughter had just completed middle school there, and my son was currently attending it during my assignment.

The impression that I had as a parent was very different than the realities that I observed as a teacher. And for the first time, I realized that parents really have no idea where they're sending their children off to each day. What the parent sees from outside the building isn't necessarily the same as what is going on within the walls of the school. This doesn't mean that all schools are bad. But it does mean that sometimes we are exposing our children to unnecessary problems that can impact their ability and desire to learn—and in extreme cases, to feel safe. How much better could our education system be if we could just eliminate or even reduce some of these problems?

On September 14, 2012, I was hired as a full-time math reduction teacher by the principal of Raven Elementary School in Baltimore County. Raven was overcrowded. The class sizes were too large, so I was hired to pull students from the first-, second-, and third-grade math classes for separate math instruction.

This was the beginning of a new chapter in my life. At the time, I didn't realize how opening this new door would close so many others that were important to me. Instead, my family celebrated that night because Mom was now a teacher in the Baltimore County Public School system.

WHY

...we need to improve the public education system.

WELCOME TO THE WORLD OF EDUCATION!

I think it's fair to say that an education system is only as strong as the weakest school within that system. But how will the school (and then ultimately the system) be able to improve if it is the system itself that is making it weak?

Baltimore County Public Schools (BCPS) is currently the twenty-fifth largest school district in the US and the third largest in Maryland. For the fiscal year 2020, BCPS had an approximate $1.7 billion budget to run 175 schools for 115,038 students and a payroll of 18,202 employees, of which approximately 9,800 are teachers.[1] I was one of those teachers up until July 15, 2019.

A TRANSPARENT SUPERINTENDENT

Back in the academic year 2012–2013, when I was first hired as a full-time BCPS teacher, the system was slightly smaller, though still a very substantial school district, ranked as the twenty-sixth largest in the country. This academic year marked the beginning of a significant change. That change was, in part, brought on by the retirement of the twelve-year superintendent, Dr. Joe A. Hairston, at the end of the 2011–2012 academic year. In March 2012, BCPS hired Dr. S. Dallas Dance as his replacement. Dr. Dance was the new superintendent effective July 1.

Dr. Dance was a controversial new hire because he was only thirty-one years old with two years of teaching experience when he assumed the role of superintendent. He had been a high school English teacher, assistant principal, principal, and administrator in the Virginia public school system, and he was chief of middle schools in the Houston Independent School District prior to accepting the superintendent position with BCPS.[2]

Therefore, Dance changed jobs about every two years and had no experience ever working in or for the state of Maryland. His lack of teaching experience concerned many Baltimore County parents (and teachers) and required a waiver from the state superintendent because Maryland requires a minimum of three years of teaching experience for its superintendents of schools.[3] To assuage the public's concerns, Dr. Dance stated, "I will tell you I am very open. I am very transparent. I want to make sure that people are part of the solutions."[4] These words would eventually come back to haunt him.

A TIME OF CHANGE (2012-2013)

There were other significant nationwide changes going on in education at that time. President Obama was in office, and Arne Duncan was the US Secretary of Education. Common Core was just beginning. The academic year of 2012–2013 marked the first year that the Common Core standards were being used, and the curriculum thus aligned to those standards for first-grade students in Maryland. Many other significant changes in education practices and policies were on the horizon—both as a result of a national movement and under Dr. Dance's vision and initiatives. These changes, along with the changes in demographics of the student population, would drastically influence my teaching experience over the next seven years.

I officially became a BCPS teacher in September 2012, about three weeks after school had started for that academic year. Starting after school was already underway, especially as a new teacher, was tough. In fact, most of my first year teaching was grueling. I knew that going back to college for a master's degree would be difficult and expected a new job to be challenging, but what I had not anticipated is how hard it would be to start a new career and have to prove myself all over again. The last time I had to do this was when I was a single twenty-two-year-old with no other responsibilities. Now I was almost forty-five years old. I was a wife and mother to three children, the youngest of whom was in third grade.

I quickly realized that life wasn't going to be getting easier for my family; rather, I felt as if I was drowning and failing at everything—especially as a mother. My hours teaching at Raven were 9:05 a.m. to 4:05 p.m. But as a new teacher of three different grade levels and three different curriculums, I was routinely spending at least ten hours a day at the school, Mondays through Thursdays, and on Fridays, I would frequently stay until 7 p.m. to plan and make copies for the upcoming week. I then had at least a half-hour commute home, and I would typically work one full day on the weekends to make materials, grade papers, and communicate with parents.

A BLUE RIBBON SCHOOL

When I began teaching at Raven in September, it had just been named a National Blue Ribbon School. I had learned this during my interview, a fact that certainly made the job offer more appealing to me. The National Blue Ribbon Award is given to public and private schools that have superior academic achievement and meet other criteria. At this time, Raven had about 780 students (the majority of which were African American) and had achieved 96 percent proficiency and above on Maryland School Assessments (MSA) in both math and reading.[5] According to a news release issued by BCPS, "Among schools statewide with similar demographics, [Raven] has ranked first in both math and reading."[6]

I would soon learn the strategies that Raven used to help ensure those success rates. MSA was the state standardized test later replaced by the Partnership for Assessment of Readiness for College and Career (PARCC). PARCC is undeniably a much more rigorous exam than MSA; the strategies used to boost Raven's MSA scores were ineffective with PARCC.

Raven's principal at the time I started was a little like a petite drill sergeant. She was a strong, energetic force who appeared to hold very high standards for herself and her staff. As a new teacher, I had to be observed on four separate occasions each year for three years before I could earn my tenure in Baltimore County. Observations are customary in the public school system. I haven't met another teacher who is comfortable with formal observations and who believes that they accurately measure the instructional effectiveness of a teacher. That's because teachers have to plan a lesson that "shows off" everything, which, in theory, a teacher should include; however, in practice, this can be unrealistic.

The observation lesson is pre-planned by the teacher and then approved in advance by the administrator who will be conducting the observation. When the administrator observes the lesson, she or he literally checks off boxes on a checklist and writes comments on specifics—good and bad. Every observation should include recommendations for how a teacher can improve on their delivery, classroom management, facilitation of discussion, higher-level questioning, etc.

BECOMING A "BETTER" TEACHER

In all honesty, I struggled with the observations and adjusting to Raven during my first year. There was a huge learning curve. My internship had been in Baltimore City, and I quickly discovered that the Baltimore City and Baltimore County public school systems are noticeably different. Raven, in particular, had very high standards for its teachers, as evidenced by its ability to become a National Blue Ribbon School.

There was no doubt in my mind that the teachers at Raven worked harder than any teachers I had ever worked with as a student teacher and as a long-term sub. There were almost always teachers at Raven early in the morning and late at night. The parking lot was rarely empty. The principal had a reputation for "grooming" new teachers. She knew what she was doing and offered a lot of suggestions, but I let her intimidate me and influence my lesson plans too much during the pre-observation meeting. That was on me, not her.

In the end, when I was being observed, I was so nervous trying to make sure I hit on everything that she had told me that I must do, my nerves sabotaged the instruction. The lesson became hers and not mine. It wasn't until I was rated "Developing" on an observation that I realized I needed to make the lesson my own—that is, do what I felt comfortable with and teach the way I believed the students would best understand the material. That didn't mean that I ignored all of her suggestions; it just meant that I took ownership of my plan, good or bad. It was definitely for the best. I gained the principal's respect, and I gained confidence in my ability to teach.

Raven is an unusually large elementary school located in the northwest region of Baltimore County. The school was built for 684 students, but it had already exceeded capacity by about 100 students in early 2012. When I started at Raven, the principal told me that approximately 85 percent of the students were African American. Over the course of seven years, a lot of things changed about the school, including the demographics and socioeconomics of the student population.

TEACHING FOR THE TEST

My first year at Raven, I discovered what it meant to "teach to the test," which explained how so many students received good grades and scored so successfully on the MSA. Despite the beginning of Common Core in grade one, MSA was still administered and measured in the spring of 2013.

Raven drilled information into the minds of its students through the repetition of questions that mirrored how those questions would be asked on BCPS unit assessments. I learned this early on during one of my pre-observation meetings. I had included a question in my lesson plan that assessed the skill, but the principal interrupted our meeting to look up exactly how this question would be formatted on the unit assessment. She then had me change the question to mirror the one on the upcoming BCPS unit assessment (with different amounts), including something as minor as using the same character font and border around the question. Each lesson had to be formatted in this manner.

Routinely, students were given BCR (Brief Constructed Response) questions to practice in order to prepare for unit tests. The questions were worded exactly like the ones on the unit test. They were given one BCR question that the teacher had already completed as a model, one to answer with the teacher using the model, and a third to answer independently. All three questions were worded precisely the same except for the numbers and the names of people or objects referenced in the problem.

Students would then use the teacher's model as a guide to answering the other two questions. Also, before each unit exam, students would have a homework review where each question was worded identically to and presented in the same order as on the upcoming unit test. The only difference was the numbers used in the problem. By the time students took their unit tests, they were very well prepared. They at least recognized what the question was asking and how to go about solving it. As a result, grades reflected a higher level of understanding than the true ability level for many students. Students weren't learning how to think; they were learning how to regurgitate information.

In order to help prepare students for the standardized state tests (MSA), Raven held "voluntary" review classes before school, which students were encouraged to attend. They used MSA review booklets as sample questions—all perfectly ethical. I helped to run these classes during my first year. It wasn't that difficult to drill-down the types of questions that could be asked and teach various testing strategies to help select the correct multiple-choice answer. The result was that many of my students who had no number sense at all scored "proficient" on the MSA using these strategies.

By the end of my first year at Raven, I had learned how to play the game—one that most schools play—but I still believed that more emphasis should be placed on understanding versus achieving a certain test score. I had learned many valuable teaching skills from an array of excellent teachers and administrators. Most of all, I had gained confidence in my ability to effectively plan a lesson that was engaging to students while managing to challenge them to a higher level of thinking.

I found that children were more attentive if they were actively involved in a learning process that *appropriately* challenged them, as opposed to just repeating information or carrying out repetitive steps. I formed lasting, meaningful relationships with many students who continued to feed my passion for becoming a great teacher—one that I would want my own children to have. Near the conclusion of the year, the principal asked which grade I would prefer to teach the following year, and I requested to be a fourth-grade math teacher. She assigned me that role for the start of the 2013–2014 academic year, and I ultimately stayed in that position for another six years.

A TYPICAL YEAR

Over the course of those six years teaching fourth-grade math, I taught students of all ability levels—from the advanced class to ones with students far below grade level and in need of special supports. The majority of students in fourth grade performed at least one grade level behind in both math and reading. But I focused my efforts on growth—academic and personal. I wanted all of my students to believe in themselves and enjoy learning so they would want to work hard and get a good education.

In a school like the one where I've spent most of my time teaching, a teacher's impact extends far beyond anything academic. In many cases, you become almost like a parent figure. For the past seven years, I've probably impacted my students as much on a social/emotional level as I have on an academic level, not necessarily because that was my goal, but out of circumstance and necessity.

A typical homeroom ranged in size from twenty-four to twenty-nine students. I usually had several English language learners (ELLs), at least one homeless child, one or two students who had a parent currently incarcerated, one in foster care, most living with one parent, most living in apartments, most receiving free and reduced-price meals, and most below grade level. Things that my own family and I took for granted were not so for my students.

The principal left Raven after my second year (2013–2014). Dr. Dance instituted many new practices like the integration of technology and curriculum changes, as well as modifications to the grading policy and discipline policies. A lot of those changes were met with criticism for their hasty implementation and resulting negative consequences.

CORRUPTION IN THE SCHOOL SYSTEM

Dr. Dance became "the first superintendent in the 170-year history of the school system to be convicted of a crime."[7] Dance, who once told the public that he was very transparent and open, had been under investigation for failing to disclose that he had earned $147,000 for doing consulting work for SUPES Academy, an Illinois-based company that won a no-bid $875,000 contract with BCPS shortly after he was hired. "The statement of facts to which he agreed in pleading guilty said Dance told a SUPES official he would fire an employee if she stood in the way of SUPES getting that contract."[8] Dr. Dance was originally sentenced to five years in prison, but in April 2018, a judge suspended all but the six months, plus 700 hours of community service.[9]

After Dance officially resigned on April 30, Verletta White, former Chief Academic Officer (CAO) for BCPS since 2013, was named the interim superintendent. She was later rejected by the Maryland State Department of Education (MSDE) as the permanent superintendent because she, too, failed to disclose outside income that she earned while working as the school system's CAO. She had worked as a consultant for a Chicago-based Education Research & Development Institute (ERDI) and was paid about $3,000 from them to attend conferences.[10] Ms. White claimed that it was an honest mistake, but in light of Dr. Dance's deception and indictment, she couldn't get past this accusation and regain the public's trust.

EDUCATION'S DECLINE

Raven became a different place over the course of my seven years. According to a 2018–2019 report card issued by the MSDE to each school, Raven scored 55 percent, or three out of five stars, as a combination of academic and school quality ratings by the MSDE. Specifically, Raven earned 7.8 points out of twenty for Academic Achievement; 17.1 points out of thirty-five for Academic Progress; 7.4 points out of ten for Progress in Achieving English Language Proficiency; and 22.7 points out of thirty-five for School Quality and Student Success.[11] Only 28.6 percent of its students scored proficient in math, and 24 percent scored proficient in English Language Arts (ELA) for the academic year of 2018–2019.

The demographics changed as well. For the school year 2019–2020, BCPS reported that Raven is a Title I school, as 65 percent of its student body receives Free and Reduced Meals (FARMS). According to the MSDE's report card, as of August 2019, approximately 69 percent of the 799 students were African American, 18 percent were Hispanic, 5.5 percent were white, 3.6 percent were Asian, and 4.1 percent were other. Over 16 percent are considered English Learners (ELs), which means they are not proficient in reading, writing, or speaking English.

Furthermore, a once-celebrated Blue Ribbon School has fallen victim to discipline problems on a routine basis. BCPS reported (under the school data profile) that during the 2019–2020 school year, only 74 percent of the students and 78 percent of staff felt safe. During my last two years, I frequently witnessed or encountered students cursing at their teachers, throwing furniture and laptops, and hitting other students.

The faculty themselves became victims of student violence, including a special education teacher who had her finger intentionally broken, a former assistant principal who had her fingernail ripped off, and a school counselor who had bruises all over her abdomen from being punched while trying to restrain a student. Of the six fourth-grade teachers (of which I was one), three were pushed or struck by a student at least once. In fact, two staff members told me that they transferred out because they were afraid to be pregnant while working there.

There was no doubt that the school climate drastically declined during my seven years at Raven. I was told by teachers who helped open the school in 2005 that originally, learning habits and social behaviors were excellent. Students were respectful, polite, and engaged in learning, and parents were supportive of the teachers and administration. By the end of 2019, Raven looked and felt like a completely different place for the students and their teachers. The school office frequently had students lining the benches and pacing about as they awaited a counselor or administrator to address their behavior issues.

Students could often be seen wandering the hallways after escaping the classroom. Teachers visibly looked exhausted from the strain of trying to teach a curriculum that far exceeded the ability level of a majority of the student population and from fatigue in dealing with the same behavior issues time and time again without any consequences imposed for those actions. I frequently saw many teachers shaking their heads and rolling their eyes in the hallway as they escorted their classes to the bathrooms just to ensure that students didn't vandalize the bathroom or assault another student in the absence of supervision.

Raven was certainly not an easy school to teach at, but I was always aware that there were schools with far greater academic and behavioral challenges. At the end of 2019, the MSDE gave it a rating of 55 percent. I would say that on a scale of one to five, with five being the worst, Raven fell around a 3.5. I'm basing that on other schools that I have worked at and visited and on feedback from my colleagues who have taught elsewhere. Unfortunately, I do not believe the demise of Raven is unique; rather, I think it is representative of a national trend in our public education system, which is why I share my experience in that particular school with you. The national facts speak for themselves:

• Forty-one percent of fourth-graders and 34 percent of eighth-graders scored proficient or above on the 2019 Math National Assessment of Educational Progress (NAEP).[12]

- Thirty-five percent of fourth-graders and 34 percent of eighth-graders scored proficient or above on the 2019 Reading NAEP.[13]
- More than 70 percent of elementary teachers believe disruptive behavior has increased over the past three years.[14]
- The number of Americans enrolling in teacher training programs to become an educator has dropped by a third since 2010.[15]

PASSIONATE TEACHERS

Of all the teachers whom I worked with, trained with, and observed, those at Raven were among the very best. Their passion and commitment to help students (most from disadvantaged backgrounds) by giving them a solid education was undeniable. I, too, was part of that group of educators who would wake up in the middle of the night thinking about students who I knew were struggling and pondering an idea that I thought might reach them. As did other teachers, I gave up my personal time and resources to supplement what the students lacked and to help them wherever possible. I counseled those who were being pulled in the wrong direction by their peers and comforted those who faced struggles at home beyond the emotional capacity of any child.

Tragically, the talents and efforts of the teachers cannot outweigh the forces of destruction brought on by misguided federal and local education policies. I believe that most politicians and school board members who create them lack the experience in the classroom necessary to realize the full impact of their decisions. Teachers often aren't made aware of the intent behind the practices that they are told to implement and rarely have the opportunity for honest feedback without fear of retribution.

THE BEGINNING OF A COURAGEOUS CONVERSATION

We have to join together in an open and honest conversation to discuss what is and is not working within our educational system. It doesn't matter whether you have a child in the public school system or not. We are all adversely affected by a poor educational system, now and in the future. And for that reason, I share with you the following subsections on my perspective as a teacher:

- Common Core
- Technology in the Classroom
- Grading Policies
- English Language Learners
- Discipline

These sections obviously do not encompass all of the problems in our schools, but I believe that each one of these areas needs to be critically examined if we really want to increase academic achievement for *all* students and improve the public education system and environment. I have specifically chosen these because, as a teacher, I personally experienced the effects of educational policies with regard to each one of these topics. Each section, therefore, gives a background on the topic and shares my experiences and opinions.

My intent is not to provide all of the answers, but to raise some questions that we should all be asking so that together we can find better solutions. For this reason, at the end of each section, I have listed some potential questions that you may want to use to begin the conversation. I deeply believe that until we voice our concerns and acknowledge the problems, we can't effectively begin to work toward a solution.

In between each one of these subsections is a personal story of a particular student whom I had the privilege of teaching. Each one of these students impacted my life probably more than I impacted theirs. **Please do not skip these stories.** They are essential to understanding the need for improvements in our education system. If public education continues to decline, those with financial resources will have an alternative—private schools. But these children and many others will *not* have a choice. Public school is their only option, and education is often their only hope for a better life. We owe it to all children and their parents to make public education a "better" choice.

Raven, its staff members, and all student names have been changed to ensure anonymity. Academic results and demographics for the school are actual data taken from the websites of the Maryland State Department of Education and Baltimore County Public Schools.

Suzanne and her students promoting a class project, "Pay It Forward," December 2016

COMMON CORE

A Common Complaint

What do you feel when you hear the words "Common Core"? To some, it's like fingernails down a chalkboard. Those two words conjure up more fear and anger from parents than probably any other school terminology or topic.

I first heard these words myself at the end of 2010, in my last year of a graduate education program at Goucher College. While none of my professors openly criticized it, you could tell there was a feeling of tremendous apprehension in the air, similar to that feeling right before a forecasted hurricane.

HOW COMMON CORE WAS DEVELOPED

Common Core was officially launched in 2009 by the National Governors Association (NGA) and the Council of Chief State School Officers (CCSSO), presumably because these state leaders and state commissioners of education "recognized the value of consistent, real-world learning goals" and wanted "to ensure all students, regardless of where they live, are graduating high school prepared for college, career, and life."[16]

But unofficially, Common Core was conceived in 2007 when David Coleman and Jason Zimba wrote a paper for the Carnegie Corporation suggesting that education standards could be more specific, rigorous, and focused.[17] Coleman and Zimba had developed that belief during their time working together in a business they formed called The Grow Network. The Grow Network was a company that "found a niche in the burgeoning field of testing by producing reports" that would interpret results from the many standardized tests created through The No Child Left Behind Act.[18]

Zimba had discovered that every state had its own educational standards and that those standards varied widely from state to state. In addition, a student's proficiency level was determined by each state.[19] This means that a student might be considered proficient in Florida according to their standards and statewide testing, but that the same student might not be considered proficient in Maryland due to different state criteria. "But what most worried Coleman and Zimba—and many education experts—was the sheer number of standards in most states. The common critique was that most American grade-level guidelines were "a mile wide and an inch deep" in stark contrast to fewer but more intense expectations in high-achieving countries like Japan and Singapore."[20]

Coleman and Zimba's paper got the attention of the CCSSO and the NGA, and eventually, the CCSSO contracted with Student Achievement Partners (a new organization formed by Coleman and Zimba) to develop the path and lead the charge in developing fewer, yet more rigorous standards. Three people: Jason Zimba, Phil Daro (a former high school algebra teacher), and another individual named William McCallum (head of the math department at the University of Arizona) crafted the Common Core math standards.[21] All three are undoubtedly brilliant people with impressive backgrounds, but those backgrounds do not include teaching elementary children.

Zimba started drafting the Common Core math standards in September 2009. He started with a blueprint written by Achieve (a non-profit organization), College Board, and ACT. The blueprint set the expectations of every student by the end of high school. Then they worked backward from there and consulted with state officials, mathematicians, and teachers.[22]

RACE TO THE TOP

By June 2010, the NGA and the CCSSO released the final Common Core State Standards.[23] But it was President Obama's "Race to the Top" initiative that likely encouraged widespread adoption of the standards and simultaneously gave critics ammunition against those standards. Race to the Top was a competitive grant under the American Recovery and Reinvestment Act of 2009. It was a $4.35 billion grant, "the largest-ever federal competitive investment in school reform."[24]

Race to the Top incentivized states to adopt the standards by including "adopting internationally benchmarked standards and assessments that prepare students for success in college and the workplace" as one of four criteria to demonstrate school reform.[25] "Race to the Top applicants who agreed to adopt the Common Core standards had a small number of points (40 out of 500) added to their score, since the Core standards align with Race to the Top's goals."[26] "Thanks in part to financial incentives dangled by the Obama administration, more than forty states had adopted them" within a year of the final release.[27] As one of my graduate school professors said, when money is being offered as a reward for adopting the standards, it questions the integrity of the standards, and they no longer stand on their own merit.

Now there is no doubt that we need to make improvements in education because data was showing and continues to show that students in the US lagged behind several other developed nations. The Programme for International Student Assessment (known as PISA) is one of the largest international tests that is given every three years to measure reading, math, and science literacy of fifteen-year-olds across dozens of developed and undeveloped countries.[28]

The PISA 2018 results showed that the US performed slightly above the OECD (Organisation for Economic Co-operation and Development) average in reading and science, but below average in math, with no significant improvement or decline in any of the three subjects since 2006,[29] meaning our scores are remaining relatively stagnant.

According to the National Center for Education Statistics, among the thirty-seven OECD members, the US mathematics literacy scores were "lower than the average in twenty-four education systems, higher than in six, and not measurably different than in six."[30] On a scale of one to six with six being the most advanced, only 8 percent of US test participants scored a five or above, while 27 percent scored below a proficiency level two.[31] But perhaps most disturbing is that "[i]n the United States, socioeconomically advantaged students outperformed disadvantaged students in reading by ninety-nine score points..."[32]

So, I wholeheartedly agree that the US is lagging behind in some areas and needs to make changes to its education system to work toward strengthening our student academic performance among all student populations. But was Common Core the solution? Over the past seven years, I have been asked my opinion on Common Core by more parents than I can keep track of, and as a parent myself, I've questioned the legitimacy of Common Core, especially in regard to the math component since that's what I am most familiar with.

As I said earlier, the three individuals who wrote the math standards are brilliant and certainly have a superior understanding of mathematics. But how much experience do they have with the public education system, with elementary-aged students, and with the neurological/ developmental capabilities of young children? Have these three individuals ever been exposed to students at all socioeconomic levels, including those from disadvantaged homes/backgrounds? There are a lot of other variables to consider that impact the academic needs of our diverse student population. For example, you have to consider children who are English language learners, those who struggle with reading, and those who have difficulty maintaining attention.

There's also the financial incentive that was offered to states that adopted the Common Core standards as part of President Obama's Race to the Top. I completely understand the idea that if the federal government thought the Common Core standards were going to improve education, they would want to get states on board with the standards as quickly as possible, and what other way to speed up that process than by offering a financial reward? However, when money is the reason for adopting an initiative, it doesn't mean that it was adopted for the right reasons. While it would have taken much longer, wouldn't it have been better to test out the Common Core standards and a curriculum that aligned to it, discovered the strengths, and corrected the flaws before full-fledged implementation? If the standards were successful and proven with concrete data, they would have sold themselves.

INTRODUCING THE STANDARDS TO TEACHERS AND PARENTS

Even if you completely agree with the standards themselves, many teachers and parents would say that the implementation of those standards was flawed. Teachers were given the standards, and school districts were scrambling to write a curriculum that aligned to them. In Baltimore County, when Common Core and the matching curriculum were fully rolled out in 2013–2014, teachers were told by the county, "We're building the plane as we fly it." Who the hell would want to fly on that plane? I know it's a metaphor, but these are children we are talking about—we need to have it right *before* we start teaching it.

I was in a meeting where a school administrator said, "This year [in reference to the curriculum] was a mess, but the county will hopefully get things straightened out for next year." Well, there is no next year for fourth-graders or first-graders or students in any grade. A student has one opportunity at each grade level, and it is presumed that the student will learn what he or she needs to in that grade to be adequately prepared for the next one. It needs to be right the first time.

Not only did teachers not get time to learn the new standards and curriculum, but parents were completely left in the dark. One of the biggest complaints I've heard from parents is that they can't help their children at home with their school work because the parents themselves don't understand the way it's being taught. Under Common Core, I taught fourth-grade students how to multiply and divide using concepts and strategies that are completely different than the methods that all three of my own children learned in elementary school not that long ago. For example, below is a grade-four Common Core standard that relates to multiplication:

CCSS.MATH.CONTENT.4.NBT.5

Multiply a whole number of up to four digits by a one-digit whole number, and multiply two two-digit numbers, using strategies based on place value and the properties of operations. Illustrate and explain the calculation by using equations, rectangular arrays, and/or area models.[33]

This standard essentially requires that a fourth-grade student learn how to multiply using four different strategies: an array, an area model, an expanded form algorithm, and a standard algorithm. Parents are likely only familiar with the standard algorithm, and there's not a lot of information out there for parents to learn about the other strategies, particularly when it was first rolled out. Had Common Core had time to develop properly, there would have been educational websites and resources set up for parents to understand the conceptual reasoning behind the standards and help with learning how the standards have changed the curriculum and how it is currently being taught.

Instead, parents are frustrated. They can't help their children and, at times, feel there is no other choice but to pay for a tutor to help their child. Again, this goes back to my concern that the elite authors of those math standards hadn't had experience with disadvantaged populations. Most parents whom I've worked with cannot afford a private tutor for their children and, frankly, shouldn't need one if the curriculum and instruction are solid *and* their children are appropriately placed at the correct grade level to match their abilities.

STANDARDIZED ASSESSMENTS

Assessments are another issue, a major complaint of both teachers and parents. Proponents of Common Core say that the newly aligned exams to measure progress under Common Core are only replacing what used to be the year-end standardized tests. In Baltimore County, prior to CCSS, students were given the MSA, the Maryland State Assessment.

I have administered both the math MSA and the math Common Core-aligned assessment PARCC (Partnership for Assessment of Readiness for College and Careers). I have to agree with the proponents of Common Core that MSA measured how prepared the student was for the test questions and not a student's true mathematical understanding and ability. It was very easy to "teach to the test" for the MSA exam.

In contrast, the PARCC exam is much more difficult to prepare for. The questions are wordy, the content is extensive, and scoring often includes the student's ability to justify their mathematical reasoning—not just on the accuracy of the answer itself. In essence, a high score on the PARCC exam truly measures a student's ability, unlike a high or average score on the MSA exam. But PARCC did not simply replace MSA in a one-to-one fashion. The MSA exam used to take up only a few days in the school year. The PARCC exam requires more than just a few days.

For grade four, the math portion of the exam is four sixty-minute sessions. The ELA (English Language Arts) portion is three ninety-minute sessions. Unless a school doubles up on two sessions given within the same day, the PARCC test will, at the very least, interfere with seven instructional days (that's one and a half school weeks). Then, unlike MSA, the PARCC exam is given on the computer.

In order to get students ready for taking the exam on the computer using the various technological tools, teachers have to give up more instructional time to devote to computerized practice problems so that students are comfortable with the device before the exam. For example, in math, students have to learn how to use the computerized math tools (like a protractor) and formulas to type a fraction. Many schools devote additional instructional time to practicing typing on the computers throughout the school year in preparation for the PARCC exam because most elementary students don't know how to type, yet they have to type sentences and paragraphs for many of the responses. As a result, I would argue that we lose more instructional time with the Common Core assessment than we ever did prior to Common Core.

Furthermore, the Common Core-aligned assessment (PARCC) provides very little insight to teachers because the results of the exam aren't timely. The PARCC assessment is so comprehensive that results aren't available until late summer (the summer after the students you've taught have finished with you), which means the only benefit to teachers is to look at the results for the students coming into your September class. Results for a group of students whom you weren't teaching when the test was taken are not as meaningful. You don't know anything about the instruction that the students had in preparation for the test or their state of mind at the time it was administered. It's all an afterthought.

BENEFITS OF COMMON CORE

On the flip side, there are many things that I do like about Common Core. First, I agree with one of the basic premises behind a common, national set of education standards. Today's student population is mobile and fluid. People today frequently change jobs and careers that may require them to relocate. That means their children will be relocating too.

In my experience, children from lower socioeconomic communities are more transient. At Raven, students were enrolling and withdrawing throughout the school year. In my opinion, school should be the one constant in a child's life. A child moving from Maryland to Missouri should easily be able to adapt to the same grade in their new school if the standards are the same. A child shouldn't miss out on any piece of learning or instruction just because they moved. Not only should the standards be the same, but I believe the proficiency levels of each child in the US should be measured the same way. This will help correctly place a child who has moved at their ability level and will serve to benefit colleges and universities on their student selection.

Secondly, I like that Common Core attempts to develop a deep conceptual understanding of math. If the curriculum and the instruction are good and aligned to the standards, a child can understand how mathematical algorithms are developed through repeated reasoning. As I pointed out, fourth-grade students learn multiplication by learning arrays, then area models, then algorithms based on understanding place value. If a child can learn and understand each of those components, the algorithm will make sense in eliminating any memorization of steps.

I've actually seen students discover the algorithm on their own because they successfully understood all of the building blocks (conceptual pieces). There's frankly nothing more exciting for a teacher than to see "the light go on" in the student's head when they make that discovery. And even many of those who didn't figure the algorithm out on their own have commented, "Oh, that makes sense," by the time they learn it. Although most of my teaching experience has been working with elementary students, I have to believe that this greater conceptual understanding will benefit students when they get to higher levels and more abstract mathematics.

COMMON CORE = ONE SIZE FITS ALL

However, as much as I love the conceptual focus, I have a concern related to the emphasis placed on deep conceptual understanding. It is extremely difficult for students with below-average math abilities. A child with limited number sense has difficulty understanding when to use the operation of multiplication (as opposed to using addition or division). Learning four different strategies for multiplication compounds their confusion. Multiple strategies and representations become confusing for these children, and teachers are being told *not* to use phrases and tricks to help students remember the steps.

For example, rounding is a very difficult concept for students with limited number sense. Prior to Common Core, teachers would teach students how to round a number by performing three simple steps, and then using the phrase, "Five or above, give it a shove. Four or below, let it go," to help them remember it. With enough practice, most students could repeat these steps and get the rounded number. Common Core teaches rounding using number lines and number-sense understanding—great conceptual ways to explain it, but very difficult for students with little number sense to understand.

At my school, math teachers would spend a full week teaching rounding, practice it for weeks afterward, and still, about half of the students would be unable to calculate a rounded number. Here's the problem: rounding is used to estimate sums, differences, and products to help check your answers. If those students could learn the quick tricks to be able to round, they then might be able to apply that skill to estimate, which is a higher and useful skill. But the fact that they can't seem to learn rounding through conceptual understanding holds them back.

ACCOUNTABILITY TO THE STANDARDS

Again, I embrace much of the reasoning behind Common Core. But if you are going to set rigorous standards like Common Core, then you **must** hold students to those standards **and not allow them to progress to the next grade level unless they've met those standards.** The Common Core standards are very specific, and the progression of those skills is based on mastery of the prior standards. My experience in Baltimore County is that students are pushed from one grade level to the next *without* having demonstrated an understanding or completion of grade-level expectations. Other BCPS teachers routinely expressed the same concern.

The boy referred to in the first chapter is a real-life example. He had started his elementary education in Baltimore City but was enrolled in Baltimore County in second grade. I could see in the first week that he was lacking many fourth-grade skills, and I did everything that I could to fill in the learning gaps. I used Pearson's prescribed research-based interventions and brought him up for SST (Student Support Team). The fall MAP test (Measure of Academic Progress, part of NWEA) showed that he was on a first-grade math level. He could not correctly take thirty-two tiles and group them into three tens and two ones. He had no one-to-one correspondence or place-value understanding. He was also reading well below grade level. His mother agreed with me and supported my recommendation for him to repeat fourth grade, but the system ignored that recommendation because so many of his peers were even further away from meeting the grade-level standards.

If we are truly intent on raising the academic standards (to a level like Common Core), then let's hold students accountable to those standards, but make sure that they are developmentally appropriate, that the curriculum aligning to those standards is solidly built (not in the "construction phase"), and that there are supports in place to help teachers fill in the gaps and meet the individual needs of their students. Allow teachers to use their professionalism to determine how best to meet those needs.

IMPACT ON PROFICIENCY LEVELS

The best measure of whether or not Common Core has been successful may be in the data. The 2018 PISA results ranked the US as thirteenth out of seventy-nine countries in reading, thirty-seventh out of seventy-nine countries in math, and eighteenth in science.[34] Another measure of performance, the National Assessment of Educational Progress (NAEP), reported that 2019 results show that 41 percent of fourth-graders and 34 percent of eighth-graders scored proficient or above in math and 35 percent of fourth-graders and 34 percent of eighth-graders scored proficient or above in reading.[35] Looked at another way, approximately 59–66 percent of our fourth- and eighth-graders are not proficient in math and reading.

These results indicate that we need to do better. I'm not suggesting that we completely throw out Common Core. But maybe we need to build in better supports for the teachers, students, and parents. They deserve to have a plane that's fully built and tested before they are a passenger, and if we can't do that—then let's consider another form of transportation!

QUESTIONS TO ASK IN CONVERSATIONS ABOUT COMMON CORE

- What is the neuroscience behind the standards at each grade level—in other words, are the standards developmentally appropriate at each grade?
- How can we differentiate the curriculum to meet the diverse needs of our students and still have it aligned to Common Core standards, or do we need to differentiate the standards themselves?
- How can we ensure that a district's curriculum and its supporting resources/materials are aligned to the standards?
- What more can we be doing to provide extra support to children outside of school (at home), and/or what can we do to help the parents understand the curriculum so they can support their children at home?
- How honest is the district in regard to students that are meeting the standards and being promoted to the next grade level?
- Is there a better way to recognize progression through the school system rather than (honestly) what we're currently doing—promoting students based on chronological age?

NADIA

Nadia was a student in my class during my first year as a fourth-grade teacher. She stood out for a few reasons. First of all, the obvious—Nadia was one of only two Caucasian children in my class, and when I say Caucasian, I mean that her skin was the color of freshly fallen snow! She was very pale, very thin, and had whitish blond hair and pale blue eyes. The second reason that she stood out was her spirit. She was always smiling and enthusiastic. She consistently worked hard, and it was obvious that she loved school. You might have thought her size and skin color would make her feel uncomfortable as the minority in a mostly African American school, but not so. She embraced diversity. She showed equal affection for all of her classmates and seemed oblivious to the fact that she looked different than almost all of them.

Nadia physically looked frail. Her teeth were very pointed and yellow, and she was so thin and pale that at times she appeared malnourished. Nadia had told me that she now lived with her grandparents. She said her mom was sick and had stayed in Ukraine, where she was born.

At the end of the first quarter, Nadia's grandmother came in for a conference. An older feeble-looking woman with a kind face and voice told me a story that I'll never forget.

Nadia was the oldest of three girls. She was born in Ukraine, along with her two siblings. When Nadia was around four years of age, her father brought all three girls to the United States to live. Nadia's mother remained in Ukraine for a reason that the grandmother didn't share with me. Nadia and the girls lived with their father here in the US, but the father really was not properly providing for them.

The father was found leaving the youngest two girls in Nadia's care for extended periods of time. At age five, Nadia was responsible for preparing the meals for herself and her sisters. She also bathed the girls and got them to bed each night. At some point, the grandparents must have discovered this, and they eventually ended up getting custody of the girls when Nadia was around eight. Listening to the grandmother tell me this story, I sensed some guilt—Nadia was robbed of her childhood.

And yet, I would have never guessed what a tragic beginning this little girl had because she never gave the slightest hint of the sad life that she had recently lived. I realized that school was probably a safe harbor for Nadia. It was the place that always kept her safe, warm, and fed. It also relieved her of the responsibility of caring for her younger sisters while she and they were in the school building.

Once, I had a chance to observe Nadia at school in the company of her siblings. All three girls were beautiful, but the sisters appeared much healthier than Nadia. They visibly weighed more, and their hair and teeth looked in better condition. It was obvious by seeing Nadia with the girls that she was like their mother—and like any mother, she had put the needs of those she cared for above her own.

A few years later, I learned from Nadia's youngest sister that all three girls were back living with their father. I hope that he is now fulfilling his responsibilities as a parent. She, as well as all children, deserve to be a child for as long as possible—and for some children, school is the only place that can protect them from the adult world.

TECHNOLOGY

User Error or Buyer's Remorse

As I was writing up one of many technology referrals for a student who was playing a game on his computer when he was supposed to be completing an online assignment, I couldn't help but wonder if the $200 million that my school district spent on student devices was worth it. Imagine if instead they had put that money into hiring more teachers to reduce class sizes; bought supplies so that teachers didn't have to use their own money to buy glue sticks, markers, and tissues; fixed the roof above my classroom so that I didn't come into a soaking-wet floor and mold inside my cabinets; or perhaps maybe even invested a small portion of that money to purchase microphones so students could hear their teachers? Were one-to-one devices for elementary students really the best use of the funds?

I'm not the only one with these thoughts. Many parents and teachers have questioned the same thing. What has prompted school districts to invest so much money into this kind of technology? Is it enabling better instruction? Is it improving academic performance?

STANDARDIZED TESTING REQUIREMENTS

"In 2010, the US Department of Education awarded $330 million to two different consortiums for states in order to develop assessments for the Common Core State Standards."[36] One was called The Smarter Balanced Assessment Consortium (SBAC), which included twenty-one states. The other testing consortium was called the Partnership for Assessment of Readiness for College and Careers (PARCC), which served fourteen states plus the District of Columbia.[37] The SBAC assessment requires internet connectivity and technological devices because it is an adaptive test, meaning that each test changes which question is asked of the student depending on how the student has responded to prior questions.[38] Questions increase or decrease in difficulty based on the student's knowledge. Schools that use this type of assessment must have the technology available to the students, at least for testing purposes.

PARCC is not an adaptive test, but rather a "fixed" test, which means that all students taking PARCC get similar questions.[39] Initially, some students took PARCC on computers, and others took the PARCC assessment using traditional paper and pencil medium. But PARCC was designed to be a computerized test[40] and is now most often administered that way.

In essence, most standardized assessments today require schools to have wireless connectivity, enough devices, and sufficient bandwidth for testing purposes. "Test officials say computers are a more secure way to administer a test, allow for faster scoring, and enable more innovative questions. Proponents say online testing is an important way to prepare students for a workplace reliant on technological skills."[41]

TECHNOLOGY SUPPORTING EDUCATIONAL NEEDS

But the push for technology in education actually began long before Common Core and the related assessments. In 1994, President Bill Clinton signed The Goals 2000: Educate America Act, which included a technology component. Later, President George W. Bush created the No Child Left Behind Act of 2001, which wanted to improve student academic achievement through the use of technology.[42] Thus, as far back as 1994, technology was thought to have benefits in improving education, but it was twenty years later when it became a priority, essentially because of Common Core assessments.

According to the US Department of Education, the Office of Educational Technology believes that technology should be embedded into the tools, resources, and practices of education because technology has the ability to bridge the equity and accessibility gap.[43] Using technology, all learners can access information, experiences, and resources where geography, economics, and individual abilities previously were barriers. Technology also has the ability to target the specific needs of students to provide more individualized instruction. But, as the US Department of Education pointed out, there are many challenges that have to be overcome in order to realize the potential of technology-enabled learning.[44]

BALTIMORE COUNTY'S TECHNOLOGY INITIATIVE

BCPS was at the forefront of implementing technology in the schools and curriculum but has encountered many challenges and controversies along the way. In March 2014, the BCPS School Board approved a $205 million plan to provide laptop computers to 150,000 students and teachers over a seven-year period.[45] The superintendent, Dr. Dance, made student one-to-one devices a key initiative referred to as STAT, Student and Teachers Accessing Technology.

Under STAT, during the first year (beginning in the 2014–2015 school year), all teachers (approximately 8,500) in the county and students in grades one through three at ten "experimental" schools were given devices for $6.8 million under a contract with Daly Computers Inc. out of Montgomery County.[46] The devices converted to tablets, included software, and included additional equipment for teachers such as docking stations and twenty-four-inch monitors.

The ten experimental schools were referred to as "Lighthouse" schools. For year one of implementation, only elementary schools were Lighthouse schools. Lighthouse schools not only were the experimental group but also served to "showcase" or demonstrate to educators around the county and the public in general how the devices could be integrated with instruction. At the same time, schools in the county were choosing Teacher Leader Corps (TLCs), one or two teachers at each grade level or by department to tour the Lighthouse schools. TLCs were to seek out professional development, bring that information back to their schools, and share it with their administration and peers. I was the TLC chosen for the fourth grade at my school; thus, I toured two of the Lighthouse elementary schools, Fort Garrison Elementary and Rodgers Forge Elementary. Both are very different in terms of size, demographics, and socioeconomics than Raven.

In the spring of 2015, I toured Fort Garrison during the school day.

I observed three primary-level classrooms. It is important to note that although the school was in session and we were told this was a typical day, the teachers and administrators at Fort Garrison were expecting our arrival. During our tour, I saw students actively engaged in various classroom activities and tasks. Students were independently moving around the classroom with their devices and working at various stations throughout the room. All students seemed very engaged and on task. Most students appeared to be collaborating with at least one other student. The teacher's small-group instruction appeared uninterrupted by the activities within the classroom. Overall, I was very impressed and excited for the devices to come to our school the following year. In my mind, I was already planning how to incorporate them into my daily math lessons.

Later that same spring, I observed Rodgers Forge Elementary on a night where the school, as a Lighthouse school, was open to the public for purposes of showcasing how instruction was changing. The teachers were all present, and a few of the Rodgers Forge students had volunteered to be there as well to demonstrate some aspects of instruction and the use of technology. Once again, I was enthusiastic about getting these devices in my classroom.

MY EXPERIENCES (AND OPINIONS) WITH ONE-TO-ONE STUDENT DEVICES

In December 2015, my elementary school received devices for each student. As part of the introduction, teachers discussed the learning purposes for the devices and taught students how to handle and care for them. Students were told that they had a responsibility to appropriately use their devices according to the directions of their teachers, how to safely use the internet, and how to secure their information.

As a fourth-grade math and science teacher, I have always taught two distinct sections of students. For the 2015–2016 school year, I had an advanced math class in the morning (as my homeroom) and a below-grade-level math class in the afternoon. After seeing how the two groups used the devices, I had two very different opinions on them. I found that in subsequent years, these opinions were generally reinforced.

Overall, I loved the use of the devices with the more advanced students. These students handled the devices carefully and respected and followed the rules concerning when and how they could use them. I developed a website that each class could access through the school's grading and reporting software. I integrated the website into many of my lesson plans, allowing time for students to use it to reinforce a skill that was previously taught or to get extra help. The device allowed me to really target some of their individualized needs.

I encouraged my students to use the website at home for extra practice or to help them catch up when they were absent. In fact, after determining that all of my students in the advanced class had internet access at home, I was able to assign specific sections of the website for students to preview an upcoming lesson. This is essentially called flipped learning or front-end learning, where students are introduced to the lesson at home before they come to school. It allowed me to quickly assess their understanding of the topic at the beginning of class so that I could group the students according to their level of understanding and really spend the majority of the class time either extending their learning or providing remediation.

However, I could only do this with the advanced group for two reasons. One, because not everyone in the lower-ability class had access to the internet at home. But the main reason was because a large majority of the students in the lower-ability classes would not complete homework—especially if the homework didn't require anything tangible or concrete to turn in for a grade. Just telling students to watch a learning video and try some online problems wasn't enough to motivate most of them to actually do it.

Over the past few years, I encountered many other problems with the devices—particularly with students at lower-ability levels. The devices often became a distraction from learning rather than a tool to enhance learning. Students would often use the device to play a game or use it to search out and view pornography—even in fourth grade. BCPS had tried to block what was deemed harmful websites for children, but somehow, the students always managed to get around these firewalls of protection.

Teachers did their best to prevent students from inappropriately using the devices. However, it is impossible to see the individual screens of twenty-six students around the room, many of which are moving around as recommended in a learner-centered environment. The learner-centered environment encourages teachers to use small-group instruction to meet the individual needs of each learner for the majority of the class period. So, for approximately three-fourths of the class time, teachers are seated at a table instructing and helping a small group of students who rotate out while the remainder of the class is working collaboratively or independently. Under this model of instruction, the teacher cannot be roaming around the room to monitor screen-time use.

Furthermore, to be honest, student devices enable teachers who are already bad teachers to be even worse. There are some teachers who use the devices as "babysitters," even with policies in place to help prevent misuse. Parents need to be cognizant of how much time their child is spending on the device at school. Ask your children: "Did you use your device in math class or ELA class today? What did you use it for? Did you use the device at any other time in school today? Why?" Devices can be great, but they add responsibility to the teachers and the parents.

STUDENT RESPONSIBILITY

The students should also have a responsibility associated with having a device. Many students were irresponsible in how they used and handled the devices. Seriously, not a day went by at school when I didn't hear the sound of at least one device crashing to the ground, and almost always, that sound bothered me more than it bothered the student who dropped it. In fact, I witnessed students who purposely threw their devices when they got angry. Each device cost the school system $1,366 over four years,[47] but it cost the students (and their parents) nothing—and sometimes, when you get something for free, you tend not to appreciate it as much.

Even when the damage was intentional, such as plucking off the keys, using a pencil/scissors to scratch the screen, or sticking a small object into the charging outlet—the student and his or her family never compensated the school for damages. Initially, when the devices were given out, there were no negative consequences for the student who was intentionally irresponsible. Eventually, probably in part to the number of damaged devices, each student had to sign a technology agreement at the beginning of the year. If that agreement was violated, then the teacher had to write up a technology referral, which amounted to not much more than a lunch detention and/or possibly losing use of the device for a short period of time.

Yet teachers had consequences for a student's irresponsibility. Each time a device was damaged or not working properly, a "Request for Service" ticket had to be completed online to initiate a repair. Initially, my school had a technology liaison who was responsible for this, but due to an abundance of needed repairs, that responsibility was passed down to the teachers. Teachers are already overburdened with responsibilities, and technology troubleshooter and repair manager now became additional ones.

DEVICES AND INSTRUCTION

Despite any of these problems, we need to ask: "Do devices improve instruction and learning?" As an elementary math teacher, I found that devices were not always the best option for instruction, practice, or assessment. BCPS spent millions on online curriculums and math programs that would make use of the technology.[48] But was the technology purchased for the online curriculums, or were the online curriculums purchased to justify the cost of the technology? Other teachers (including ones from other elementary schools) and I found that in many cases, the online curriculums didn't improve instruction or learning for several reasons.

The fourth-grade online curriculum that I used was not always aligned to the district's curriculum, which was aligned to Common Core. Word problems were often too wordy and used vocabulary beyond the capabilities of below-grade-level readers and some of the limited English proficient (LEP) population. Many students, particularly those who struggled academically, had difficulty going from reading a problem on the screen, to solving it on paper, and back to providing an answer on the computer, especially when they had to scroll down to finish reading the problem or question. And by the fourth year, the computers were in such poor condition that often students would lose a connection, get kicked out of a program, or have the battery die (particularly for my afternoon class). Consequently, teachers always needed a backup plan, even if only for a handful of students.

ELEMENTARY STUDENTS AND SCREEN TIME

Instruction aside, I have one last significant concern with elementary students using one-to-one devices. Young children are already spending too much time outside of school looking at screens—either on their phones, televisions, iPads, or computers. If children are engaged in this type of independent activity, it means they are not collaboratively playing, working, and socializing with other human beings. Hence, they're not developing communication and peer-relationship skills. Let's not further take away opportunities for children to learn these important life and social skills by putting them in front of a screen in school for any more time than necessary.

We also need to examine the cost-benefit of incorporating technology into the elementary schools on a one-to-one level. I believe that devices are necessary and should be provided to each high school student in order to prepare them for college and/or a career. Devices allow high school students to communicate better with their teachers and to self-manage their own assignments and grades—which, again, helps to prepare them for the world beyond college. Unfortunately, under Dr. Dance's S.T.A.T. initiative, high school students were the last to get a device after elementary and middle school students. They didn't get devices until 2018. My question is, are one-to-one devices at the elementary level worth the excessive cost?

ARE DEVICES WORTH THE MONEY?

In the spring of 2019, five years after the ambitious S.T.A.T. program began, BCPS decided to scale back. As of fall 2019, first- and second-grade students now shared one device for every five students, and the county switched from HP laptops to Chromebooks (which are less expensive) in all of its elementary schools.[49] Every middle and high school student in the BCPS system still had a laptop and could take it home, which "gave students from low-income families access to technology at home for the first time."[50]

What was the reason for the scale-back? Insufficient results. "Despite the saturation of technology, Baltimore County ranks near the bottom of the state in passing rates on standardized tests. The scores are generally flat for students in grades three through eight, many of whom have had the computers for at least three years."[51] So maybe, one-to-one devices at the elementary level either do not significantly improve learning or just aren't being used correctly to improve instruction.

These are my thoughts: Consider having quality, portable devices to be shared at the elementary level (say five students for each device), and use the savings on equipment, maintenance, and online curriculum programs to reduce class sizes. Hire more teachers to lower the pupil-to-teacher ratio. Every teacher I've ever spoken with has said that nothing is more effective in improving education than a lower number of students in each class. Let teachers really be able to focus on the individualized needs of their students, and let students develop social and collaboration skills through regular peer interactions—not interactions with a screen.

Fewer devices in the classroom would make it more feasible for the teacher to monitor the activity on students' screens and reduce the number of repairs required, which translates into cost savings and savings on instructional time that's currently wasted when the teacher has to stop instruction to address technical problems.

TECHNOLOGY FOR TEACHERS AND COVID

Student devices can be a worthwhile investment, but their purchase is a substantial commitment that takes away financial resources from other technology items for teachers, such as interactive displays, microphones, and classroom cameras with recording software. These technologies would provide benefits to instruction and safety throughout the entire day, whereas elementary student devices provide limited benefits for only part of the day.

The COVID pandemic has brought education technology front and center. Some may now be thinking that there is more of a need for student one-to-one devices to enable distance learning. This is true, but it is only a temporary need, and not every student needs the school to provide the devices. Many elementary students already have access to a home computer or iPad that they could use for distance learning. Rather than giving a device to every student, lend one just to those in need. The financial savings on devices could then be used to provide hotspots or devices with cellular capability to those students who lack internet access at home. Without that internet access, devices are useless—further enlarging the equity gap.

Teacher technology is certainly more necessary during COVID. Some districts have installed cameras in classrooms that can record teacher instruction live to allow students who are learning from home to participate in the discussions. This is a great tool for the hybrid model of instruction and has so many benefits beyond distance learning.

Teachers can record their lessons so that students can review them at home at a later time. Essentially this is like giving everyone a free tutor and would also benefit parents in understanding how skills are being taught—addressing the confusion behind Common Core. The instructional recordings can also be used by teachers for self-reflection or shared among peers for training and professional growth.

The bottom line is that school districts are on tight budgets, and they must constantly be analyzing how to appropriate funds. When making decisions about buying technology or online curriculums, let's do it for the right reasons. The district must ask: "Will this increase a student's ability to learn, and will it help the teacher with instruction?" If both answers are yes, then the district or school needs to carefully plan the integration of that purchase, including the infrastructure to support it. We need to make sure that schools aren't making these huge financial purchases just so that students can take a computerized test once a year.

QUESTIONS TO ASK IN CONVERSATIONS ABOUT TECHNOLOGY

- How much time on a device is actually needed to benefit the student's learning?
- Is the amount of time that students spend on the device at school age-appropriate?
- How much instructional or planning time can be saved because of the devices?
- Do teachers have the appropriate technology available in the classroom to help them engage, instruct, and manage the behaviors of their students?
- Are the students responsible enough to be using and caring for the devices?

- How can students be held accountable for device use and care?
- Is there a more cost-effective method with possibly better-proven results?
- Does the school/district have the infrastructure to support the technology?
- What support do the teachers have for this technology?
- What effective tools are in place to help ensure that students aren't misusing their devices?
- How are you ensuring equal access to this technology outside of school?
- What technology do teachers need to facilitate in-person and distance learning?

AVI

Avi was a tall, lean boy from India who was once a student in my advanced mathematics class. He had excellent work habits—always focused and attentive, very methodical in his work, and very responsible. These traits far exceeded most of his peers' behaviors, especially the boys. He was more mature than the average ten-year-old. Avi was a really sweet child—kind and respectful to everyone, students and teachers alike. I got to know him very well because he was in my homeroom as well as my math class. Sometimes he liked to hang out with me during recess, and he always took advantage of an opportunity to enjoy a "lunch bunch" with a few other students and me.

Avi was very bright, but it was mostly his work habits that made him stand out in a class of such outstanding abilities. At the end of the first quarter, both parents and Avi himself attended the Friday Conference Day. As with all of my parent conferences, I started off on a positive note, discussing all of the strong qualities that I had witnessed so far in Avi's abilities and behavior. Unlike some parent conferences where I struggled to come up with something positive, it was very easy to compliment Avi on both fronts—personally and academically. At the time, he had around a 91 percent in my class, which reflected grades on assignments and assessments above a fourth-grade level.

As I was talking, Avi's mom politely smiled and nodded (she never spoke during the entire conference). However, as soon as I finished talking, Avi's father asked in a very stern voice, "Why isn't he doing better? What can he do to improve his grade? Is he playing around in class?"

I looked over at Avi and saw him just shrink before my eyes. This boy who typically seemed older than his age now appeared like a scared, embarrassed young boy. I had noticed a change in his demeanor from the very beginning of the conference. He wasn't smiling, he didn't say anything, his shoulders were slumped over, and he had almost no eye contact with anyone in the room. When his father asked these questions, Avi's insecure, fearful body language became even more pronounced.

I tried unsuccessfully to explain to the father that Avi was part of a very challenging class in which the curriculum and expectations were above grade-level standards. But it was clear that the father had expectations much higher than any curriculum, and I sensed that Avi would never live up to them.

After that conference, I felt very sad. To see a bright, happy, kind child cower in fear of his father made me feel helpless. I never saw any signs of physical abuse, but there appeared to be an abuse of power in that family and a failure to recognize the gifts of this amazing child. Any parent should have been grateful to have him for their son.

Luckily, when Monday morning came, Avi was the same happy, confident student whom I had known prior to that conference. I was wondering if he would be embarrassed, but fortunately, it didn't appear so. It was obvious that school was his escape from a home life that I would never be able to fully understand. Setting high standards and expectations for your children is admirable and responsible parenting. But expectations need to be achievable, and the character of that child needs to outweigh all other expectations.

During the last week of school, I engaged the students in various activities that focused more on their character than academics. One of those activities was something that I referred to as the "Lollipop Moment."

The idea was based on a TEDx talk by Drew Dudley. The basic premise is that most of us think a "leader" is a title that only belongs to a few people—those who have had a powerful impact on changing the world for a large number of people. He, on the other hand, redefined leadership as being about lollipop moments—a moment when someone said or did something that you feel fundamentally made your life better. Drew explained this by sharing a personal story in which he was handing out lollipops to incoming students at college. That one seemingly insignificant act caused a scared girl, who was doubting herself and ready to go back home, to stay and give college a chance. A moment that he didn't even remember because it seemed insignificant to him turned out to be one of the most important moments in someone else's life.

After I played the six-minute TED talk for my students, we had a talk. I said that each of them has been or would be the catalyst for a lollipop moment in someone else's life, just as someone would be in their life. Then I gave each student a lollipop with the instructions to give their lollipop to a person who has created a lollipop moment for them. It could have been the lady who works in the cafeteria, a friend, a parent, a teacher, or a coach. The kids were so excited to hand out their lollipops as a way of recognizing someone who made a difference in their life.

At the end of class, Avi quietly came up to me and handed me his lollipop. He said, "Mrs. DeMallie, you are my lollipop moment." That's all he needed to say.

On the last day of school, I took all of the students outside for an extended recess. It was a beautiful day to begin our summer vacation. I didn't have too many students to supervise because attendance was low that day, so I sat on a bench opposite the playground. Avi came and sat next to me. He said he didn't feel like playing on the equipment; he just wanted to be with me.

I asked Avi if he had anything fun planned for summer. He said, "No."

I asked him if his family would be going on a vacation. He said, "No."

I asked Avi if he had any friends in his apartment complex to play with. He said, "No."

I said, "Well, Avi, maybe you can play some games inside with your family. You said you have an older brother and sister. Maybe you could play card games or backgammon like my family likes to do."

Avi said, "No. My family doesn't play games. My brother goes to school. He is becoming an engineer. My sister and my parents work. I will just spend time by myself on the computer, not doing anything fun like in your class."

This broke my heart. As excited as I was for summer break, I realized that for many children, like Avi, summer vacation isn't filled with the fun family time that my children could look forward to. School is actually a break for many of these kids.

I was very sad to say goodbye to Avi at the end of the day. I know he will be successful, but my hope for him is that one day, he has a family who will bring him the happiness that families should have together.

A few years after I taught Avi, an email popped up through BCPS's school course/grading software. It was from Avi to me. It just said, "Hi, Mrs. DeMallie. It is your student, Avi. Do you remember me?"

I replied, "Absolutely, Avi. I will never forget you!" He is my lollipop moment.

It was often very difficult to reconcile my students' home life with mine (summer 2015).

GRADING POLICIES

Would you rather your child bring home a report card filled with As, knowing that those grades didn't include any assignments that she or he failed or didn't complete, *or* a report card that includes some Bs and maybe a few Cs, but reflects all grades on all assignments?

This is part of an issue that many teachers and parents are grappling with, including myself as both a teacher and a mother. The issue has arisen because today's education leaders have started another movement that revolves around a fundamental question: how should students be assessed?

HISTORY OF THE GRADING SYSTEM

The history of the grading system goes back to the late eighteenth century when, in 1785, Yale broke their seniors into four categories: Optimi, second Optimi, Inferiores, and Perjores.[52] "By 1837, Yale was also recording student credit for individual classes, not just at the completion of college studies, using a four-point scale."[53] However, students never saw their grades.

After observing "increasing [student] attention to the course of studies" and the belief that public rankings and evaluations encouraged "good moral conduct," Harvard and other schools began to implement a form of grading as well.[54] By the late 1800s and early 1900s, the number and size of schools were growing at a fast pace. "[G]rades became one of the primary means of communication between institutions," which meant that they needed to have meaning beyond the school itself that was issuing the grade.[55] Mount Holyoke appears to be the first institution to use an A through F grade system in 1898, and the 100-point scale became very common by the early 1900s.[56] By the 1940s a concern over uniformity pressured many schools to use the A through F four-letter system (the E was dropped around the 1930s) and percentages, but there were still many inconsistencies and concerns about issues such as aptitude curves.[57]

It's fascinating that over eighty years later, we are still confronting and debating many of the same issues. I find it ironic that the education world is focused on increasing the rigor of the curriculum and increasing the number of assessments given to students, yet we are withdrawing many components of feedback from the grading system to the point where there is a "no-grades" movement, and Ivy League school Brown University will not use Ds in its grading scale, nor does it report failing grades.[58]

GRADING PURPOSES

What is so wrong with the traditional reporting system that schools are taking a 180-degree turn? Well, there are reportedly a few reasons that revolve around an essential question: what is the purpose of grades? According to the article "Teaching Students to Think," the most effective grading practices provide "accurate, specific, timely feedback designed to improve student performance,"[59] and this opens up a flood of other questions:

- Do grades motivate students to learn and improve their academic performance?
- Do our grading practices accurately reflect a student's understanding or mastery of the standards?
- Among schools and within the same schools, are we consistently using the same criteria to determine a student's grades, and are there biases built into the grades?
- Are grades equitable among the diverse population of students in today's classrooms?

Butler and Nisan (1986) found that "[grades] may encourage an emphasis on quantitative aspects of learning, depress creativity, foster fear of failure, and undermine interest."[60] The same study found that grades motivate students in ways to avoid getting bad grades, but not necessarily in a way that stimulates a desire to learn. This could infer that to avoid a bad grade, rather than study or practice a skill, a student might copy the homework, plagiarize, or cheat on an exam. If not caught, the student then earns a grade that doesn't reflect anything about their knowledge or understanding.

Other studies show that grades can "dampen existing intrinsic motivation, give rise to extrinsic motivation, enhance fear of failure, reduce interest, decrease enjoyment in classwork, increase anxiety, hamper performance on follow-up tasks, stimulate avoidance of challenging tasks, and heighten competitiveness."[61] However, Butler (1988) found that students who normally receive good grades do not seem to experience the same negative effects and have shown continued motivation to complete additional assignments.[62]

Thus, my takeaway from the research is that if you are consistently receiving low grades, you will be less motivated to work hard in school, whereas if you are generally receiving good grades, you will be motivated to work hard, presumably with the desire to continue earning more good grades. So, is it right to completely overhaul the grading process for students who are not doing well in school in hopes that they might be more motivated to work harder? And in the process, are you punishing the students who already work hard and do well in school?

Along the same lines, do grades provide feedback that helps students to improve upon their future learning and understanding? Studies have investigated the relationship between grades (evaluative feedback) and personalized written comments (descriptive feedback). Butler and Nisan (1986) found that students receiving *only* descriptive feedback performed significantly better on follow-up quantitative and problem-solving tasks compared to students that just got grades or no feedback at all.[63]

I would say, why not give both (a grade and written feedback)—as I did many times to my math students. But other research has shown that when students receive both a grade and comments on an assignment, those comments tend to be ineffective in improving the results on follow-up tasks, presumably because students focus on the grade and not the comment. Therefore, descriptive comments by themselves are the best feedback for improving understanding and future success on a follow-up task.

As a teacher, I think this is very valuable information and should be considered when returning assignments, conferencing with a student, or just giving feedback. But I do not believe that it necessarily means we need to completely abandon grades on some assignments and at the completion of a marking period. Don't we need some measure to let parents and older children know where they stand in regard to grade-level or course-level standards?

DO GRADES REFLECT A STUDENT'S KNOWLEDGE?

What about the purpose of a grade to reflect that student's level of understanding? Can't a grade just be a rating of ability rather than a motivator or an enhancement to future learning? "Research has shown that grading is a solid predictor of student-success outcomes, but it is not always an accurate representation of what students actually know…"[64]

Here's how this topic is being debated. Take, for example, two students: Student #1 and Student #2. Assume that both are in the same class and were graded on the same assignments and assessments as follows:

Student #1's Grades: 100, 95, 90, 0, 86, 93, 0, 87

Student #2's Grades: 80, 75, 82, 77, 79, 80, 70, 75

If we calculate an average grade for each student by summing each student's scores and dividing that sum by the total number of assignments, Student #1 would earn 68.9 percent (a letter grade of a D) and Student #2 would earn 77.3 percent (a letter grade of a C). But if you look at their individual scores, who do you think has a stronger understanding of the material?

If you ignore the zeroes, Student #1 clearly has demonstrated a stronger understanding. It can be assumed that the zeroes resulted from missing assignments or perhaps incomplete work, both of which could be due to apathy or poor executive function skills (i.e., organization and planning). Proponents of the no-zero policy believe that Student #1's grade should only reflect his or her understanding of the curriculum, and missing or incomplete assignments should be ignored.

THE NO-ZERO POLICY

This is the debate that became the catalyst for the no-zero policy that many school districts are implementing. The no-zero policy sets the lowest possible grade for any assignment or test at 50 percent. Even if a student intentionally neglects to complete an assignment or fails to turn in the assignment, the teacher is prohibited from giving the student a zero in the grade book. Many districts are adopting this policy, including Baltimore County and Prince George's County in Maryland, Fairfax County in Virginia, and Philadelphia School District in Pennsylvania.

Proponents of the policy say that a zero or grades below 50 percent make it too difficult for students to bring up their grade point average (GPA) and therefore, the GPA doesn't truly reflect the student's ability. Some say, "The new grading systems are more fair and end up being more conducive to learning, encouraging students to catch up when they fall behind rather than just giving up…and such failures can put students on a path to dropping out before graduation."[65]

Opponents disagree with the premise and the outcomes. According to three hundred members of the Edutopia audience who responded to a Facebook post question, "Is Our Grading System Fair?" a no-zero grading policy "allows students to do minimal work and still pass, pushes students forward who haven't mastered the content, and doesn't teach students the real-life consequences of not meeting their responsibilities."[66] Tom Bannon posted, "We are creating a generation of entitled people who are hitting the colleges and the job market with major holes in their abilities to survive." Lara Morales added to the thread, "Zeros don't create holes…kids choosing not to do their work creates holes."[67]

As with many broad policies, I can appreciate both sides of the argument, but overall, I have strong feelings against this policy both as a teacher and a parent. As a teacher of elementary school students, I feel that elementary school should build the foundation of a lifelong learner, including the development of habits of mind (problem-solving and life-related skills). As such, students need to learn early on the importance and responsibility of completing all assignments. If we don't establish this connection early in education, I fear a dangerous pattern and mindset will develop. "I don't need to do this assignment," or "I don't need to study; I'll just take the 50 percent." It sets up an entitlement culture where students see the teacher as a person who "gives out" grades, rather than seeing themselves as a capable person who earns the grades. Students with this mindset aren't associating their grades with their actions, which sadly means they don't understand the incredible power they have to control their own destiny through education.

I have also witnessed students who really put a lot of effort into an assignment but failed, and those who never picked up a pencil for the assignment or simply pushed buttons on a computerized test and ended up with the same grade—50 percent. What message does that send to both students? We've already looked at research that shows that grades, in particular low grades, do not motivate students. I would argue that the effects of the no-zero policy go further than not motivating; they actually discourage effort.

As a teacher, I have another fundamental problem with the no-zero policy. Proponents of this policy argue that grades that include zeroes are not meaningful because they don't truly represent the ability of the student. However, the same claim can be made about grades that include a 50 percent as a replacement for a grade less than 50 percent. How can grades that have been artificially inflated under the policy accurately represent the learner's ability?

You may say that a 20 percent and a 50 percent are both failing grades, so why does the inflation matter? I would say there is a big difference between those scores. A student who earned a 20 percent is far from attaining grade-level understanding, but one who scores a 50 percent is closer to at least developing an understanding of grade-level standards. This may sound like an unrealistic situation, but when you teach in a school where the majority of the school population is below grade level, and you need to target specific interventions to meet students at their ability level in order to help them, the delineation matters.

More than once, I sat in a Student Support Team (SST) meeting trying to convince a parent that their child was struggling in school and had significant gaps in their level of understanding. The parent focused on an overall grade that was often inflated by the 50 percent adjustment (due to the no-zero policy). This policy causes some students to earn Ds and pass a course, rather than fail the course as a consequence of their true ability. A policy that prevents failing grades actually causes educators to fail.

The system is failing our students and their parents when we fail to accurately report the deficiencies in a child's understanding. Again, what good are the rigorous standards under Common Core if we don't accurately report a student's inability to meet those standards and if we don't hold everyone (students, teachers, administrators, parents, etc.) accountable for not meeting the standards?

Accountability and responsibility are the primary reasons that I strongly oppose this policy as a parent. I feel it is my obligation to teach my children to be responsible for their own actions. I have three children. One never had any issues with missing assignments. One had a few missing assignments in middle school but cared enough about the effect on his grades to correct the problem on his own. I'm certain that if the no-zero policy had been in effect when he was younger, he would have perpetuated some habits like procrastination because the effects of those bad habits would have been abated.

I have another child who, unfortunately, was in middle school when these policies started. She struggled with organization and, in general, was apathetic about school. I strongly feel that this policy and other grading policies that we will cover enabled many of her poor learning habits because there were rarely any consequences as a result of not completing the work on time. How is this helping our children?

Think about it like this: the worst thing that can happen if a student fails an assignment or even fails a course in school is a low GPA and, possibly, rejection from a college (which might not be a bad thing if a student has trouble completing assignments). If this child goes into adulthood and fails to show up for their job or complete a job assignment, he or she will likely get fired, which will impair future job opportunities and suffer serious financial consequences, which could affect an entire family.

I believe we are letting our children down by not teaching them the importance of completing responsibilities while they are still able to learn from their mistakes without life-altering outcomes. After all, I've never met an employer who will pay an employee 50 percent of his or her salary for not doing any work.

My arguments and those of other opponents of the policy follow the same logic that caused Leominster Public Schools in Massachusetts to rescind their no-zero policy. Sky View Middle School principal Tim Blake reported to the *Sentinel & Enterprise News*, "We really felt that after years of doing it that way, kids just weren't learning to be responsible."[68] Theresa Mitchell Dudley, president of the Prince George's County Educators' Association, said that "42 to 69 percent of high school teachers who responded to a recent survey voiced concerns about some of the key recommended changes."[69] She went on to say, "We have no problem being fair to students…But if they are not doing the work and not performing, and we give them a grade they did not earn, how does that make them college and career ready?"[70]

BODY OF EVIDENCE—ASSIGNMENTS TO INCLUDE IN GRADE CALCULATION

In addition to the no-zero policy, districts are changing what assignments are allowed to be considered in the computation of a grade. Baltimore County (BCPS) refers to this as a Body of Evidence, "a collection of aligned instructional tasks, such as assignments, assessments, homework, presentation, products, and observations used to determine if a student has met identified curriculum goals."[71]

Effective July 1, 2016, Baltimore County changed its Grading and Reporting Policy to specify that grades should be calculated based on a "body of evidence" that included assignments, tests, discussions, and projects but *not* homework, effort, attendance, and behavior.[72] Parents and students protested so much that the policy was revised in November to specify that tests, projects, and other major assignments should make up a third of a student's grade while "minor summative assignments" should represent the other two-thirds.[73] Minor summative assignments could include classwork, discussions, and "significant homework" assignments.

As with other new BCPS initiatives, this policy wasn't clearly explained to teachers ahead of the rollout, nor was it clearly explained until close to the end of the first quarter in 2016. Teachers avoided conversations with parents about the composition and calculation of grades during their back-to-school meetings in September, because honestly, teachers themselves didn't understand the policy. The irony is that this policy was intended to make grades more equitable, yet the lack of clarity in the policy heightened the level of inconsistency in grades among teachers and schools. While this is unacceptable for all students, imagine how this could affect seniors in high school as they are getting ready to apply to colleges. An upheaval of this magnitude could easily distort grades on a high school transcript.

The "body of evidence" under new grading policies should be multiple representations of a student's ultimate understanding and demonstration of the standards in their grade-level curriculum. "Many school systems are moving toward 'standards-based grading,' which emphasizes evaluating students on what they ultimately learn rather than on work habits, student effort, punctuality, or homework."[74]

Assignments and "exit tickets" (short assessments given at the conclusion of a lesson) that are part of the routine instruction are considered practice items as the student is working toward mastery of the skill. This also means that teachers could no longer deduct points for missing names, missing labels (like units of measurement), or late turn-ins. Those deductions and practice-related assignments were no longer permissible in the calculation of the grade. This is where homework is a gray area. Normally, homework is intended to practice a skill. If this is the case, homework should not be graded.

GRADING HOMEWORK

As an elementary teacher, I was instructed *not* to grade homework. Prior to the new grading policy, I used to assign two points for each homework assignment based on completion and effort, not accuracy. I graded it this way because some students had a lot of support at home in completion of the assignment, while others had none. Some students had parents at home who spoke no English at all and therefore weren't able to assist their child with the homework. Others had parents who would check the answers on the homework and have their child redo any incorrect problems. The two extremes made it unfair to grade those assignments for accuracy. But when you take away a teacher's ability to assign *any* grade at all for the homework, you take away many children's incentive to do the homework.

I found this to be particularly true for students in the below-average classes. In fact, on average, only 30 percent of my students in the below-average classes would attempt to do the homework once it stopped counting toward a grade, and yet, these children needed the extra practice the most. Not only was this frustrating because I only assigned homework that I felt would help improve their understanding, but it made going over the homework answers in class a waste of time for two-thirds of the students. It was precious time that we could not afford to lose. As much as I tried to explain to the parents and students the connection between doing your homework and improving test performance, many didn't get it. I even had a parent once yell at me, "Why are you telling me my child isn't completing the homework when it isn't graded?"

Ideally, we would want students to be intrinsically motivated to do their homework in pursuit of understanding, but the reality is that it doesn't always work that way. I think we are expecting a higher level of thinking from elementary students to make that connection on their own. (If some of their parents aren't making that connection, why would they?) I have heard many educators question the value of homework and emphasize voluntary reading, playing games with their families, and outdoor play over time spent on homework assigned by their teachers.

I agree that at the elementary level, those things are very important, but most of the children I taught came from homes where those things weren't happening. Some children were alone in apartments until their parents could get home from work around dinner time. The children weren't allowed to play outside while their parents weren't home. These children spent most of their after-school hours playing video games indoors—so why not give students a minimal amount of homework to practice some skills that they desperately need to learn?

ASSIGNMENT REDO OPPORTUNITIES

The same "standards-based philosophy" is the premise behind allowing students to redo assignments and turn them in late without penalty. Kevin Hickerson, the president-elect of the Fairfax Education Association, supports policies that encourage students to keep trying and redoing assignments "because, in the end, all teachers are about making sure that students have had proficiency or mastered a concept."[75] In Baltimore County, redoing assignments was part of the 2017 grading policy changes. As a teacher, I understand the idealism behind the policy—it may motivate students to improve their understanding if they have another opportunity to demonstrate it and improve their grades.

And there are times where I have witnessed a student who is really not in the best mental state to take an assessment on the day it is given; either they don't feel well, something happened at home to upset them, they are excessively tired, or they didn't take their medication. In those cases, a redo is necessary to get an accurate measure of their understanding (and in some cases, I gave redos for this reason, before it became a policy).

But the practice of offering multiple redo opportunities to an entire class is cumbersome for a teacher, in particular when the teacher has no choice but to give the redo during regular instruction time. This was the case at my school, and I would guess at many schools where students have no other transportation to or from school other than the school bus. This presents a dilemma—redos can't be given outside of instruction time without inequity toward some students. Unfortunately, instructors then have to weigh the benefit of a redo versus the cost of that lost instruction time.

From a teacher perspective, redo opportunities often necessitate second editions of assessments because it wouldn't be fair to allow students a second chance to answer the same question, particularly if you have gone over the answers to those questions in class. The teacher's responsibilities then are doubled: (1) to create a new assessment and (2) to grade the original assessment and the redo assessment.

From a parent perspective, I appreciate an *occasional* opportunity for my child to retake an assessment. However, as was my concern with the no-zero policy, I do not want my child to assume that there will always or often be the possibility of a redo. I feel that it sends a message, "Don't worry about doing it right the first time; you can do it again." Life just doesn't work that way. When you interview for a college or a job, you have one opportunity to leave an impression. No matter what job you have, you often have one chance to prove your capability and sincerity.

Imagine a server at a fast-food restaurant. That server may be the first impression a customer has with the eating establishment. A bad first impression may lose that customer forever. Even in cases where you can redo an exam—like the SATs, the CPA exam, or the Bar exam—there is a cost associated with a redo in terms of money, time, and potentially a lost opportunity in the interim.

As a parent, I want my child to understand that redos are not guaranteed, and you should strive to get it right the first time. I have heard plenty of students, including my own child, say, "It's alright; if I don't do well the first time, I'll take a redo." That's not the message we should be sending when trying to foster responsibility and accountability in our young people.

EQUITY ISSUES

We still haven't addressed the issue of equity with respect to traditional grading policies and new grading policies. Joe Feldman, CEO of the Crescendo Education Group and a former high school teacher, principal, and central office administrator, believes that equity is the most compelling reason to move to a standards-based grading approach.[76]

Feldman has found that teachers have inconsistent grading criteria, including how they weigh the scores, penalize late work, count extra credit, allow for retakes, include homework, etc.

Feldman believes these inconsistencies have implications for equity in schools because many times, these practices punish students with fewer resources.[77] For this reason, Feldman proposes eliminating extra credit, participation grades, and group work grades and recommends redo opportunities where the teacher only records the higher score. Other practical strategies to eliminate problems with equity include grading student work without looking at the student's name (much like a blind study) and using rubrics to ensure consistency.[78]

As a teacher of a very diverse group of students, I can agree with some of the concerns surrounding equity. That's why I graded homework only based on completion and effort (demonstrated by showing his or her work to support the answer). As a parent, I can also appreciate some of the concerns with consistency. They are both valid concerns. But I don't necessarily believe that we need to completely eliminate all components of the traditional grading policy and recreate a new one.

Grading assignments without regard to the name of the student and using rubrics are very easy things to implement that have benefits beyond ensuring equity. Allowing for some retakes is manageable and is justifiable when a student has shown evidence (that is not subjective) of improvement. But, to ensure consistency, teachers within a school should agree on the criteria to justify a redo (which could include consistent homework completion) and timing of the redos to avoid disruption to instruction.

And if you are really interested in grades reflecting mastery of a standard, then why only record the higher of two scores in a redo? If the student scores lower on the redo, then maybe that student didn't retain the information, which means they really didn't learn that standard. The same is true with the no-zero policy. "Giving" an unearned 50 percent distorts the reality of the student's ability and effort. **We can't alter grading policies just to prevent students from failing, because ultimately, that will only increase the achievement gap as students are pushed through the system and enter college without the skills and work habits necessary to be successful.** As Ethan Hutt, an assistant professor of teaching and learning, policy, and leadership at the University of Maryland, College Park, says, "Students do need to learn to be conscientious, responsible, hardworking and to seek help."[79] In his experience, those are the students who succeed. In my experience as a mother and a teacher, I agree.

QUESTIONS TO ASK IN CONVERSATIONS ABOUT GRADING POLICIES

- How is the grading policy affecting the accountability and responsibility of the student in regard to assignment completion and effort?
- What does your school do to ensure consistency in the grading policy at each grade level and within the school as a whole?
- How do you ensure that within a district, all schools are applying the grading policies consistently?
- How closely do the students' grades align with their abilities?
- Is there a way to record an average based on all of a students' true grades and one that adjusts for the no-zero policy? This way, parents and students could see how effort impacts the grades. For the GPA calculation, maybe you use the adjusted grade for the first half of the year and the traditional grade (without the adjustment for the grades below 50 percent) for the second half of the year.

- What policies are in place to help ensure grading equity? Are these policies being applied consistently? How do you know?
- Should districts have different grading policies for their elementary, middle, and high schools?
- Do or can students receive descriptive feedback as an alternative to evaluative feedback—even if only on certain assignments or at certain times within the marking period? Perhaps for the first quarter?
- What opportunities are provided for redos, and what can be done to limit their interference with instruction time?
- Should the redo grade be the final grade, or should teachers only accept the higher of either the original grade or the redo?
- What incentives can a school/district put in place as a prerequisite to qualify for a redo that will ensure students have "earned" the opportunity (possibly a 95 percent homework completion rate and/or good behavior)?

ROBIN

Robin was a petite African American girl with dark, expressive eyes, dark hair, and a beautiful, large smile. However, shortly after the school year began, I noticed that Robin was smiling a little less each day. That smile began to be replaced by an attitude toward me and her work. She began occasionally distracting other students, and she became more off-task. She was spending more time being social than doing her work. I was beginning to get the impression that Robin was just one of "those" students who didn't care much about school.

I communicated with Robin's mom by writing notes back and forth in her planner and talking with her on the phone. Her mother was very concerned about Robin academically and genuinely wanted to help her daughter to be successful in school. She was also very supportive of the efforts that I was making in class to send the right signals to Robin about the importance of work and effort.

One day during class, I could see how embarrassed Robin was when it was her turn to give an answer. I had already noticed from her work that her math skills were low, but it was evident by her embarrassment how much she recognized her own struggles. This is when I first realized how much Robin really cared. She wasn't apathetic about school at all. The off-task behaviors were just attempts to distract herself and those around her from the fact that she couldn't do the work. It was a revelation that made me see Robin in a whole new light.

I pulled Robin aside one morning after I had dropped the rest of her class off at the library, and we sat and talked. I told her my reasons for wanting to become a math teacher and shared my personal struggles with math as a child. I explained that every day became worse than the day before. Every time I was in class, I would feel like I was going to throw up because I was just so lost that I didn't know where to begin. I told Robin how bad I had felt about myself, but then, I just started trying and asking questions when I didn't understand something. Gradually the math started to make sense to me.

For the first time since the very beginning of the year, I saw those beautiful eyes of hers looking at me again, this time with tears in them. She knew at that moment that I understood her and believed in her. I also think that she could sense my authenticity, which seemed to earn her trust. I went on to tell Robin that I could see that math was hard for her and that I really wanted to and could help her, but only if she gave me a chance and worked with me. She agreed, and from that moment on, I had a completely different student in my class. Her mom noticed the change as well and called to ask if I knew why Robin now liked school. I shared with her mom our conversation.

Robin went on to finish up the year with a much better understanding of math than she had when she began fourth grade. But I'm not taking credit for it. It was all because of her. It was her attitude and effort.

I will never forget Robin because she was the first student whom I saw such a dramatic change in, and yet I would never have suspected at the beginning of the year that Robin would be "the one." The one who really stands out at the end of the year. The one whom I really helped. The one for whom I made a difference. What Robin taught me was not to ever judge a student based on how you see them acting in class and to never judge their abilities based on what you see at the beginning of the year. Sometimes it's the students who seem like they don't care who may care the most. You never know what's keeping a student from engaging and being successful.

At the end of the year, we had an awards ceremony that parents could attend. Robin's mother came up to me afterward and was crying. The surrounding communities had been redistricted, and next year, Robin would be attending a new elementary school. Her mother said she wished that I would be going to the new school because I had made such a difference for her daughter. Funny thing was...it was actually her daughter who made a huge difference for me.

ENGLISH LANGUAGE LEARNERS

Look Past the Policies

This past fall, I substituted for a fourth-grade teacher in an elementary school. As I was walking around the classroom to make sure that everyone was on-task, I noticed an Asian boy sitting silently at his desk but not doing any of the same work that the rest of the class was assigned. I stopped to ask him why, but one of his classmates told me that he didn't speak any English, and clearly that was the case by his lack of response to any of my questions. So I asked his tablemates, "What does your teacher have him do?" The answer was, "He keeps busy with a workbook." That workbook appeared to be on a kindergarten level.

Now, I admittedly did not know the background of this situation. I didn't know how long the student had been in this class, in this school, or even how long he had been in this country. What I did know was that a young boy who appeared to be the same age as his classmates—ten—sat the entire time I was in that classroom without having any communication with his peers or me and without doing any grade-level work. Ironically, as lonely as this may sound, he isn't alone. Every day, there are many students who don't speak English at all or have limited English speaking ability who are attending our schools and spending at least the majority of their day as passive "onlookers" in the education process.

I know this because I, too, have had some of those students in my classroom as a teacher. While the majority had at least some English-speaking ability, I had one who was just like this boy. She didn't speak any English, and as her teacher, I struggled to find meaningful work for her to do because children shouldn't spend seven hours, five days a week, doing "busywork." It is unfair to these children to confuse struggles in a non-native language with an inability to learn at a cognitively age-appropriate level.

According to Pew Research, in 1960, only 5.4 percent of the US population or 9.7 million people were foreign-born; but as of 2018, those figures have more than quadrupled to 44.8 million or 13.7 percent.[80] In 2018, roughly half of those immigrants come from Latin America or Mexico, and 28 percent come from Asia.[81] "Based on census data, Pew Research Center projects that the first- and second-generation immigrant segment of the American population will swell to 37 percent by 2050, compared with 15 percent back in 1965."[82]

These data and future projections are important considerations for issues affecting today's educational policies, student population, instruction, and academic performance. According to the National Center for Education Statistics, as of fall 2015, US public schools had close to five million English language learners (ELLs) representing close to 10 percent of the student population.[83]

"ELLs," sometimes called ELs or English Learners, is a broad term used to describe students who have limited English proficiency. Two-thirds of the ELL students are in the elementary grades (K–5), with the remaining one-third in grades six through twelve.[84] According to the National Education Association (NEA), "The ELL population is the fastest-growing population of public school students in the US. From 1990–1991 to the 2000–2001 school year, ELL enrollment has grown by more than 105 percent in the United States, compared with only a 12 percent growth of total student enrollment during the same period."[85]

ELLs represent such a significant portion of the student population that we can't ignore looking at how they are impacting education and how education is impacting them. But before we dive deeper into the composition of students, languages, and programs to assist them, we must take a look at federal laws that outline our responsibility to these students and influence how to carry out that responsibility.

1964—THE CIVIL RIGHTS ACT

The Civil Rights Act of 1964, while not specific to immigrants or ELLs, prohibits discrimination based on race, color, religion, sex, or national origin.[86] This law put an end to racial segregation in our schools, and while that may have been targeted to African Americans, it applies to all school students, including first- and second-generation ELL students.

1965—ELEMENTARY AND SECONDARY EDUCATION ACT (ESEA)

"This law brought education to the forefront of the national assault on poverty and represented a landmark commitment to equal access to quality education."[87] "Equal access" means that every child residing in this country is entitled to a good public education. Since its enactment, the law has been reauthorized every five years with some revisions and amendments.[88]

1968—BILINGUAL EDUCATION ACT (AKA TITLE VII OF ESEA)

Title VII, or the Bilingual Education Act of 1968, encouraged schools receiving funds to use Transitional Bilingual Programs in an effort to move students toward attainment of English proficiency.[89] Funding included grants for resources, training, materials, and parent involvement projects.[90] The act was ultimately repealed by No Child Left Behind in 2002, but the Bilingual Education Act was the first "official federal recognition of the needs of students with limited English speaking abilities."[91]

1974—EQUAL EDUCATIONAL OPPORTUNITY ACT

This act established that no state "shall deny equal educational opportunities to an individual on account of race, color, sex, or national origin, by the failure by an educational agency to take appropriate action to overcome language barriers that impede equal participation."[92]

The Equal Educational Opportunity Act was an extension of the 1974 Supreme Court's ruling on a case known as *Lau v. Nichols*. This was a class-action lawsuit brought against the San Francisco school district, alleging that 1,800 limited English proficient (LEP) Chinese students had been denied their civil rights—equal education—even though the LEP students had been given the same resources (facilities, teachers, textbooks, etc.) as their classmates.[93] The Supreme Court ruled in favor of the LEP students because those resources weren't meaningful to students with limited English proficiency.

The court's decision upheld the principle that "where the inability to speak and understand the English language excludes national origin-minority group children from effective participation in the educational program offered by a school district, the district must take affirmative steps to rectify the language deficiency."[94]

There have been many legislative amendments in regard to ELLs since the 1965 Elementary and Secondary Education Act and the 1968 Bilingual Education Act, but the basic intent remains the same: to provide a quality education and to help ELLs reach English proficiency.

ILLEGAL AND LEGAL (STUDENT) IMMIGRANTS

One other point before we look at ELL programs in schools today. It seems that most of the controversy over immigration today centers around illegal immigration. According to the Pew Research Center, among the public school population of students who are not English proficient, 72 percent were born in the US, and of the 28 percent remaining, **only 23 percent are not US citizens** (the other 5 percent were born abroad to American parents and thus are naturalized citizens).[95] Therefore, **the majority of students who need this extra support in our schools are US citizens.**

Furthermore, no matter how you personally feel about children who are not here legally in this country, the Supreme Court has ruled in *Plyler v. Doe* (1982) that states "cannot constitutionally deny students a free public education on account of their immigration status."[96] The court based its ruling on the US Constitution's Fourteenth Amendment, the Equal Protection Clause. The court explained that "education has a fundamental role in maintaining the fabric of our society" and "provides the basic tools by which individuals might lead economically productive lives to the benefit of us all."[97]

As Justice Blackmun noted, "When a state provides an education to some and denies it to others, it immediately and inevitably creates class distinctions of a type fundamentally inconsistent with the purposes of the Equal Protection Clause because an uneducated child is denied even the opportunity to achieve."[98]

COMPOSITION OF ELLS IN THE UNITED STATES

According to the National Center for Education Statistics, in the fall of 2016, 4.9 million (9.6 percent) of public school students were classified as ELLs.[99] There were nine states whose ELL population was 10 percent or higher in their public schools: California had 20.2 percent; Texas had 17.2 percent; and Nevada had 15.9 percent.[100] Eighteen states and DC had percentages that were between 6 and 10 percent while only eight states had percentages less than 3 percent.[101] Most are concentrated in urbanized areas and most are in the elementary grades—which also reflects that some have obtained English language proficiency by the time they reach the upper grades. As of fall 2016, about 3.8 million (roughly 75 percent) ELL students spoke Spanish, followed by Arabic (129,400), Chinese (104,100), and Vietnamese (78,700), and there remains a broad range of other languages spoken.[102]

IDENTIFYING STUDENTS AS ELL

When a student registers in a school, they are identified as ELL by a simple, low-cost method: a take-home survey.[103] The survey gathers information to determine if the student's primary and home language is something other than English. Then the districts must determine "if potential EL students are in fact EL through a valid and reliable test that assesses English language proficiency in speaking, listening, reading and writing."[104] Those students identified as English Learners are then entitled to services, but their parents can op -out of the district's EL program or opt out of a particular service within that program if they choose. Even then, a school district "must still take steps to provide opted out EL students with access to its educational programs, monitor their progress, and offer EL services again if a student is struggling."[105]

EDUCATION PROGRAMS FOR ELLS

Under Title VI of the Civil Rights Act of 1964 and the Equal Educational Opportunities Act of 1974, "public schools must ensure that EL students can participate meaningfully and equally in educational programs."[106] School districts can choose among programs designed for ELLs, provided the "program is educationally sound in theory and effective in practice."[107]

There are currently three service programs that districts choose from to provide services to their ELLs: English as a Second Language (commonly called ESL), Transitional Bilingual (sometimes just called Bilingual), and Dual Language (often called Dual Immersion). Each one has some pros and cons.

English as a Second Language (ESL) places students by their chronological age into a mainstream classroom. They are immersed into an English-speaking classroom along with other ELL students who may speak a different language and then pulled out for intense English instruction at a beginner's level. "ESL stresses simplified speech and uses visual or physical cues, memorization, and drills...Instruction is all about getting kids to function in English as quickly as possible and spend little time on a child's native language."[108]

According to research, this is the most widely used program, but it may be the most costly and least effective.[109] This model of instruction requires extra resource teachers who have ESL credentials, though the ESL teachers do not actually need to be able to speak the foreign language themselves. There are two notable disadvantages of this program: First, students miss out on instruction (like math and science) when they are pulled out for ESL instruction.

Second, students with very low levels of English language understanding suffer academically because they can't understand the content instruction in their non-native language. This simply means that they miss out on learning academics (such as math) that they are probably capable of learning, just because they don't fully understand the language in which those subjects are being taught. The advantages are that students are immersed in the English language, and students are not segregated from their peers or segregated by national origin, thus conforming to the Civil Rights Act of 1964.

Another ELL program is based on the transitional bilingual instruction model. "In this model, a teacher who is fluent in both English and the student's native language builds on that child's language for at least two to three years."[110] The ELL student is given instruction in their native language in all subject areas as well as intense instruction on the English language like the ESL program. The goal is to help transition the students to English language instruction within two to three years, but some believe the timeframe is insufficient for academic purposes.[111]

The primary advantage of this program is that students are maintaining or growing their academic proficiency in subject areas that are taught in their native language. This prevents the problem of falling behind academically because they don't understand the language of instruction. The primary disadvantage of this program is that the ELL students are being segregated based on national origin, a violation of the Civil Rights Act.

The Department of Justice and the US Department of Education state, "School districts generally may not segregate students on the basis of national origin or EL status. Although certain EL programs may be designed to require that EL students receive separate instruction for a limited portion of the day or period of time, school districts and states are expected to carry out their chosen program in the least segregative manner consistent with achieving the program's stated educational goals."[112] So this is a very slippery slope.

The last option for ELL instruction is the Dual Language Immersion program. Under this model, the students in the class are made up of English and ELL students. Instruction (in all subjects) is given in both languages so that part of the school day is in English, and the other part is the native language of the ELLs. This model is "designed to engage students with their native language as well as the English language in an inclusive environment…The classroom dynamics are changed to reflect collaborative learning in which ELLs help native English speakers to grasp the curriculum, and English speakers help ELLs to acquire the curriculum through English."[113]

The Dual Language model is very promising because it has a high success rate and is cost-efficient.[114] The other positives include that ELLs are not held back on achieving academic proficiency because of language issues as much as under the ESL (pull-out) model; English-speaking students have the opportunity to learn another language; and this model supports total inclusion—there is no segregation of students. However, in order for this to work, the teacher must be fluent in both languages,[115] which is difficult to achieve because our ELL population is very diverse and speaks many different languages.

Finally, the sad reality is that some of these students receive no instructional support at all and are left to flounder through our educational system. I suspect many get passed on from one grade to the next or drop out early as supported in data collected by the US Department of Education.[116] The article, "Research Talking Points on English Language Learners," reported that approximately 15 percent of ELLs receive no special instruction or program to meet their language and content-area needs, and only 8 percent of ELLs receive extensive instruction—ten or more hours of ESL instruction and modified content instruction.[117]

The point in sharing the three different instructional models is to prove that there isn't a one-size-fits-all solution. There doesn't appear to be a perfect solution that satisfies all of our legal requirements *and* meets the needs of all students (ELL and native English speaking). All three solutions come at a financial cost. Funding for all of the ELL programs is mostly derived from state and local sources because federal education funding, on average, only represents about 11 percent of total education costs incurred by the district.[118]

Research on the costs associated with each instructional model varies even across sites using the same model.[119] However, on average, a 20 percent increase in per-student cost is associated with each ELL student.[120] Among the different models, the primary source of expenses is associated with the special resources staff, teachers, and administrative staff.

TEACHER TRAINING AND CONFIDENCE IN WORKING WITH ELLS

And that poses more critical questions: Even with appropriate funding, do we have the right human resources to satisfy the learning needs of the ELL student population? How equipped are the teachers to meet the demands of the ELL students while managing the demands of their other students?

The US Department of Justice and the US Department of Education specifically state that "EL students are entitled to EL programs with sufficient resources to ensure the programs are effectively implemented, including highly qualified teachers, support staff, and appropriate instructional materials,"[121] yet the reality is that qualified teachers are a scarce resource and training is insufficient.

In 2016, thirty-two states reported not having enough teachers for their ELL students.[122] According to the National Center for Education Statistics (NCES)—only 2.5 percent of teachers who instruct ELL students have a degree in ESL or bilingual education.[123] Furthermore, the NCES (2002) found that "of the 41 percent of teachers nationwide with ELLs in their classrooms, only 12.5 percent participated in eight or more hours of professional development related to ELLs in the past three years. Fewer than 8 percent of teachers reported eight or more hours of ELL-specific professional development in seven states where more than one third (41 percent) of teachers were teaching ELLs."[124]

Insufficient training supports Renner's findings (2011) that teachers lack the confidence to meet the needs of their linguistically challenged students.[125] Most ELLs are in mainstream classrooms (using the ESL pull-out model of instruction), and the mainstream teachers are inadequately trained to support their needs throughout the day.[126] I personally recall only one training that I attended in my seven years of teaching ELL students that was specifically targeted to improve instruction for ELLs, and I don't recall any course during my master's education program that was entirely devoted to ELL instruction.

The data clearly shows that we have a large number of ELL students, limited financial resources, limited qualified human resources, and instructional programs of which none perfectly satisfy the legal requirements and meet the academic and linguistic needs of the students. The best way to measure our effectiveness in meeting the needs of the ELL students is to look at how long students are classified as ELLs (meaning they haven't achieved English proficiency), how they are scoring on state standardized tests and on national assessments like the NAEP (National Assessment of Educational Progress), and graduation rates.

NATIONAL ELL MEASURES OF PROFICIENCY

According to the US Department of Justice and the US Department of Education, "School districts must monitor the progress of all EL students to ensure they achieve English language proficiency and acquire content knowledge within a reasonable period of time. Districts must annually administer a valid and reliable English language proficiency (ELP) assessment in reading, writing, listening, and speaking, that is aligned to state ELP standards."[127] Once an EL student demonstrates proficiency, he or she is exited from the program and monitored for two years afterward to make sure that they truly are language proficient.

The US Department of Education reported, "Nationally, [only] 14 percent of ELs in grade 4 were at or above proficient in mathematics, and 9 percent were at or above proficient in reading on the 2017 NAEP. A smaller percentage of ELs were at or above proficient in reading and mathematics in grade 8."[128] Although EL performance has improved overall since 2000 in both reading and math, more recent years have shown little change. Furthermore, proficiency of ELs lags far behind their non-EL peers in every subject and grade.[129]

The Department of Education reported that in 2015–2016, 84 percent of students nationwide graduated from high school within four years compared to the ELLs' graduation rate of 67 percent.[130] These lower graduation rates translate into fewer opportunities for employment and higher wages. With that being said, we have a lot of work to do to improve the opportunities for the ELL population.

ELLS IN MARYLAND AND BCPS

While the ELL population has been increasing nationwide, here in Maryland, it is growing at an even faster rate. ELL enrollment grew 4.9 percentage points in Maryland between 1998 and 2015, while it only increased 3.3 percentage points in the US during that same time period.[131] Maryland is among the top twenty-five states with the largest proportions of ELL students.[132] Data collected by the Maryland State Department of Education between the years 2016 and 2017 show that while three-fourths of Maryland ELs speak Spanish, Maryland ELs speak over two hundred languages other than English,[133] which, if you recall the different instructional models to assist ELLs, makes a dual language program difficult to implement.

In Maryland, students identified as EL are assessed annually using the WIDA ACCESS for ELLs until they score high enough to be reclassified as English proficient. Maryland students are expected to take no longer than six years to achieve English language proficiency.[134] Yet, according to the Migration Policy Institute, in 2017, less than half (48 percent) of Maryland ELs achieved proficiency within the six years.[135] The state has a goal of reaching 74 percent by the school year 2029–2030.[136]

Just like the rest of the nation, Maryland has a long way to go before closing the education gap between ELL students and all students. For the school year 2016–2017, Maryland ELLs scored thirty-three to forty-one points lower than all students in grades three through nine that met or exceeded the English Language Arts standards as measured by the PARCC tests.[137] There were considerable gaps in the PARCC math results as well, ranging from fifteen to forty-six points.[138] But the most disturbing measure might be the graduation rates. Only 45 percent of Maryland's ELLs graduated in the 2015–2016 school year compared to the national ELL graduation rate of 67 percent and the national all-student graduation rate of 84 percent.[139]

According to the Maryland Equity Project, 95 percent of Maryland's ELL students are enrolled in eight districts.[140] Baltimore County Public Schools (BCPS) is one of them.[141] BCPS has experienced a 130 percent increase of ELL students over the past ten years, including a 12 percent jump between January 2018 and January 2019.[142] Over the past five years, Baltimore County has added about 5,000 students—"More than half of those new students, about 3,500, [were] recent immigrants or children whose families speak another language…[In 2019], such students make up 6.7 percent of county enrollment."[143] Most of the foreign-born students within BCPS are coming from Central America, but in total, they come from 116 countries and speak ninety-seven different languages.[144]

MY EXPERIENCE TEACHING ELLS

During my seven years of teaching at Raven Elementary, I saw a significant increase in the number of Hispanic students and EL students. For example, when I began in 2012, Raven had an EL population less than 5 percent. By the academic year ending in 2019, Raven's EL population represented 16.6 percent of the school.[145]

Throughout my seven years at Raven, I taught various EL students from different origins—not all were Hispanic, though they represented the majority. Three of those years, I was specifically assigned a homeroom/math class with a large concentration of EL students, ranging from 10 to 33 percent. Overall, these children and their families were kind, hardworking, and appreciative. If you read the stories of certain students who had the biggest impact on me throughout my time teaching, you will notice that four out of five are children of immigrants.

For the most part, I truly enjoyed working with ELL students. But while the majority of my ELL students were very kind and respectful toward their peers and me, those who were not could be very challenging to deal with. One of my fourth-grade ELL students lit the school's bathroom trash can on fire at least once (he didn't admit to the second lighting), was found in possession of a pocket knife, and was openly recruiting members for a gang to which he and his older brother (enrolled in middle school) allegedly were members.

Unlike children whose parents are native English speakers, it is much more difficult to maintain ongoing, consistent communication with the ELL parents and, therefore, more of a challenge to inform them of discipline issues as they occur before they become too serious. In essence, if an ELL student has a behavior problem, it's harder to figure out what's causing the problem and work with the parent to resolve it quickly *before* it becomes an issue for that child or other students.

Many of the children coming into the Baltimore County system are natives of El Salvador, Honduras, Nigeria, Guatemala, and Pakistan.[146] Some are coming from situations where they routinely observed and/ or experienced violence. For example, my ELL student who lit the trash can on fire witnessed his father's murder. Children who have grown up in this culture are bringing some of their fears, aggression, and survival skills into our American school system *without* the benefit of mental health care. If we are inviting these students into our school system, we need to be prepared to identify early on any social-emotional issues and then to provide immediate intervention to help that child assimilate and to protect the other students in school.

Academically, we are failing a majority of the ELL students. In Baltimore County, we use the ESL academic model. Incoming students are identified as ELLs through the home survey and then placed into a mainstream classroom based on their chronological age, not based on educational experience, academic proficiency, or English proficiency.

Just as I mentioned at the beginning of this chapter—I once taught a ten-year-old girl who spoke absolutely no English. She and her family spoke only Spanish. She had no school experience prior to her arrival in the US, so not only was she lacking knowledge in all academic subjects, but she had never experienced being in a school setting for seven hours a day—eating in a large cafeteria, walking in lines in the hallway, taking turns using the bathroom, using a computer, sharing supplies, and maintaining focus and effort for such a long period of time.

Consequently, she had to learn classroom social structure and behavioral expectations along with English. It was a challenge for her and for me as the instructor. I had to figure out what she knew, which was no more than basic addition of one-digit numbers, and then try to fill in the gaps enough to help her make some sense of the fourth-grade curriculum that I was teaching in whole-group instruction. I found myself taking time away from planning my fourth-grade instruction to find things for her on a kindergarten/first-grade level in Spanish (for both math and science). I also had to teach her how to behave in a school setting. She was very playful, and I'm sure quite bored since she didn't understand anything, so she would seek out the other students' attention by throwing objects at them, kicking them as she walked by, or showing them sexually explicit photos that she found on the internet.

Raven had two part-time ESL instructors. Both were talented and dedicated—using every opportunity possible to pull the EL students in small groups. Unfortunately, there are just too few of these teachers to meet the demands of this growing population. It is not uncommon for one ESL teacher to be split between two elementary schools and provide services to seventy or more students. If an ESL teacher's schedule gets disrupted due to snow days, early closings, illness, or testing, it's not always possible to provide make-up services.

The ELL students whom I taught usually were pulled twice a week for ESL instruction. That meant that they missed part of math and all of science class two out of five days a week. ESL teachers many times "push-in" to the English Language Arts classes to help the ELL students within the context of the class, but there usually isn't any assistance to the math classes or content classes like science—again, the result of heavy demands with too few ESL teachers.

I have been amazed at how quickly many of these students pick up on English. But I have to question if we couldn't be doing more for these students to expedite the English proficiency and to accelerate their academic knowledge in all content areas at the same time. Many of these students lag behind academically, and they really don't receive much support for those academic deficiencies other than what their regular teacher provides within the context of their class.

In my school, for example, 25.9 percent of all grade-four students were proficient in ELA compared to less than 6 percent of fourth-grade EL students. The gap was even greater for math proficiency, where 28.7 percent of all fourth-grade math students were proficient compared to, again, less than 6 percent of their ELL peers.

ELL students are just as bright and capable as any other student. But those new to this country often come without a strong academic foundation, and all of the ELL students have the disadvantage of learning new academic content in their non-native language. Most of these students have no help available at home because their parents don't speak English.

In fact, lots of those parents look to their children for help navigating through an English-speaking community, which requires these children to take on a lot of adult responsibilities outside of school. I had one student who rarely completed her homework. When I asked her why, she told me that she needed to help with her family's cleaning business after school. As educators, we have to understand the background and home life of our ELL students so that we can balance cultural sensitivity with their academic needs.

There are many things that I've learned on my own about ELL students and their families over the past seven years. One common problem was how to communicate basic student responsibilities and deadlines. My district provided field-trip forms and many other schoolwide notices in the child's native language, but not every form of communication is translated. As a teacher, I liked to communicate often with my parents to let them know where we were in the curriculum, how they could help at home, and to make them aware of upcoming tests and projects. This was an unmet challenge with the ELL students. Teachers need resources other than language apps on their phones to foster better communication with the ESL parents so that we can work together.

Finally, we need to be realistic about the increased demands on our districts with so many ELL students enrolling in our schools. Here in Baltimore County, enrollment at many schools is exceeding capacity, requiring trailers to take the place of regular classrooms. The high school near my home has around eleven trailers needed for additional classrooms. Raven Elementary was built in 2005, yet it already exceeded capacity when I started there in September 2012.

Parents don't realize the impact that an overcrowded school has on instruction and safety. While the classrooms may be housed in trailers, students still need to access the main school building for lunch, physical education, the library, the nurse, and usually for the bathrooms (some trailers do include a single-use bathroom). This means that the bathrooms and hallways are usually overcrowded, increasing the time to transition between classes, and often decreasing the actual time students have to eat their lunch because the cafeteria lines are so long. In a school such as Raven, where most students use a school bus for transportation to and from school, an excess number of students necessitates ending instruction earlier to prepare for dismissal.

Overcrowding also presents problems for faculty parking and student parking—as in the case of high schools. And let's not neglect to address perhaps the biggest issue with overcrowding: safety. Trailers present safety hazards for many reasons. There's no buffer between visitors and the trailers (even though the trailer doors are supposed to be locked). Students traveling between the main school building and the trailers are more vulnerable, and the school building itself becomes more at risk to intruders entering during these transitions. Trailers are not viable substitutes for school buildings that house students within the capacity guidelines. We have to come up with better solutions because ALL of the students and teachers deserve it.

I realize that some of my observations about ELLs in our schools sound negative because I'm highlighting problems that I see or have experienced. Let me be clear. **The problems are not with the children themselves; the problems are with the system**—an antiquated system that includes facilities, instructors, and curriculums not equipped for the volume and diversity of its current and future occupants. A system that also has to operate within the confines of laws, such as laws on segregation that were written to protect students, but which may have consequences that prohibit cost-effective solutions and deny ELL students opportunities to help maintain or improve their academic proficiency while their English proficiency develops.

No matter how or why these children are here, we have an obligation to educate them *as well as* the students who are already here (yes, let's not forget them in our effort to improve education for the ELL subgroup). We need ways for teachers to communicate with the parents on a regular, ongoing basis about behavior and academic issues before either one interferes with that student's or his or her classmate's ability to learn. We need to assess not only the English proficiency level of incoming ELL students but also what their emotional/social needs are and to provide the necessary assistance to the student and their teacher.

We need to consider other ELL instruction models and hire/train the appropriate instructors as necessary. We need to provide more resources (in terms of people, training, and time) for teachers who have ELL students in their classrooms with either academic gaps or low English proficiency levels. And we need to make certain that *no one's* academic needs or safety are being compromised in the process.

Some of the problems shouldn't be that difficult to address, but most require additional funds for which we need to identify a source. I don't have the answers on how to pay for these reforms. I just don't see how things will improve for *any* of our students if we don't do something; because when the ELL students' needs aren't being met, all students in that class are affected, and ultimately, society is impacted as well.

QUESTIONS TO ASK IN CONVERSATIONS ABOUT ELLS

- What can schools do to ensure that ELL students gain academic proficiency concurrently with language proficiency?

- If schools want to use the transitional bilingual program for their ELL students, what do they need to do to ensure civil law compliance?

- Can we modify the laws to protect civil liberties but allow appropriate segregation to more effectively educate our ELL students? Is it possible to build a "temporary" separate school for ELL students (just until they have language proficiency), which also would help with the overcrowding issue?

- Can we screen incoming ELL students for emotional/mental health problems and provide immediate counseling if needed?

- Can each school have a person designated as a translator to help teachers communicate with the parents on a routine basis?

- How can we provide better training and help our teachers with a large number of ELL students?

- How can we incentivize teachers to obtain the ELL credentials so that we have more ELL teachers?

- If we continue to use the ESL instructional model, can we place students in classes using another determinant other than chronological age, such as academic proficiency and/or language proficiency?

- If we use the ESL instructional model, can we provide resources (as needed) to those students to help improve their academic proficiency?

MARCOS

Marcos's story is important on many levels because it represents something much bigger than Marcos himself. It shows how judgments (on both sides) can interfere with our ability to help each other.

Marcos was a ten-year-old boy who was born in this country to illegal immigrants. I didn't know this officially for more than half of the school year. I did, however, know that neither parent spoke English. Marcos's ability to speak English was pretty good—much better than his math abilities, which were about two years behind where they should have been.

Marcos was a very kind boy to his classmates and very respectful to his teachers. He seemed young in terms of academics, and he looked young compared to some of his classmates. He had dark, wavy hair and large, expressive, dark eyes. He would listen attentively when I was giving instructions to the whole class, and he would work well with me in small-group, but he frequently lost focus and got off-task when it came to independent practice—most certainly because he had difficulty doing grade-level work.

Two days before winter break, Marcos was talking when he should have been quiet, and this continued even after he had received a verbal warning. As a consequence, I gave him what we call a "level" in his planner. Raven's behavior policy was a five-tiered system. Each tier was referred to as a level, basically indicating a form of misconduct.

Marcos only had one mark in his planner: just the warning level, and a note next to it from me to explain to the parent what prompted the level. Once it was given, the behavior was corrected, and I forgot all about it. At Raven, levels were frequently given out to students for all kinds of behaviors. As far as I knew, Marcos had never gotten one from me before, and I don't believe he had received any from other teachers yet that year.

The day after, Marcos came to school, and as part of our normal routine, I went around in the morning to make sure that students had their planners signed by their parents for the previous day. Marcos's planner had the level circled and a large note (that appeared to be in a child's handwriting) next to it saying, "My son didn't do anything wrong. You hate Mexicans." The note was in English. I asked Marcos, "Who is this note from?"

Marcos replied, "My mother." He was visibly embarrassed and appeared worried. He kept repeating, "Mrs. DeMallie, I tried to explain it to my mother. You are a good person."

I told Marcos not to worry. I said that I would call his mom and discuss it with her.

During my planning time, on the day before winter vacation, I got Mr. Bimm, another staff member in my school who spoke Spanish, to call his mom on my behalf. He tried to explain the behavior system at Raven and that I was just doing my job. He tried to defend my actions and my character—all in Spanish. I am able to understand some Spanish when it is spoken slowly and clearly, but this mom was talking so fast that I couldn't comprehend anything she was saying.

When the conversation ended, Mr. Bimm hung up the phone and said,

"She's just worried about her son. She said that her son did say Mrs. DeMallie doesn't treat people differently. Marcos had told his mom that you were very kind to him."

That was the end. I felt bad for Marcos. I felt angry at the mother because I knew that I treated all of my students the same and worked very hard to help all of them. And I was now thinking—what if there is another occasion where Marcos needs to get a note/level in his planner? Do I not treat him the way I treat all of the other students just to avoid his mother thinking I'm a racist?

Time went on. Students returned from winter break. All was forgotten on my end.

In February 2018, I noticed that Marcos had been absent from school for an extended period of time. The flu was going around, so I assumed that's what he had. One week turned into two. When two weeks turned into three, I asked Mr. Bimm to give Marcos's mom a call to check on him.

That afternoon when I was eating lunch at my desk, Mr. Bimm came into my room to break the news to me. Marcos had been diagnosed with an aggressive bone cancer. His mother said the prognosis was bad.

I literally felt sick to my stomach. Last year, a fourth-grade student had been diagnosed with the same type of cancer. She had gone through so much—surgery, radiation, chemotherapy, repeat and repeat. But she wasn't my student, so while I knew of her and talked with her, it wasn't the same. How could this happen to a little boy who was so lively in my classroom just one month ago?

Marcos never returned to school that year, but I did everything possible to keep him involved with our class. The class had made cards for him, and one day after school, I delivered the cards to his apartment along with some games and activities to keep him occupied. Marcos, his two sisters (one just a toddler), his mother, and his stepfather all lived in a very tiny apartment on the third floor of a nearby older apartment building. When I was walking the three flights of stairs to his apartment, my first thought was that he had bone cancer in his leg. He had already had surgery to have the tumor removed. He was in a cast and on crutches. It was very important that his leg stay immobile. His bones were extremely fragile. How did he navigate the steps in that apartment building to go to and from his appointments at the hospital? I didn't see any elevator in the building.

When I arrived at his door, I didn't know what to expect. His mom answered my knock. This is the same mom who had basically accused me of being a racist and not caring about her child. I didn't know how she would treat me, but her smile and gestures welcomed me inside. The apartment was small. There was only a large sectional and a television in the living room area. The walls were beige and bare. The carpet was a beige shag. I could get a glimpse of a very tiny galley kitchen; there was one bathroom and no more than two bedrooms. The apartment was very neat and clean. Only a few baby toys were on the floor.

Marcos looked bad. He looked very tired with dark circles under his eyes. His hair had already started to fall out, and his leg was in protected padding and gear. It was hard to look at him and not cry, but the sadness of the situation was offset by the joy on his face. Marcos was so happy to see me. He thanked me over and over again for coming to see him, clearly wanting some attachment to his precancer normal life.

Because I couldn't speak Spanish and his mother couldn't speak English, Marcos served as an interpreter. His mom spoke openly about his prognosis and about her fears, all while Marcos was translating it to me. This boy who once seemed so young for his age now seemed like an adult. The cancer diagnosis had transported him into an adult world with adult issues and concerns.

After a while, his mom left the room to work on dinner and I read Marcos a book. When I finished the book, he said, "Mrs. DeMallie, I am really scared."

Of course he was scared. Who wouldn't be? I knew from the translations that he was completely aware of future surgeries and the effect of the chemotherapy. I gave him a big hug at that moment, fighting back tears. I asked in a shaky voice, "Marcos, do you like your doctors?"

He said, "Yes."

I said, "Well, doctors are very smart people. They go to school for many years to learn the best ways to take care of people. You are in good hands. They are going to use all of that knowledge to take the very best care of you that they can."

I went on to let him know that it was okay to be scared and that all of us were scared. We would all keep praying.

I saw Marcos about another three or four times again at his home before the school year was over. It was the second or third visit in which Mr. Bimm came with me. As usual, I brought a little something with me for Marcos to help pass the time. I know he was bored because even when he was feeling up to it, he couldn't go out in public for fear of germs. Marcos and I were going through the things that I brought while Mr. Bimm and his mother were talking in Spanish. He was getting a medical update for me and finding out how the home and hospital schooling was working out. The mom was talking for a while and then started crying. I assumed it was bad news about Marcos's health, but Mr. Bimm looked at me and said, "Oh, wow, how do I say this?"

He said to me in English, "She is embarrassed about how she treated you. She said that she is so ashamed of the things that she wrote in Marcos's planner. Marcos was right. You are a good person."

The mom looked at me with tears in her eyes. Marcos was in the room with us. I got up off the sofa and went over to her. She stood up, and we embraced. We held each other for a while, both of us crying. I asked Mr. Bimm to tell her, "Those words don't matter anymore. You didn't know me then. You were just a mom trying to protect your son. I'm a mother too. I understand now, and all that matters is that Marcos gets well."

Each of us could have continued to talk in our own language without any translation because our words didn't matter. All barriers were broken. It didn't matter what had been said. We were both mothers, and above that, we were both caring human beings each looking out for this little boy in our own way.

On that same visit, the mother asked Mr. Bimm to look at a parking ticket she got. Apparently, on one of Marcos's visits to the hospital, the mother had gotten a $500 ticket for parking in a handicap restricted area in Baltimore City. She couldn't find an open spot, needed to park close to the hospital for her son, and wasn't able to read English. All resulted in this ticket. I suggested and Mr. Bimm translated that we both felt like she should go to court to explain the circumstances to a judge, who might either waive the fee completely or at least reduce it. The mother explained that she couldn't risk going to court because she is here illegally. She was too afraid.

On my ride home from that visit, I couldn't help but think of all the stereotypes and judgments that I may have made—if I had heard part of this story on the news. The part where an illegal immigrant gets a parking ticket because she parked where she shouldn't have. The bigger story is a mom needed to get her very sick son to the hospital for one of many chemotherapy treatments. He can't walk far. She did the best she could. End of story. Nationalities and laws don't matter at that point. Sometimes we're all just trying to do the best we can.

Immigration laws are complicated, but when it comes to children and it comes to someone's health, those two things trump all others. Craig and I both raised the $500, and I delivered it to Marcos's mom on my next visit. His mom was incredibly grateful. I know this because her eyes told me so.

Finally, one more thing about Marcos's situation. Even some of the toughest kids in my class were crying when they heard the news about his cancer. Cancer doesn't discriminate. Several of these children had been impacted by cancer in their families. One boy said his father had cancer. Some other students had a grandparent who either had cancer or had already died from cancer. They were concerned about their classmate—even those who weren't his friend.

I tried to keep Marcos somehow included in our class for the sake of the students and himself. The students wrote notes to Marcos, and once I used my cell phone to call him while he was in the hospital. I put him on the speaker setting, and everyone in the class got a chance to talk with him. In spring, Marcos dominated our thoughts, but we had some other issues starting up in our classroom. The students had come a long way in terms of behavior since the beginning of that school year. But behaviors were off across the board, even from those who normally did the right thing.

In one of our circle meetings, I asked, "What's going on? You all know the right thing to do. We've learned a lot this year. Why are so many of you getting in trouble in the cafeteria and during specials, even those of you who never used to get in trouble?"

One of my best-behaved students spoke up. She said, "When you do the right thing, you're called a nerd."

This prompted a whole discussion on "What is a nerd? What's a nerd look like? What does a nerd do?" I brought up that my oldest daughter was referred to as a nerd. She focused a lot on school. She turned down opportunities with her friends sometimes to go out and party. But in the end, she graduated valedictorian from her high school. She then got into a really good college where she wanted to go. And now, she has gotten job offers from the best places in DC to work.

This resonated with the students, even though most of them didn't have anyone in their family who had attended college. They got it. As a class, we decided to reimage the word "nerd." The students came up with the idea of wearing something to advertise that they wanted to be a nerd and then created a T-shirt.

BE A NERD.

Smart is the new cool!

Nice

Educated

Respectful

Determined

These words were part of our virtues language that we had discussed throughout the year. The vice-principal and I had these shirts printed up (thanks to a T-shirt company that gave us a really good deal), and then the students sold the T-shirts as a fundraiser to help Marcos's family with the medical costs. The students ended up raising over $800 (above cost) to hand over to Marcos's family. In May, Marcos and his mother came to school so that we could present her with the money. Each of us wore our shirts to welcome them. Once again, his mom was grateful, and I was grateful to see Marcos back in school for the first time since he got sick.

Students wearing their custom-designed T-shirts to reimage the word "NERD," May 8, 2018

The point of this story is that I learned from Marcos that we're all the same on the inside. We may look different, come from different places, and have different experiences. But we all want good health and a chance at a good life. We just have to sit down and work together so that more people can achieve those goals—which, of course, includes improving public education.

Update: Marcos's cancer progressed rapidly. The chemotherapy couldn't keep up with the aggressive tumor. In the summer of 2018, he had the bottom half of his leg amputated. He eventually got a prosthetic leg, resumed chemo, and is doing well. But that little girl

I referred to, who had been diagnosed with the same cancer just one year before Marcos, wasn't as lucky. She passed away in spring of 2019.

DISCIPLINE AND BEHAVIORS

A Courageous Conversation

On July 15, 2019, I sat in front of my computer—sad and numb. With one click of the mouse, I essentially undid ten years of hard work to become a good teacher. That one motion, submitting my resignation as a teacher from the Baltimore County Public School system—ended everything I had worked for and a profession that I basically loved.

My decision to resign was primarily due to a personal situation that was complicated by factors related to my job—distance from home, nonflexible school hours, etc. But it was the topic of this chapter that played the biggest role. You see, I was going through something very difficult at home that was emotionally and mentally draining.

The behaviors of students in my school were extremely challenging as well (you'll read about some of those soon), and it took constant patience, empathy, and vigilance to watch over my students and to keep their classroom a safe learning environment. The combination of both stressful environments—every day, all day—was just too much. I was mentally fatigued. If only I could have just been a teacher—not a psychologist, counselor, and parent to fifty students—I wouldn't have resigned.

Although my personal circumstances are unique, my professional experience is not.

DISRUPTIVE BEHAVIORS ON THE RISE

According to a recent study of nearly 1,900 elementary teachers, administrators, and staff from forty-one public school districts throughout the United States, more than 70 percent of the surveyed elementary teachers reported that disruptive classroom behaviors have increased dramatically in the last three years.[147] The survey specified disruptive behaviors as emotional disconnect/unresponsiveness, tantrums/oppositional defiance, eloping (which means leaving the classroom without permission), bullying, verbal abuse or threats, and physical violence toward students, teachers, or other school personnel.[148]

More than half of those surveyed reported tantrums and defiant behavior occurring "at least several times a week, and 25 percent reported that they see tantrums or defiance several times each day.[149] "Emotional disconnect and unresponsiveness were the next most common types of disturbances. Nearly half of teachers reported that they see these behaviors at least several times a week."[150]

It is important, as this survey did, to define the types and identify the frequency of each specific disturbance to gain insight into the extent of the problem and the potential causes. But make no mistake about it, any "disruptive" behavior is just that. It disrupts instruction. It disrupts learning. It may create safety concerns. And it most certainly prevents all of the other students in the classroom from getting the education they *deserve.*

What is going on? Why are teachers reporting an increase in behavior problems? How do these behaviors impact learning? And let's be honest—these problems are infiltrating all of our schools to some degree. It's a complicated issue, with likely an equally complex cause, but one that we must explore if we really want to improve education. That exploration begins with an understanding of federal and state guidelines and initiatives that have influenced how school districts and consequently schools themselves manage behaviors and enforce discipline policies.

BREAKING SCHOOLS' RULES REPORT (2011)

In July 2011, The Council of State Governments (CSG) Justice Center in partnership with the Public Policy Research Institute of Texas A&M University released a report entitled "Breaking Schools' Rules: A Statewide Study of How School Discipline Relates to Students' Success and Juvenile Justice Involvement." The study was conducted to "improve policymakers' understanding of who is suspended and expelled from public secondary schools, and the impact of those removals on students' academic performance and juvenile justice system involvement."[151]

This report revealed the results of a study that included nearly one million Texas public secondary school students. "Nearly six in ten public school students were suspended or expelled at least once between their seventh- and twelfth-grade school years."[152] Furthermore, the students who had experienced disciplinary actions were found to be five times more likely to drop out and six times more likely to be held back than their peers with no disciplinary actions.[153] Several other findings gained public attention:

- African American students had a 31 percent greater likelihood of disciplinary action requiring removal from the classroom.[154]
- Nearly 75 percent of special education students were suspended or expelled at least once.[155]
- Students who experienced disciplinary action were ten times more likely than their peers without disciplinary action to have contact with the juvenile justice system (23 percent versus 2 percent).[156] This connection was referred to as the STPP, School-to-Prison Pipeline.

FEDERAL SUPPORTIVE SCHOOL DISCIPLINE PROJECT (2011–2014)

This report was the catalyst to a collaborative project between the US Departments of Education (DOE) and Justice (DOJ). In the summer of 2011, Education Secretary Duncan and Attorney General Holder announced the Supportive School Discipline Initiative to support the use of school discipline practices that foster safe, supportive, and productive learning environments while keeping students in school.[157] The role of the Initiative was to coordinate federal actions in an effort to provide schools with alternatives to exclusionary discipline and to "encourage new emphasis on reducing disproportionality for students of color and students with disabilities."[158]

In October 2012, the DOJ awarded $840,000 (an amount then matched by the Atlantic Philanthropies) to the Council of State Governments to initiate and manage a School Discipline Consensus Project.[159] An overarching goal of the project was to dismantle the School-to-Prison Pipeline. To achieve that goal, the Consensus Project worked to build agreement for the need to reform school climate and discipline, research more effective ways to promote a positive school climate and manage behaviors, issue legal guidance on discipline along with providing resources for improving school climate and discipline using research-based practices, and promote awareness and knowledge.

By December 2012, the US Senate was conducting a hearing to address the School-to-Prison Pipeline. It was proposed that civil rights data collection be used to monitor school discipline data. The Discipline Project "utilize[ed] the [Education Department's] Civil Rights Data Collection system to track the total number of students receiving in-school and out-of-school suspensions/expulsions, the number of students referred to law enforcement, the number of students with school-related arrests, and the number of students expelled under zero-tolerance policies."[160] This data was to be collected for every school district in the country and was to be released in 2014.

PRESSURE TO LOWER THE NUMBERS

Under immense pressure, school districts nationwide began to revise school discipline policies, student code of conduct guidelines, and modify/reduce the consequences for behaviors that didn't meet the standards. The trend was to move away from zero-tolerance policies and to avoid suspensions and expulsions. Maryland was no exception. In 2012, the Maryland State Board of Education proposed a new regulation to "reduce the number of long-term and out-of-school suspensions for nonviolent offenses, proposed amendments to school discipline regulations, and collected data on school arrests and referrals to the criminal justice and juvenile justice systems, including specific data on referrals of special education students.

More importantly, the board proposed a regulation that requires any school system with disciplinary actions having a disproportionate impact on minorities to develop a corrective action plan to reduce the impact within one year, eliminate it within three years, and report to the board annually."[161] This put a lot of pressure on the principals to reduce suspensions and pressure on teachers to limit office referrals.

At Raven, a school predominately occupied by African American students, teachers were strongly discouraged from writing office referrals, and frankly, even when we did, there was no apparent consequence. It wasn't long before the students seemed to pick up on the fact that they could say or do anything to other students or to teachers without any disciplinary action. The Maryland Board of Education directed efforts to a more rehabilitative approach, prohibited policies that allow automatic disciplines without using discretion, and allowed long-term suspensions/expulsions only as a last resort.[162]

On January 8, 2014, US Secretary of Education Arne Duncan addressed The Academies at Frederick Douglass High School in Baltimore, Maryland. The purpose was to announce the release of a guidance package on school discipline that had been designed by both the Departments of Education and Justice. The school discipline package included several elements, including a Dear Colleague Letter from Catherine Lhamon, head of the Education Department's Civil Rights Division, and Jocelyn Samuels, head of the Department of Justice's Civil Rights Division. The letter provided information on how schools and districts could meet their legal obligations to administer student discipline equitably, i.e., without discriminating on the basis of race, color, or national origin. According to Secretary Duncan, "Racial discrimination in school discipline is a real problem today, and not just an issue from forty to fifty years ago."[163]

Another key element introduced in the package was the Guiding Principles document. This document outlined voluntary action steps for local educators and leaders to promote a positive school climate and equitable discipline practices. Secretary Duncan said, "Schools should remove students from the classroom as a last resort, and only for appropriately serious infractions, like endangering the safety of other students, teachers, or themselves."[164] He referred to data collected by the Civil Rights Division showing a disproportionality of suspensions and expulsions to African American students and students with disabilities. To emphasize his point, Secretary Duncan cited Civil Rights Data Collection (CRDC) data from the 2009–2010 school year showing that South Carolina had suspended 12.7 percent of students compared to North Dakota, where suspensions were as low as 2.2 percent.

Secretary Duncan said, "I am absolutely confident that students in South Carolina are not six times more likely than their peers in North Dakota to pose serious discipline problems worthy of an out-of-school suspension. That huge disparity is not caused by differences in children; it's caused by differences in training, professional development, and discipline policies. It is adult behavior that needs to change."[165]

The Guidance Package therefore had three guiding principles summarized as follows:[166]

1. Schools and districts should build a positive school climate to prevent misbehavior and support the students who have underlying causes for misbehavior.

2. Students should have clear expectations and be held accountable, but schools should provide different levels of supports and interventions for students based on their needs.

3. School leaders should continuously monitor data and use that data to evaluate the impact of their discipline policies to different student groups.

Concluding his remarks, Secretary Duncan recalled that back in 2004, Baltimore City Schools had handed out more than 26,000 suspensions in a school system of approximately 88,000 students. Last year (2013), Baltimore City School suspensions had dropped by about two-thirds, to 8,600. "In just the last year [2013–2014], the number of suspensions district-wide fell by almost 25 percent to a modern-day low."[167] Frederick Douglas High School was part of the dramatic Baltimore City turnaround, including a substantial increase in graduation rates. This turnaround was rewarded with $4.2 million in school improvement grants.[168]

RELEASE OF CIVIL RIGHTS DATA ON SCHOOL DISCIPLINE (2014)

On March 21, 2014, the US Department of Education Office for Civil Rights officially released the data that Secretary Duncan had cited in his Baltimore address. They issued Brief No. 1, a data snapshot of school discipline, restraint, and seclusion, based on data collected between 2011 and 2012. Some highlights are as follows:[169]

SUSPENSIONS AND EXPULSIONS

- Black students (particularly males) were suspended and expelled at a rate three times greater than white students.

- Black girls were suspended at higher rates than girls of any other race or ethnicity.
- Students with disabilities were suspended out of school twice as often as their peers without disabilities.
- ELLs received a **lower** than proportionate rate of out-of-school suspensions.

ARRESTS AND REFERRALS TO LAW ENFORCEMENT

- Black students, who represent 16 percent of the student population, represented 27 percent of the referrals to law enforcement and represented 31 percent of students subjected to a school-related arrest.
- Students with disabilities, who represent 12 percent of the student population, represented a quarter of those arrested and referred to law enforcement.

Pressure continued to mount toward each state to lower the number of disciplinary actions specifically for African Americans and special education students. Maryland amended its Code of Maryland Regulations (COMAR 13A.08.01.11) in February 2014, and each local school board was required to review and revise its student discipline regulations and policies (COMAR 13A.08.01.11A).[170]

BCPS revised its student disciplinary policies and procedures for the 2014–2015 school year, which included decreasing the length of suspensions and increasing minimum education services for those expelled. The zero-tolerance policy was eliminated. Data showed that during the period of 2012–2014, BCPS's overall suspension rates dropped from 8.3 to 4.9 percent, but that African American student suspension rates dropped from 13.3 to 8.5 percent.[171] Since those rates still indicated a disproportionality, BCPS had to present an action plan to reduce that disproportionality in the next year.[172] As with many other schools around the country, BCPS looked to other behavior models and practices to proactively reduce behavior issues in the classroom.

RESTORATIVE PRACTICES

Restorative Practices (derived from Restorative Justice) became the new buzz phrase that BCPS school administrators started passing down to their staff. It was presented as a new behavior management plan that would foster a safe, collaborative, positive environment for students and that would address their social-emotional needs. According to a Guide for Educators and the International Institute for Restorative Practices, Restorative Practices are "processes that proactively build healthy relationships and a sense of community to prevent and address conflict and wrongdoing."[173]

They are meant to build and thus improve relationships between educators and students so that as part of the same community, the members can work together to resolve conflicts, restore order and balance, and therefore prevent harmful behavior. "Restorative practices allow individuals who may have committed harm to take full responsibility for their behavior by addressing the individual(s) affected by the behavior."[174] Thus part of taking that responsibility is recognizing how your actions affected another and then taking corrective action to repair the damage and prevent it from reoccurring.

Restorative Justice (RJ) originated in the criminal justice system back in the 1970s. Its purpose was to help offenders and victims reconcile. Victims and criminals were able to express the harm that was caused and what each experienced using dialogue expressed in circles, mediation, or conferences. Research shows that restorative justice in the criminal justice system can result in reduced recidivism, especially among juvenile offenders.[175]

Some studies have reported that Restorative Justice in school has shown positive gains in school performance, learning, and climate variables.[176] It has reportedly produced significant reductions in suspensions ranging from 40 percent to 90 percent.[177] But even supporters of RJ have challenged the research. The research lags the extent of implementation, and RJ has been implemented without proper understanding and training.[178]

Here's how Restorative Justice is typically practiced (referred to as Restorative Practices) in the schools and how I saw it practiced within Baltimore County. The most widely used visual representation of RJ is the circle process. This involves students and the teacher sitting on the floor in the outline shape of a circle. We called it a circle meeting. Circle meetings most often occur at the beginning of the day but can also occur spontaneously throughout the day. At Raven, we held most of our meetings after the morning announcements. The purpose of the circle is to provide everyone within the circle an opportunity to speak and be heard in a safe environment. "Circles can be used as a tool to teach social skills such as listening, respect, and problem-solving."[179]

Another common practice in schools is referred to as a Restorative Conference or community conference. This occurs when a conflict has occurred and all of those affected by the behavior meet to discuss why it occurred, how they were impacted, and more effective ways to deal with that type of situation in the future. An adult—such as a school administrator, guidance counselor, or educator—and the students themselves are all involved in this type of conflict resolution meeting that should occur *immediately* when the conflict arises. If the teacher is part of that conflict resolution meeting, then their instruction is disrupted for Restorative Justice activities both before and after altercations in addition to having their instruction interrupted for the altercation itself.

There are other formal and informal types of practices. Another commonly used informal practice that was used in my school was the virtues language. These are specific words like respect, determination, honesty, courage, etc., that educators are supposed to teach the students and consistently use to describe what is expected of the students and to recognize the behaviors in a positive way. For example, if my class was waiting quietly in line to use the school hallway bathroom, I might say, "I really appreciate your orderliness in the hallway and how respectful you are being of the other students who are learning in their classrooms." In this way, not only are you teaching the students the vocabulary of these words but you are using a positive behavior approach—as opposed to correcting those students who are misbehaving. This may sound like common sense, but it actually takes a conscious effort to implement consistently and faithfully.

In my school, all of the teachers were given laminated cards to wear on their lanyards. The cards had the virtues vocabulary words listed on one side and then restorative questions on the other side to use in conflict resolution conferences. Examples of questions would be: How do you think your actions impacted others? How did you feel when you did this?

Another very important aspect of Restorative Practices that, to me, is the umbrella of it all is referred to as social-emotional learning (SEL). SEL teaches students skills such as "recognizing and managing emotions, developing caring and concern for others, establishing positive relationships, making responsible decisions, and handling challenging situations constructively and ethically. These are the skills that allow children and adults to calm themselves when angry, make friends, resolve conflicts respectfully, and make ethical and safe choices."[180]

These are skills that my own children learned mostly at home or in their neighborhood through routine interactions, conversation, unstructured play, and organized sports. Unfortunately, many of the children whom I've worked with in the past few years aren't developing these skills outside of school. There are potentially a lot of reasons for this, but the bottom line is that now the school is trying to teach these social skills in addition to academic ones because students can't work collaboratively and get along safely without these basic fundamentals.

Restorative Practices are one alternative that schools are trying to replace removing students from the classroom. It's used to both prevent and address bad behaviors. The American Psychological Association (APA) found that zero-tolerance policies fail to make schools safer because schools with higher rates of suspension and expulsion "appear to have less satisfactory ratings of school climate, to have less satisfactory school governance structures, and to spend a disproportionate amount of time on disciplinary matters."[181]

While I agree with their statement, it poses the "chicken and the egg question" for me. Are zero-tolerance policies causing the schools to be less safe and have more discipline problems, OR are the schools less safe with a high number of discipline issues that require the implementation of zero-tolerance policies?

The real question is: Has RJ **proven** to be effective in the classroom, not just in the prison system? If so, are school personnel being sufficiently trained on how to implement the practices? Are we asking too much of teachers who just want to teach? And finally, how do these practices impact academics? Here's what the research says.

RESEARCH ON RESTORATIVE PRACTICES

One of the proponents of Restorative Justice, Samuel Song, found that Restorative Justice is not well defined in the academic world. Disagreements are common on the definition, the terminology to be used (justice vs. practice), the application, even on whether or not it should address racial equity explicitly or not—or just address it naturally.[182] Furthermore, "despite the popularity of RJ in school practice, it has been understudied, especially in schools. This is concerning because practice appears to be far ahead of the research on effectiveness and successful implementation and sustainability, when, in fact, research should be facilitating data-based decision making using RJ."[183]

According to Song, most of the research that has been done is not peer-reviewed and focuses only on a single school evaluation, meaning just examining the school using RJ rather than comparing students who participated in RJ to similar students who didn't participate. Those studies that are peer-reviewed are conceptual and exploratory. "Another limitation of the research literature is that no studies have demonstrated a reduction in the disproportionality gap in exclusionary discipline between majority and minority students,"[184] which is, of course, a major impetus in the implementation of Restorative Practices. The bottom line is that research is limited and needed BEFORE we start taking time away from academics for this disciplinary intervention program.

The RAND Corporation, a non-profit research organization, conducted more reliable, randomized control studies on Restorative Practices in Pittsburgh and Maine. The Pittsburgh study was commissioned by the National Institute for Justice—an agency that is part of the US Department of Justice.

The Pittsburgh study was conducted in school years 2015–2016 and 2016–2017 to study the effects of Restorative Practices on the classroom, school climate, and suspension rates.[185] Results were mixed:

- In year one, suspension rates fell at all of the twenty-two schools using Restorative Justice, but they also fell at twenty-two comparison schools that didn't use RJ.[186]
- During year two, 12.6 percent of students at the RJ schools were suspended, compared to 14.6 percent of students at the non-RJ schools.[187]
- Teachers rated an overall improvement in school climate, but students reported that teachers struggled more to manage classroom behavior.[188]
- The number of school arrests was similar at the RJ and non-RJ schools. Arrests among RJ schools did not decrease.[189]
- "The academic performance of middle schoolers actually worsened at schools that tried restorative justice. Math test scores deteriorated for black students in particular."[190]

The Maine study was a "randomized controlled trial of the Restorative Practices Intervention conducted in fourteen middle schools [later reduced to thirteen schools] throughout Maine."[191] The study did not examine suspension rates or academic results. It did, however, reveal the difficulty in implementing Restorative Justice day-to-day in the classroom, but students reported feeling more connected to their peers.[192]

The mixed results of both studies point out the necessity of comparison studies. We just don't have enough of these credible studies yet to draw any conclusions about the effectiveness of Restorative Justice in the schools, and if it is determined to be a research-based effective strategy, educators need thorough and ongoing training. According to Song and Swearer (2016), "One-time-only or even multiple-time professional development workshops are not sufficient without ongoing support."[193]

Educators are unclear on the definitions and specifics of Restorative Justice. We are not psychologists or social workers. None of my graduate courses in education covered anything close to the psychological and sociological expertise that teachers are expected to have and use regularly in their classrooms today. And really, should that expertise be expected from teachers? Do we expect the school psychologist and school social worker to be able to teach language arts, biology, or PE to their students? Do we hold the school psychologist accountable for academic progress in addition to school discipline data? The answer is "no" for a reason.

MY EXPERIENCE WITH DISRUPTIVE BEHAVIORS

We need to go back to the data—back to the survey that shared teacher's concerns over growing behavioral disruptions in their classrooms.[194] Let me share examples of behaviors that I either experienced in my own classroom or witnessed in other areas of the elementary school where I taught (in order from mild to most severe): calling out; refusal to do any work; refusal to follow basic directions; damaging or destroying other students' work or property; vandalizing the bathrooms with profanity; eloping; throwing pencils, books, or computers; using human feces to write on the bathroom mirrors; profanity toward other students; profanity toward teachers and substitutes—teachers often told to "Fuck off"; stealing from students and teachers; threatening to beat up a student; slapping, punching, or kicking other students; slapping, punching, or kicking teachers/administrators; stuffing paper towels down the toilets or sinks; throwing desks and chairs within classrooms and in hallways; pulling students around by their hair; knocking a student to the ground and jumping repeatedly on top of their head or face; lighting the bathroom trash can on fire; and bringing a knife to school.

These are just some of the behaviors that I personally experienced or witnessed. It does not include other poor behaviors that occurred out of my view within the school, at bus stops, or on the school buses. Most of these behaviors, with few exceptions, occurred at Raven on a daily or weekly basis.

There are a few things that I want to point out by sharing these behaviors. First, I don't think most parents have any idea of what is going on inside their child's school on a regular basis. I was shocked to learn that many of these behaviors occurred in a nearby middle school where my daughter attended. The result was that she suffers from anxiety and has hated school ever since.

Second, we can't just excuse or ignore defiant and disrespectful behavior because it's considered nonviolent. Secretary Duncan and Attorney General Holder stated that "95 percent of out-of-school suspensions are for nonviolent misbehavior—like being disruptive, acting disrespectfully, tardiness, profanity, and dress code violations."[195]

Out-of-school suspensions seem extreme. But behaviors classified as disrespectful can include repeatedly cursing at a teacher, noncompliance, and throwing objects. At a minimum, they interfere with instruction, but perhaps more importantly, they undermine the teacher's authority and create a culture of disrespect. What emotional harm occurs when students have to witness their teacher being told to "Fuck off"?

How can the other students feel safe in the care of their teacher if they watch that adult berated by a student and see the teacher powerless to do anything about it? Why is any student allowed to take away another's rights to an educational environment that is safe and fosters learning? If those other children feel that their teacher is being threatened—a teacher whom they likely look up to as an authority figure—how safe do you think they feel being with that disruptive student in the classroom, alone in the bathroom, or seated next to on a school bus?

Unfortunately, I saw the frequency and severity of behavior issues escalate over the course of my seven years at Raven. Remember, I began teaching there in September 2012 and ended in July 2019—all during the course of Supportive School Discipline Initiative, Civil Rights data tracking, changes in the Code of Maryland Regulations in education, BCPS changes in its Student Conduct Policies, and implementation of Restorative Practices. Yet, I saw fewer and fewer consequences resulting from such behaviors in school. So much so that, at one point, many teachers stopped writing up the office referrals because it wasn't worth their time.

When a consequence was imposed, it was often seen more as a "reward" than a deterrent. Students loved getting lunch detention in the office because they usually didn't like the cafeteria. Students sometimes left with a toy or stress ball that they would then "show off" to their classmates. Sometimes they were given a "Flash Pass" that allowed them to leave the classroom anytime they were feeling anxious or needed a break. Sometimes students just enjoyed a break from instruction when sitting for long periods of time in the office, waiting for a counselor or administrator to speak with them.

Raven had a mentor program, which matched a teacher mentor with a troubled student for the entire year. The program had admirable intentions and some success but was also criticized because it provided a periodic reward/celebration for the mentees and the mentors. Those celebrations such as ice cream, hot chocolate, a book, etc., should have been rewards for improved behavior; however, students exhibiting no improvement were allowed to participate.

Yet, school policies made it increasingly difficult to reward students who were always doing the right thing. Teachers were no longer allowed to bring in any food (purchased or homemade) for the students, which typically had been one of the greatest motivators. Eventually, even end-of-the-year celebrations (supposedly for good behaviors) had to be inclusive of everyone regardless of whether or not it was earned. What message are we sending to those students following the rules and to those who are not?

NUMBERS DO LIE

Despite an increase in the number of problematic behaviors in the classrooms both at my school and throughout Baltimore County, the number of suspensions declined. According to Project Baltimore, which compiled ten years of in-school and out-of-school suspension data, "In 2007, Maryland had 181,578 suspensions. By 2017, it plummeted to 76,719."[196]

Clearly, *numbers do lie* because what appears like a declining problem was being masked by teachers and administrators afraid to report the truth. Lead researchers of the EAB survey reporting growing behavior issues in elementary schools suggested that disruptive behavior was "more widespread than…realized, and it may be that teachers are suffering a little bit in silence because of some of the efforts to stem discipline referrals and suspensions."[197]

BEHAVIOR PROBLEMS' IMPACT ON LEARNING

And what is the impact on learning due to all of these behavior problems in our schools? We have already discussed how the US academically lags behind other developing nations in regard to math and science. There is no doubt in my mind that education is disrupted and negatively impacted by even the most minor of behavioral disturbances. The EAB elementary educator's survey reported, "Teachers estimate[d] losing nearly two-and-a-half hours of instructional time each week as a result of behavioral disruptions, which adds up to nearly three weeks of lost instructional time each year."[198] How can this lost time not be negatively impacting academic achievement?

A study of Philadelphia schools, who banned suspension for nonviolent "conduct" offenses, found a substantial negative effect on academics. "Achievement decreased by three percentage points in math and nearly seven percentage points in reading after three years."[199]

"A not-yet-peer-reviewed doctoral dissertation *examined* several California school districts that banned suspensions for nonviolent 'willful defiance': Los Angeles, Oakland, San Francisco, and Pasadena. It found no effects on reading but a harm to math achievement large enough to take a student from the fiftieth percentile to the thirty-ninth after three years."[200]

In Maryland, only one-third of students in grades three through eight scored proficient or above on the 2019 PARCC math tests, a decline of 1 percentage point, and the worst math performance since 2015 when the PARCC test was first administered.[201] English proficiency rose by 2 percent, but only 43.7 percent of students in Maryland tested proficient or above on the 2019 tests.[202] Within my school district, Baltimore County's math scores reflected a four-percentage point drop in grades three through eight from the prior year. "Overall, only 26.5 percent of its students passed the math test in elementary and middle school."[203] One must question: are the behavior problems in the classrooms and new discipline policies and strategies in the school districts contributing to the decline in academic performance of our students?

Restorative Practices takes a lot of time away from instruction if implemented with fidelity in a high-needs school. Many schools in Baltimore County are asking teachers to spend up to thirty minutes a day in circle meetings each morning. Raven requested a ten to fifteen minute meeting each morning, but we frequently required spontaneous meetings and conferences at other points during the school day.

Additionally, because there were so many behavioral problems at Raven, such as vandalism and fights, teachers could not allow students to use the bathrooms by themselves. Our administration required teachers to escort the whole class to the bathroom. This ended up occurring three or four times each day, which made us lose another fifteen to twenty minutes of daily instruction. Behavioral issues and preventative discipline strategies easily cost the students thirty minutes each day of instruction without an actual occurrence of a problem.

Another recent initiative in Baltimore County is for every classroom to have a "Calming Corner." That is a designated area in the classroom where a student can go to (without having to get permission from the teacher) to relax and calm themselves down. In the Calming Corner, there are stress toys to play with, posters for breathing exercises to do, and other stress-relieving types of remedies. Some students will just say, "I feel sad," and go to the Calming Corner. While students are supposed to be in the corner for a short period of time, self-monitored by a timer, they routinely "escape" to the corner to "escape" work. In essence, students who have legitimate anger/mood issues or those taking advantage of the "escape" mechanisms are able to miss out on even more classroom instruction.

There is no doubt in my mind that discipline problems and preventative discipline strategies are infringing on instruction time and negatively impacting academic achievement. But this isn't to say that some children, perhaps many children, don't need these extra social and emotional supports. **They absolutely do.** The question then becomes, is the school the best place to get those supports? And if there is no other option, then should the school extend the school day, offer this as an extra class like PE or music, or offer it before or after school, so that teachers don't lose that instruction time?

BEHAVIOR PROBLEMS ARE STILL AN ISSUE

Finally, I shared all of this background information with you so that you could begin to see the complexity of the discipline issue in today's schools. A February 2019 Gallup poll in the US said that 54 percent of adults believe teachers are "unprepared" or "very unprepared" to handle discipline issues in the classroom.[204]

In 2011, the US Department of Education and the Department of Justice made a broad statement that the disciplinary actions against African Americans and special education students were dispropor-tionately high.[205] They were absolutely correct. They were excessively high. But rather than using that data as an opportunity to exam-ine potential causes of *all* behavior incidents from *all* students, they focused on racial inequities and racial discrimination.[206]

This resulted in education systems drastically altering discipline policies and school systems reporting much lower numbers for suspensions and expulsions, but behavior issues were not extinguished or even mitigated. If racial inequities were the *only* problem, why then have schools seen an increase in the number of behavior issues? Why are students and teachers reporting mixed results on changes in school climate? Why have teachers' perceptions and public perceptions' of behavior management decreased? What have we missed? There is obviously more that we need to consider.

ADDRESSING EQUITY CONCERNS

We shouldn't ignore the possibility that racism has been a factor in past school disciplinary actions. As such, suspected cases of inequity need to be investigated on a case-by-case basis using a process that is transparent and easily accessible to students and their families. We should also consider putting in place safeguards to proactively prevent future cases of racism. Schools could install cameras in the classrooms and common areas to record teacher and student interactions. Those recordings could not only be used to verify a disciplinary incident but could then provide information to school psychologists and coun-selors about circumstances that tend to trigger behavior problems.

But just as we can't ignore the possibility of racism, we can't ignore other potential causes for behavior problems that clearly still exist in our schools. And we have to make sure that we don't solely focus on the child with a behavior problem and neglect to consider the negative impact that those disruptions have on the other students, who become victims when they are denied their right to a full, uninterrupted day of learning. As a teacher, this was the most disheartening aspect of the behavior problems in my school.

Over the past few years, I have had several African American parents express to me concern over the changing culture in the school and increasing number of behavior problems that their child either had to witness or fall victim to each day. A few parents have even asked me to write a recommendation as part of an application to move their child out of the public school system using a scholarship aimed to help students from disadvantaged communities have access to better educational opportunities. I know of one recipient. Unfortunately, most of my students didn't have another choice for an education. That's why we need to explore other ideas. Because from what I have seen, simply focusing on decreasing the number of suspensions and expulsions hasn't helped.

"READING" EACH STUDENT'S STORY

I view each one of my students as a book. They all have a different cover. My cover is a middle-aged, white, female. But the cover never really tells you much about the story. You have to read the pages to really learn what the book is about. Each one of my students has a different unique page that makes up their story. A page that explains their biological makeup; one that describes their home life; one that describes their previous school experiences; one that describes their family's past; one that describes their social experiences; one that describes their emotional experiences; and so on and so on. If you are trying to find out why a student or group of students is demonstrating any area of concern—you must read the pages!

That's also why educators need the help of a multitude of professionals to help assess the needs of the students. We cannot read their "story" alone. We are not psychologists. We are not counselors. We are, for the most part, well-intentioned, caring professionals who had a passion for learning and want to share that with our students. We are trying to add a page to their book that produces a better ending.

POTENTIAL BEHAVIOR INFLUENCES—A COURAGEOUS CONVERSATION

In the spirit of truly wanting to help all children, we have to honestly share our thoughts and experiences. With that goal in mind, I share the following observations and thoughts regarding the *potential* cause of some behavior problems. Over the past seven years, I have encountered a lot of frustration and aggression in some of my students. As the rigor of academics has increased, I've seen an increase in frustration of students that are below grade level. Many of these students exhibit perfect behaviors when I am able to meet them at their academic level and build in supports.

This is what I try to do during small-group instruction. But teachers are required to provide students with instruction and assess students on grade-level standards—whether the students are ready for those skills or not. So these students who keep getting passed on to higher grades despite not meeting grade-level standards are constantly getting feedback on graded assignments and report cards that they are failures. I'm not suggesting that we give them or their parents a false report on where they stand, but something needs to change to help minimize that frustration and sense of worthlessness.

Many research studies have supported parental involvement as a predictor of academic achievement regardless of demographics or standardized achievement scores.[207] My experience in the classroom with students of all ability levels and demographics has revealed that families or what I would call a "supportive home network" are the same predictor of positive school behavior. I believe, as a teacher, that good behavior has nothing to do with skin color, gender, economics, or even IQ. Of all the students whom I've ever taught, my most well-behaved and kindest students have come from families with two parents that are actively involved in their child's life—that is, they have conversations with their child, eat dinner with their child, do activities with their child, ask questions about school, and know what's going on in their child's life.

According to KIDS COUNT, a project of the Annie E. Casey Foundation, data collected for the period of 2013–2015 shows that the national average of children living in two-parent families is only 68 percent.[208] Asians exceed the national average at a high of 84 percent; Hispanics or Latinos are close to the average at 66 percent; non-Hispanic white children are at 77 percent; and non-Hispanic black children fall well below the average, at 37 percent.[209]

But in my experience, "two-parent families" doesn't necessarily mean that two parents have to be living together in the same household. I have met divorced parents who work together and are both actively involved in the child's academic and personal life, and I have observed all types of supportive families: grandparents, aunts, uncles, gay parents, adoptive parents, and foster parents. A supportive family does not necessarily mean a traditional biological mother and biological father. It just means people who care, love their children, and instill good values in the children at home, including holding their children accountable for their actions—that is, not jumping to blame other children or the teacher for their child's behavior.

We can't magically change a one-parent household into a two-parent household or change an uninvolved parent into an involved one. But maybe we can work to improve communities so that people within that community support each other when there is a need for extra support. Perhaps we could pair the older generations with the younger ones. I had a student whose father was incarcerated. His grandparents stepped in to help his mother. This student was a very sweet boy who genuinely seemed to want to do the right thing; he just needed help managing his anger over the loss of his father. We need to start thinking outside of the box—outside of the classroom—as the place where children can get the emotional and social support they need. Help take the burden off of the schools, so that schools can get back to focusing on academics.

Until we get there, we need more support in schools. In the 2019 Gallup poll, six in ten participants rated "access to mental health services" for students as "very effective" among six possible solutions to address the discipline problem.[210] I, too, believe that mental health services are needed by true mental health professionals in our schools—not teachers and or even guidance counselors. Unfortunately, I've witnessed too many children with mental health needs that are not being met. I have had students who hear voices in their head, intentionally hurt themselves, and cannot control their anger. We need to identify mental health issues sooner and improve access and cost for treating the problems.

There is one final suggestion I would like to make—teacher microphones. I will talk much more about this topic later, but when classrooms have access to teacher microphones and speakers, research shows that behavior problems decrease, and students are more likely to be engaged.[211] I used a wireless teacher microphone and had a portable speaker in my classroom when I taught at Raven.

I experienced the dramatic calming effect that this simple technology had on the atmosphere in my classroom because I never had to raise my voice to address the students. Students who came from environments where they routinely heard a lot of yelling never heard that from me, and the tone of my voice was more soothing because I didn't need to strain it.

This technology made a huge impact in my classroom, so much so that the behavior specialist working in my school once asked me what I was doing differently, because she witnessed how students (who had been involved in behavior problems elsewhere in the school) were even-tempered and on-task in my classroom. I know that using that microphone made the difference. This inexpensive idea deserves consideration.

Educating teachers at Raven on the benefits of auditory learning issues and use of voice-enhancement technology—including improved behavior, January 2018

As I said earlier, school discipline is a complex issue, and something so complex likely requires many strategies and ideas to work toward a solution. But in order to get to that solution, we have to work backward and identify some of the causes of the behavior problems, and that means that we need to better understand each individual student and their family. We must look beyond their "cover" and read each of their "stories" to implement practices and policies that may help to prevent disruptive and dangerous behavior from occurring.

But when prevention is ineffective, there must be consequences that discourage recidivism. I agree that out-of-school suspensions should be rare because, in most cases, that's just a day off for students who likely don't want to be in school anyway. But what about in-school suspensions or "reflections" that offer a professional counseling component (from an actual psychologist, not a teacher) and a restitution component, like a school community service project?

This would serve a few purposes: temporarily remove the disruption from the classroom, get the troubled student some professional help in identifying his or her poor decisions, make a corrective action plan for the future, and send a message that bad behavior has consequences. I'm afraid if we don't send the message that certain behaviors are unacceptable, we are just deferring that prison pipeline to a time when these students enter the real world.

QUESTIONS TO ASK IN CONVERSATIONS ABOUT DISCIPLINE

- How can we get to know each student's story so that we can better understand that individual and proactively prevent potential discipline issues rather than reactively respond after they have occurred?
- How can we create better family supports within the community to help single-parent families?
- How can we reward the students who are always doing the right thing and use that as an incentive for the others?
- Does research justify using Restorative Practices in the school system, and if not, should we continue with it?
- How can we build in safeguards to prevent racial discrimination?
- How can we build in more psychological and social supports

within the schools where it's needed to relieve teachers of this responsibility?

- How can we ensure that students are academically challenged at the appropriate level—within their reach—so they don't feel like failures and are able to work independently?
- How can we make sure that classrooms are a place where all students can focus on academics without the disruption of behavior issues?
- How can we send the message to students and parents that behavior problems have consequences—so they learn this before they get into the real world?
- How can we make all students and teachers feel safe at all times and in all places in school?
- How can we reduce the "menu" that teachers must serve—that is, all the responsibilities and roles that they must play—to allow teachers the time and energy to focus on academics?

NITA

Of all the students I've ever known or taught, there is one who frequently stands out in my thoughts and has even guided some of my decisions over the past few years. Her name is Nita. I met Nita in September 2013 when she began fourth grade, and I became her homeroom and math teacher. Nita was a little girl with hair almost down to her waist that she wore most of the time in two braids. She had large, expressive brown eyes, light brown skin, and a smile that went from cheek to cheek—a smile that I saw every day, except for one.

Nita was born in India and then raised there by her grandparents up until about a year before I met her when she was summoned by her parents to join them in the US. She was around eight or nine years old at the time. Her parents had come to the US when Nita was an infant. Her mother came to work on a green card, while her father had a temporary Visa. Mom had a background in technology. I'm not sure what Dad's background was, but I do know that he held various jobs in the US, such as a restaurant manager. Both parents came to the US, hoping to establish a better life for their daughter. When they felt ready, they sent for Nita to join them.

When Nita arrived in the US, she didn't know any English. She was enrolled at my school and put into third grade based on her age. So when she started my fourth-grade class, she had been in the US and spoken English for less than one year. The class that she was put into was a mixture of abilities ranging from below average to high average. At the beginning of the year, Nita seemed to fall in the average ability level. Her English was already very good. I would have never known that she had only begun learning English less than a year ago. There were some sounds that she had a hard time enunciating and some vocabulary words in word problems that she needed me to explain to her. But other than those few exceptions, it was apparent that she was very bright and more obvious that she loved learning and school.

Almost every day, Nita arrived at school beaming with excitement to be there and to learn. Her locker was near the classroom door, where I stood to greet the arriving students. I noticed that she would always make eye contact, cheerfully respond to my greeting, and frequently would ask, "What are we going to learn today?"

Nita's confidence grew as much as her academic ability during the first few months of fourth grade. Not only did she develop a solid foundation of math skills, but she confidently defended her answers. She wasn't embarrassed when she pronounced or used a word incorrectly. She would just listen to the corrected version and then repeat it herself, all while maintaining that big smile.

Nita's class was among the first fourth-grade classes to be taught a curriculum that aligned to the Common Core standards. She was a student who devoured this new approach with a focus on conceptual understanding. She actually articulated her love of the new teaching style by telling me one day, "In India, they teach things very quickly. We are shown how to do something, and then we learn something else. I love the way you teach us. I love understanding why we are doing [solving] the problem this way. School is much better here than in India."

Nita absorbed information like a sponge absorbs water. Her eyes followed me everywhere, and her mind was just as focused. She often could solve a new kind of problem on her own, based on what she already knew, using logic and intuition. She was clearly very bright. By November, I had her on my radar to recommend for the advanced class next year.

I spent a lot of time with Nita because she would often join me for lunch, chose to hang with me at recess, and helped me clean up the classroom after school while waiting for her bus to arrive. These opportunities gave me time to learn about her family, her hopes, and her dreams. She told me that she really didn't know her mother very well. She had visits with her parents when she was living in India, but since birth, she had been living with and was raised by her grandparents. She told me that she loved the US, she loved our school, and she had aspirations to become a doctor—specifically a cardiologist. I tried to encourage her to do so because I knew that she had the drive and intelligence to make it possible. Nita also would ask me about my family. She wanted to know if I lived in a house and she wanted to know about my own children. She had the opportunity to meet my oldest daughter when Katie came to spend a day with me while she had off from school. Nita admired Katie. She told me that Katie was smart and pretty. She wanted to be just like her.

Nita's optimism and enthusiasm were contagious. However, there was one day when she arrived at school without her typical smile. She came into the hallway, went to her locker, and started to put her things inside without looking my way or saying anything to me. I immediately noticed her avoidance and said, "Hello," hoping to initiate some contact. She politely responded, but there was nothing more. I knew right away that something was very wrong. I approached Nita so that I was in close proximity and could privately ask her if everything was okay. Other students were arriving at the same time, putting their things into their lockers, and I didn't want them to invade our conversation.

Nita turned to me looking very tired and sullen. She whispered, "My mom and dad cannot afford to keep my baby sister. They are sending her back to India to live with my grandparents. I could hear my mom crying all night long."

Nothing could have ever prepared me for that conversation. I usually could think of something soothing to say to students when they shared troubling information about home with me, but I had never heard of a parent needing to give up their child. All I could really do was listen to her and reassure her that it was okay to feel sad. I felt numb myself, almost in a state of disbelief. There was nothing that I could do to make the situation better. The helplessness that I felt was probably similar to how Nita was feeling.

That night, I returned home to my house, where everyone had their own room, their own clothes, and their own bed. It was hard to reconcile in my head how it could be so different for Nita's family. I couldn't begin to imagine how her mother felt.

The next day, though, Nita arrived with the same smile that I was used to seeing each morning. Resilience is the only word to describe it.

The saddest day of the year for me was in December when I got an email notification that Nita was going to be withdrawn from Raven in February. She and her parents were moving to Missouri. Mom's work assignment had ended, and her father apparently couldn't find employment in the area. I could tell that Nita was also sad to be leaving her school mid-year. She had perfectly adjusted to her new life in the US and to her school. It was a challenge for me not to share my disappointment with her. Instead, on Nita's last day, I invited her back to my classroom for lunch with me.

Nita and I dropped off the rest of the class in the cafeteria and then went back to the classroom together. We made small talk on the way, but the sadness that we both felt was obvious. When we got back to the room, we took our lunches to the back table that I used for small-group instruction. I watched as she opened up her lunch. It was a heart-shaped Dunkin vanilla crème-filled donut. Not only was this an odd thing for a student to eat for lunch, but it immediately caused additional concerns.

You see, two weeks before—on Valentine's Day—I had brought to school Dunkin Donuts to celebrate good behaviors. I had leftover donuts at the end of the day, and some of the kids had asked to take them home. Nita had been one of those students. She had taken home what appeared to be the very same donut that I now saw her eating. She saw my face, and being incredibly perceptive, she said, "This is not the donut you gave me. My mother bought this for me this morning."

I said, "Okay," but that explanation didn't make any sense. I couldn't imagine Dunkin Donuts selling that specialty donut two weeks after the holiday. However, I tried not to let my concern ruin our last lunch together. Instead, I handed Nita some cards that I had asked the students to make as a send-off, wishing her well. Nita looked at the cards with their handwritten notes and signatures and smiled. She said, "I will miss my friends."

I reassured Nita that she would make new friends in her new school, just as she had done when she came from India to Raven. Surely the transition would be easier than everything that she had been through since arriving in the US. I said, "You can put the cards up on your wall in your bedroom to remind you of your friends here."

Nita said, "I do not have a bedroom. We have one room. We all sleep together."

Once again, I was awoken to the reality of how different life is for my students than for my family and me. Near the end of our lunch, I handed Nita a letter and a present. The present was the game named Mancala. I had one in my classroom to use for indoor recess. Earlier in the year, I had shown Nita how to play the game, and she always enjoyed it. I had tried to find another one in a store to buy for Nita to take with her, but couldn't find one, so I gave her the one that my family had at home. Nita was extremely grateful. She didn't mind that this wasn't a new game; actually she seemed to prefer that it had formerly been used by my family. She opened the letter and read it.

Nita and I parted ways at the end of the school day. In some ways, it was like any other day; she helped me clean up the room and chatted until her bus was called. But this time, I gave her a hug goodbye, and I haven't seen her since. We have, however, maintained a relationship and periodically communicate. Her mother gave me permission and encouraged me to continue emailing with Nita.

That spring, we emailed back and forth several times. Nita was unhappy with her new school. She was disappointed because apparently her new class was much further behind than the class she left. In an effort to keep up her skills and maintain instruction at her ability level, I emailed a few of my lessons to her so that she could continue to learn as if she had stayed at Raven. She and her mother were grateful. Of course, our class wasn't the same after she left. No one in the class was ever as enthusiastic about learning as Nita had been, and I really missed seeing that smile at the beginning of each day. For a while, it was hard for me to be as excited each morning when greeting the students.

In June, I started to really worry about Nita after her ESL instructor at Raven told me that Nita's new school was rated poorly. My mind then started wondering about the neighborhood she might be living in and what her parents would do with her during the summer months while they would be at work. I assumed money was still a hardship.

I talked with my family about offering to have Nita live with us for the summer. I didn't know how my own family would feel about it. They would have to share their time with me and their things in our house, but they unanimously voted to extend the invitation. She wasn't a stranger to them because I had talked about her all year.

Having everyone's approval, I emailed Nita's mother and extended the invitation, which included us paying for her transportation to and from Missouri. I wasn't sure how her mom would take this offer. I sensed that her family had a lot of pride, and I was worried that they might somehow be offended. Nita's mother thanked me but said that her grandparents and the baby were coming this summer to visit. Nita would be spending time with them. I was excited to hear about her plans, but disappointed that she wouldn't be with my family. It would have been really good for my children to be with someone their age who doesn't expect a lot and gives so much in return. In many ways, Nita's maturity exceeded that of my children even though she was a year younger than my youngest child—surely the result of her environment and experience.

I did not hear from Nita again until late that summer, 2014. She emailed me to say that her summer was not going well. Her grandmother had died. Her father was very sick and in the hospital. Her mother spent a lot of time in the hospital visiting her father. Nita (now only ten years old) was taking care of the baby and the grandfather all day. Hearing that this child was dealing with so many adult issues made me grieve for the loss of her innocence. In my own house, I had been dealing with teenagers and preteens not wanting to get up in the morning, not cleaning up after themselves in the house, and not wanting to go on day trips and excursions with me. What did I do wrong to make my kids so ungrateful for what they had? If only they could have lived for just a day the life that Nita lived every day.

I responded to Nita's email but never heard back for a few years. I had even presumed that maybe her father died and the family went back to India to live. But in the summer of 2017, I tried once again sending an email to her old email address and I received a reply shortly thereafter. Nita's parents were well. Her baby sister was now a young girl, and the entire family now lived together in Virginia. It was welcome news.

Nita and I have corresponded a few times since our reconnection. Each time, she shares with me her educational progress. She now is proudly attending a school for gifted children. Each time I encourage her to continue her education and offer to help her with college applications when the time comes. I truly hope that, someday, I'm sitting or standing at Nita's high school graduation. It would mean the world to me to see her graduate! I know that she's destined for great things. She is a gift to this country, and I hope that she becomes a citizen one day.

Nita represents the best of education. This is a child who started on an educational path without an attachment to her family, without knowledge of the language we speak, and without the resources that most people take for granted. But her determination, gratitude, optimism, enthusiasm, and resilience have cleared all the obstacles in the way of what is certain to be a bright future. Education has rescued her, and because she has embraced that opportunity, she will be successful. Nita has proven there are no excuses. To this day, I carry Nita's former school ID in my purse. It serves as a reminder for what an educational opportunity can mean to a child and why we must not let them down. Public education must be improved!

HOW

...to go about improving the public education system.

YOU CHOOSE THE "WHY"

I'll Show You the "How"

As compelling as Nita's story is, she is just one of about fifty million children in the K–12 public school system who deserve a better education. Each one of those children is another reason why I am asking you to join the conversation.

The first part of this book focused on the reasons **why** we need to improve the public education system. I specifically explored topics that, as a teacher, I feel need the most attention. You may agree with me or not. The point is, everyone needs to openly and honestly share their opinions and ideas.

But understanding "why" public education needs to improve without understanding "how" to initiate that change is ineffective. Therefore, the remainder of this book will focus on **"how"** you can use your own voice to speak out on the issue that is **most important to you**—the one that pulls at your heartstrings, has personally affected you or your family, or one that you feel is most problematic in your classroom. It could be one of the issues that I discussed, or it may be something completely different. The important thing is that if you are going to take on the challenge of education reform, the issue must be meaningful to you.

Fifteen years ago, I began my own battle to make a change in the classroom. My mission began with just trying to help my son, Christopher, and eventually expanded nationwide.

Christopher approximately age 2½

The experience that I will share with you is intentionally told from a personal perspective because, as you will read, making a change in education isn't easy. The more passion that you have and the more personally you have been affected by the issue, the greater likelihood that you will sustain the energy necessary to lead to a more impactful outcome. My story is not a prescription but is a guide that will hopefully lead you in the direction that you decide to go.

Step 1

ADMIT THERE IS A PROBLEM

- You can't begin to solve a problem until you first admit that one exists.
- Don't keep making excuses for things that you know are wrong.
- Don't accept an inefficient policy or practice just because it's always been that way.

NOVEMBER 2004

As soon as I walked into my friend Angel's house, I broke down and sobbed.

Angel had offered to watch my children while I attended a fall conference with Christopher's kindergarten teacher, Ms. Benson. Christopher is my middle child. He is three years younger than his older sister, Katie, and four years older than his younger sister, Megan.

Katie (8½), Megan (1½), Christopher (5½)

Christopher was enrolled in kindergarten at the same church where he had previously attended preschool, right up the street from our home in Towson, Maryland. Throughout preschool, teachers had shared with me concerns about his language development. He often had trouble using language to communicate his wants and ideas and had difficulty using language to name familiar objects, people, animals, and places. As a three-year-old, he could not count beyond nine, and sometimes he needed directions repeated before he would follow them. He consistently misused pronouns (he, she, him, and her) and never correctly used the pronoun "I."

At home, in a neighborhood filled with young children, Christopher would often prefer to play by himself. More than once, I witnessed some neighborhood boys making fun of his speech and teasing him because he couldn't count to twenty when they were playing Hide and Seek. I also saw regression in toilet training and basic self-help skills like putting on shoes, pants, or a coat. Despite being physically able, he seemed to need everything done for him.

At one point, the preschool teachers had recommended that I have his speech tested through Baltimore County's Child Find program, a special education service provided by the Baltimore County Public School (BCPS) system. Child Find identifies children who are suspected of having an educational disability and thus may be eligible for special education services.[212] We began the screening process in March 2002, when Christopher was three years and four months old. By July 16, it was officially determined that his speech articulation patterns appeared below developmental age expectations and could impact communication skills within the education program. An IEP Team (Individualized Education Program) identified Christopher with a 04-Speech and Language Impairment. Consequently, he would be eligible for one-hour speech therapy sessions lasting thirty-six weeks.

The following fall (2002), Christopher began the three-day four-year-olds' preschool program and the special education services through BCPS. His speech was difficult to understand, even within our own family. He also started to develop a kind of stuttering habit where he would repeat a whole word many consecutive times within the same sentence. He was receiving speech therapy once a week at a local elementary school by a certified speech and language pathologist (SLP). As of November 14, 2002, the SLP documented that Christopher was imitating and producing the "k" sound and "g" sound in the initial medial and final positions of words, but he still had not mastered producing these sounds at a sentence or conversational level. He hadn't made any progress on the "j" sound. However, by period three (March 28, 2003), she reported that he had mastered all twelve of his objectives on his IEP. But she noted, "He continues to experience mild, inconsistent disfluencies in a variety of settings."

Hindsight is everything. Looking back now, I saw some improvement—but not enough. His speech was still very difficult to understand, and his frustration became more evident. He seemed to recognize his own difficulty in communicating and understood that others noticed it as well. To make matters worse, Katie—once his translator at home—was now in school full-time (in first grade). She was no longer as available to help him communicate, exacerbating Christopher's feelings of frustration and isolation.

I remember one time in particular when I was putting him to bed, and he was trying to tell me something that had happened at school. I couldn't understand what he was saying, and I kept asking him to repeat it. After requesting this three or four times, I said, "I'm sorry, Buddy. I just don't understand what you are trying to tell me." Unfortunately, I could understand his reply. He said, "That's okay. It doesn't matter." In that moment, I felt his pain, frustration, and sadness. There was no doubt that something was getting in his way from being able to express himself, and I can't imagine how frustrating and demoralizing that must have been. Communication is so much more than words. It connects ideas and thoughts with people. When it doesn't occur or requires so much effort, there's much more than just the words that are lost. We lose that sense of belonging.

Suzanne and Christopher at preschool, May 7, 2004

On June 4, 2003, Christopher's annual IEP meeting was conducted. At this time, it was agreed to draft a consultative IEP to monitor Chris's speech skills and fluency. Craig and I had decided to have Christopher repeat a year of preschool (the fours') to postpone kindergarten for a year until he would be five years and nine months old. We had hoped that an extra year would provide time to improve his speech and to develop his confidence.

First day of school, September 2004

Now here it was, November 2004—about a third of the way through Kindergarten—and clearly, something was still very wrong. Deep in my heart, I had ongoing concerns about him, but I felt too ashamed to express them. What kind of mother thinks that their child is anything less than perfect? If a qualified speech pathologist believed he no longer needed services, who was I to question her? Was I just expecting too much, or was I being unfair in comparing him to his older sister, Katie?

When Ms. Benson handed me the report card, I saw the concern on her face. Christopher was struggling with several skills, including reciting the alphabet, reciting days of the week in order, printing his last name using upper- and lowercase letters, working from left to right, counting beyond ten, and sequencing numerals eleven to twenty. He could not detect phonemes, the basic sounds that are the building blocks of words. He knew many sight words but struggled with reading. He couldn't say or sing his alphabet—he didn't even want to try—and when he was urged to try, he had no idea what was to be sung in the section, "L—M—N—O—P." He used pronouns incorrectly. He confused similar-sounding words. His speech was not understandable to many of the other students, and he knew it. He was reluctant to share during circle time. He withdrew himself from his peers, and he had complained, "School is too hard for me."

I asked Ms. Benson for advice. What should I do? She said that I could wait it out and see if it is developmental, wait it out to see if the public school system would identify a problem when he entered first grade (and thus offer services as part of the special education system), or I could pay to have private educational testing done now. If it were her child, she would choose the private educational testing but warned me that it was very expensive. Ms. Benson also told me something that I still think about to this day. She said, "Christopher knows something is wrong." He recognized that things were hard for him. He recognized that he had trouble communicating. He responded by quietly removing himself from the situation. She said, "Children that are bright but have a learning difficulty often recognize that there is a problem."

In an odd way, I felt a release—like the burden of me thinking these things and keeping them all to myself was now taken away because someone else saw the problems too. I wasn't just a mother who was expecting too much from my child and unfairly comparing him to another. The problem had been recognized, but now it needed to be identified. What was causing the problem, and what could be done to help?

On December 14 and 21, 2004, Christopher met with Claire A. B. Freeland, PhD, a licensed clinical psychologist for a psychoeducational evaluation. He was six years and one month old. Dr. Freeland administered the Wechsler Intelligence Scale for Children—Fourth Edition (WISC-IV), the Developmental Test of Visual-Motor Integration (VMI), NEPSY, the Oral and Written Language Scales (OWLS), the Comprehensive Test of Phonological Processing (CTOPP), the Woodcock-Johnson III Tests of Achievement (WJ-III) Form A, and the 2001 Achenbach Child Behavior Checklist for ages 6–18 (CBCL/6-18).

Among Dr. Freeland's noted behavioral observations was the following:

> He is a tall-for-his-age, handsome boy who understands the reasons for testing. He says that school used to be easy, but the work is getting too hard…When he is engaged in hands-on tasks, he is reasonably still in his chair. When tasks are purely oral, Christopher fidgets; he pulls his arm out of his sleeve, leans against the wall, and changes position frequently…He responds readily, gets his point across, and expresses his needs and wants. He asks questions and makes spontaneous comments. Sometimes it seems like Christopher knows more than he can express in words. His syntax is young; for example, he confuses "her" and "she." Christopher also seems uneven in his auditory processing. He needs some directions repeated.[213]

On many of the tests, Christopher performed within a range normal for children his age, including intellectual functioning, verbal comprehension, nonverbal, abstract reasoning, and visual-spatial functioning. He scored above average in concept formation and exhibited very superior visual attention on the NEPSY Attention/Executive scale. A lot of the test scores by themselves seemed okay—nothing to be concerned about—but not all of them.

OWLS (Oral and Written Language Scales) is a test used to evaluate language skills. "The Listening Comprehension subtest requires the child to choose from four options, the picture that most closely matches a given sentence and measures understanding of statements that emphasize challenging vocabulary, complex sentence structure, and ambiguous word meaning."[214] On this test, Christopher scored slightly below average in the twenty-first percentile, indicating mild underlying weaknesses in auditory processing.[215]

The last set of tests were the most revealing. Dr. Freeland administered the Comprehensive Test of Phonological Processing (CTOPP). It measures three aspects of phonological processing, phonological awareness, phonological memory, and rapid naming. Christopher's Phonological Awareness composite fell at the low end of the average range (twenty-seventh percentile). He exhibited emerging word segmentation and sound matching skills, each at the twenty-fifth percentile. His ability to blend sounds to form words was solidly average (fiftieth percentile). Christopher demonstrated a distinct area of weakness in the Phonological Memory composite tests. He scored in the third percentile.

The Phonological Memory tasks included Memory for Digits and Nonword Repetition, which were extremely weak, fifth and ninth percentiles, respectively. These results indicated "that while Christopher exhibited the ability to retrieve familiar information with automaticity, which is required for fluent reading, his ability to segment and sequence sounds was less well developed, and his immediate auditory recall was an impediment to developing reading skills."[216]

Dr. Freeland met with Craig and me on January 4, 2005, to go through all of the tests and their results. She concluded our conversation with the suggestion that I have Christopher's hearing tested. I didn't understand. I told Dr. Freeland that he had his hearing tested every year as part of an annual physical, and he had his hearing tested by Baltimore County as part of the Child Find process for identification of special needs services. She explained, "I'd like you to have a specific auditory test to measure his central auditory processing. During testing, I often had to repeat directions to him before he would start."

She also pointed out that academically, Christopher showed mild weaknesses in auditory processing and in phonological memory. He scored at least within the average range in every area tested, but at the low end of average in phonological awareness and decoding skills.

At this point, we didn't know why Christopher was struggling, but all of our concerns were out in the open. It was a relief to admit that something was wrong, and I realized that you can't begin to solve a problem until you are honest that a problem exists. Now, we just needed to identify the root cause of our concerns so that we could begin the appropriate intervention. Dr. Stephen Seipp, an audiologist, would provide that clarity.

Step 2

IDENTIFY THE ROOT CAUSE OF THE PROBLEM

- Every problem has a cause; you just have to find it.
- It is easy to blame a problem on lack of finances—don't fall into this trap. Money may facilitate a solution but likely isn't the problem itself.

JANUARY 5, 2005

"Neurology can be changed," he told me—in an attempt to offer consolation.

Those are the words that stuck in my mind and played over and over, after we left the doctor's office. Dr. Seipp had conducted hearing tests specifically for auditory processing—that is, how Christopher's brain interpreted and responded to auditory signals. Preliminary results appeared to reveal a processing deficit.

Less than a week later, the final results arrived in the mail. The good news was that testing did *not* indicate a global Auditory Processing Deficit; however, it did show slowed temporal resolution/auditory processing speed. Temporal resolution is an important underlying skill, which can have some impact on learning. The acoustic signals that make up the spoken language are based primarily in time. Learning these time-bound acoustic signals requires an auditory system that can detect the smallest segments of the spoken language. An inability to detect these very small differences can create problems with phonemic recognition, spelling, and subsequent difficulties reading efficiently.[217]

Results also indicated that Christopher had a strong right ear preference. When two different signals were presented in each ear at the same time, Christopher "heard" primarily only in the right ear and did not process the left ear effectively. A right ear preference is typical for children his age since the auditory neurology isn't fully mature until the age of approximately twelve to thirteen years, and the neural pathways for the left ear are much longer than the right ear. However, the differences between the left ear and the right ear for Christopher were *much larger* than would be considered typical.[218]

Both the slowed temporal resolution and the strong right ear preference could be contributing to academic difficulties, in particular with reading. Both of these issues could be a simple delay in the maturation of the neural pathways, but to make this assumption would be risky since the differences could also be due to "neural wiring." Either way, Christopher was experiencing learning difficulties, and the earlier the intervention, the better.

In a follow-up meeting, Dr. Seipp was very reassuring. He said that when children have difficulty understanding or learning, there are those who act out and those who withdraw themselves. Christopher was withdrawing himself, and those are the children who tend to get overlooked. He explained to me that more than anything, Christopher didn't want to disappoint me. That's why it appeared that he didn't want to do his work or read to me. Removing himself from the task removed the possibility of humiliation, embarrassment, and disappointment. Dr. Seipp was able to provide this insight because he himself was diagnosed with an Auditory Processing Deficit in college, after struggling academically his whole life.

Furthermore, he reiterated that neurology can be changed. There were things that we could do to help with development of the neural pathways, including programs, such as Fast ForWord and Earobics, which help to develop auditory listening skills and temporal resolution, particularly with phonemics and phonics. He recommended preferential seating in class to help with noise reduction and to favor that strong right ear preference.

I shared all of the reports, information, and recommendations from both Dr. Freeland and Dr. Seipp with Christopher's teacher and the school's director. They immediately implemented all of the suggestions. I would soon learn that it doesn't work this way in the public school system.

At home, I transformed our kitchen into a classroom. Every morning, we would go over the alphabet, the days of the week, and counting to one hundred. I wrote the alphabet on sentence strips in sections that coincided with the phrasing in the alphabet song. We would sing it together as I pointed to the letters. I made a one hundreds chart using different colors to highlight the patterns in a base-ten number system. I tried to incorporate as many visual aids as possible, capitalizing on

Christopher's superior visual abilities. Fortunately, Christopher did not seem to realize that all of this was being done for him. I had told him that we needed to teach Megan these things to get her ready for preschool. He believed that he was teaching his little sister (she was only two at the time), and that gave him a sense of purpose and boosted his self-esteem.

Christopher and Megan, summer 2006

Addressing the reading problems was more of a challenge. Christopher hated to read to me. It was very difficult for him, and I think what Dr. Seipp said was probably true—he didn't want to disappoint me. The best that I could do was to try to ease his anxiety through incentives, breaks, and a more relaxed atmosphere. Sometimes we would take turns reading; I would read one page, and he would read the next. Other times, I would promise to do something fun as soon as he finished. He loved to take nature walks and look for bugs, so we did *a lot* of walking around the neighborhood. One time I set up a tent in the yard and filled the tent with pillows and books. That became our reading spot, one that he enjoyed and still remembers.

Another suggestion that we implemented was getting him some speech and language therapy. Christopher did *not* qualify for speech services through Baltimore County anymore, so this meant that we had to pay for these services out of pocket. On March 3, 2005, Christopher began sessions with a licensed speech and language pathologist (SLP) who was also a designated "off-site" Fast For-Word provider. She charged $90 for a 45-minute session once a week. After an informal evaluation, she found that he had difficulty producing multi-syllable words, /s/ in blends and in many words, /l/, and the /r/. These problems had *not* been noted on any of his IEP reports.

The SLP also acted as a facilitator when Christopher began using the Fast ForWord program, an online program that develops increased phonological awareness and language comprehension.[219] It is designed to build oral language skills and processing speed through an animated training exercise. The cost for this program was around $2,000. Basically, a child must use the program for two hours of uninterrupted time each day. The child wears a set of headphones and uses a mouse to click on and respond to sounds through the headphones. The child cannot take any breaks during that two-hour period, and it's physically exhausting for the listener because it requires intense concentration.

As soon as school ended, we purchased the program and began using it every morning.

Christopher's kindergarten graduation, May 2005

I learned a lot from the speech therapist. Most importantly, I learned not to overtly correct Christopher or interrupt him when he said something wrong. Rather, I would wait for him to finish and then simply repeat it using the correct pronunciation or grammar as part of our conversation. That way, he wouldn't feel like someone was always correcting him; but he would hear how it should have been said. This is referred to as rephrasing. When I started doing this, I saw an *immediate* reduction in his frustration. The rephrasing strategy took away the criticism and feeling of inadequacy.

I also learned how Christopher was misinterpreting the sounds that he heard. Because his temporal processing speed was slower than it should have been, he wasn't necessarily hearing sounds in the correct order that they were said. For example, he could have heard the word "fits" as "fist." I would sometimes get a glimpse of this when he would be talking. He would confuse similar-sounding words like "potato" and "tomato" as well as "instruction," "construction," and "destruction." He said the word "lemonade" as "elenomade." I learned that sometimes it wasn't that his speech was unclear, but it was simply that he was saying words as he had "heard" them, which reminded all of us to speak more slowly and clearly—enunciating each part of the words.

By September 2005, Christopher was ready to start first grade at Stoneleigh Elementary School, a public school. He had concluded the Fast ForWord program and his speech and language therapy sessions. We had seen improvement in all areas—social, psychological, language, and reading—but we didn't want to assume that everything was fine and stop there.

Craig and I had requested an IEP meeting with Stoneleigh back in March 2005, hoping that Christopher might qualify for some accommodations, including speech therapy sessions and preferential seating (yes, in the public school system, your child has to qualify to be seated in close proximity to the teacher). Under federal law, parents have the right to an independent educational evaluation from qualified professionals of their choice, at their own expense. That's what we had done. We submitted the results from Dr. Seipp's audiological tests, the results from Dr. Freeland's psychoeducational evaluation, and a letter from our SLP discussing her observations, outcomes, and recommendations for Christopher. The IEP team had ninety days to review the results. However, an IEP team *only* has the obligation to consider the information of the private testing. The team is *not obligated* to accept the findings of that testing.

As a parent, IEP meetings are overwhelming whether you or the school is the initiator. At our IEP team meeting, the school administrator (the vice-principal), the school audiologist, and the public school psychologist spent the majority of the meeting trying to convince me that my son didn't have a problem and did not require any special services. They threw at me numbers and percentages, trying to disclaim what I had been told privately by a well-respected audiologist who specialized in children, by a private experienced kindergarten teacher, by a private speech and language pathologist, and by a private child psychologist. The public school officials chose to discuss the numbers that were average to above average, and to "skim over" the ones that indicated a problem—even a score of 3 percent on phonological testing. I felt like we were under attack. And I wondered if the school was playing a defense strategy because, after all, Christopher once had an IEP from BCPS for speech services, and the team had concluded that he had met all of his speech goals and released him from that IEP obligation. Despite being a somewhat timid person, I finally interrupted.

"I understand that you all are focused on the numbers in the testing reports, but my child is not a number to me. I don't really care what the numbers say. I don't need a number to tell me that something is wrong. I know my child better than anyone else, and I know in my heart that something isn't right. I'm just asking you to help me, help him."

I really wanted to look strong, but I couldn't help but get choked up when saying this. We had been through a lot, all using our own resources. I can't begin to imagine how desperate a parent would feel who didn't have the support or couldn't afford the help that we had given Christopher. I didn't feel like I was asking for that much from the public school system, one that is partially funded by my taxes.

The room quieted. It was then that I believe the team administrator spoke, and we all agreed to carefully monitor Christopher's progress and to resume discussions if need be later. He would **not** be eligible for accommodations based on their standards.

As a parent, numbers and statistics do not matter because your focus is, and should be, on your one child. When your children are little, you are their only real advocate. You, the parent, are the one who spends the most amount of interactive time with your child. You celebrate their successes and quietly grieve for their failures. You know their frustrations. Many times, their frustrations become your own frustrations. And without any education or psychology background, you know in your heart when something is not right.

School officials cannot allow themselves to "feel" for each child and think with their heart the way a parent can. They have limited resources to offer, and so they must, out of fairness to each child, focus on the numbers. Every time they issue an IEP for a student, they are legally obligated to provide services to that child. It was much easier getting Christopher the help he needed in a private kindergarten setting. But continuing with private school wasn't financially an option for us, and I don't believe it should have been necessary for the few basic accommodations that we were requesting. Every child deserves an *opportunity* to achieve their full potential, and every child needs an adult in their corner to make sure they get that opportunity.

Step 3

DO THE RESEARCH

Educate Yourself

- Read as much research as you can find. Learn everything you can about the problem and its source.
- Speak with the experts on the topic. Depending on the problem, that could be doctors, teachers, school administrators, local politicians, or other parents.
- Speak with the students themselves about the problem. How do they feel? How is this problem impacting their ability to learn or their desire to learn in that environment?

IGNORANCE CAUSES FEAR

Ignorance isn't stupidity; it's just a lack of knowledge.

When a doctor diagnoses a child with a problem that a parent knows little to nothing about, that ignorance heightens the parent's anxiety, makes them feel helpless, and allows their imagination to run wild with all of the worst scenarios. You begin to fall down that "hole of helplessness." That's exactly what I experienced after Christopher was diagnosed with an Auditory Processing Deficit. Eventually, I channeled all of that energy in a different, more useful direction. I began to educate myself—to learn everything that I could about how what a child hears is processed by their brain, how acoustics in a classroom can make a difference, and how a child's ability to understand what they hear impacts their ability to learn. The results were truly shocking!

HEARING ISSUES WITH CHILDREN

A study in Putnam County, Ohio, found that 43 percent of primary-level students failed a minimal, 15 dB HL, hearing screen on any given day of the week.[220] This staggering statistic is easier to comprehend when you break down the prevalence of hearing impairments between permanent and temporary. According to the *Journal of the American Medical Association* (JAMA), 14.9 percent (more than seven million) of US schoolchildren ages six to nineteen have a low or high-frequency hearing loss of at least 16 dB in one or both ears.[221] A "unilateral hearing loss in children impacts speech perception, learning, self-image, and social skills."[222] An additional 10–15 percent of primary-level (kindergarten through second grade) children suffer a temporary hearing loss from fluid relating to middle ear infections,[223] one that commonly extends for weeks or months.

This is referred to as a conductive hearing loss. Dobie and Berlin (1979) found that children with mild degrees of conductive hearing loss have greater difficulty understanding higher frequencies (consonants) in degraded listening conditions and lose the majority of transitional information (final position consonants and plural endings) that contribute to speech intelligibility.[224] "Recurrent OME in children has been linked to compromised speech, language, intellectual, attentional, learning, psychoeducational, and psychosocial development."[225]

Christopher did not have a permanent or temporary hearing impairment. He was diagnosed with an Auditory Processing Deficit (APD), meaning that his brain had trouble "making sense" of the auditory signals that his ears were detecting, particularly sounds that were coming in through his left ear. The ears just detect signals and then send those signals to the brain for sound discrimination, recognition, identification, and ultimately, comprehension. It is estimated that around 5 percent of school-age children, or 2.5 million children, have APD, although many more children may go undiagnosed or misdiagnosed[226] because the symptoms are so similar to Attention Deficit Disorder (ADD). Since auditory processing involves the discrimination and identification of sounds in order to comprehend them, it was important that the sounds he heard were clear and distinct and equally accessible to both ears. For that reason, the closer that he was to the teacher's voice, the better.

Even children with normal hearing are ineffective listeners, especially in poor acoustical environments, until the mid- to late-teenage years.[227] Dr. Seipp had told me that a child's neurological auditory capabilities were not fully developed until the teens, but I really didn't understand the extent of that statement, nor did I understand how the typical classroom would fail to support those immature auditory needs. Children do not hear and process what they hear in the same way as an adult.

Multiple studies have shown that the "human auditory brain structure is not fully mature until about age fifteen; thus, a child does not bring a complete neurological system to a listening situation."[228] This means that children are slower at processing the sounds they hear and cannot always "fill in the blanks" for sounds and words that are missed or muffled. Everyone experiences times when they miss part of a word or sentence, particularly in a situation where there is background noise, reverberation, or they are simply too far away from the speaker's voice. However, most often, adults can automatically fill in the gaps and make sense of what they are hearing.

Sometimes this is so automatic that an adult isn't consciously aware that it's happening. This process is referred to as auditory or cognitive closure. Children can't do this, particularly the younger they are, because their brains simply do not have the "historical" data or life experience to fill in the missing pieces. This is the reason that children need more favorable listening conditions than adults to gain the same level of comprehension.

Therefore, whether a child has a hearing impairment (permanent or temporary), an auditory processing problem, or completely normal hearing—the auditory environment is *crucial* to the unique needs of its listeners in order for those listeners to comprehend what they hear. This meant that I needed to understand the basics of acoustics and, in particular, those in the classroom since students spend up to 75 percent of their school day engaged in auditory learning.[229]

ACOUSTICS

Acoustics measure the impact that the physical environment has on auditory learning. There are three major components of acoustics: ambient noise, reverberation, and the signal-to-noise ratio. Ambient noise is simply the background noise in a room, such as the hum from computers and HVAC equipment, pencils tapping, chairs scraping the floor as students adjust their seats, and any whispering or side conversations. Reverberation is commonly thought of as an echo. When sound can't be absorbed because of hard surfaces, it bounces (or reverberates) around. The longer that it takes sound to reverberate, the harder it is to hear, particularly if you have multiple sounds (including that background noise we just talked about) reverberating.

Signal-to-noise ratio (SNR) is the important measure of acoustics and speech intelligibility. SNR is measured as the difference between the teacher's voice and the background noise. For example, if the teacher is speaking at 60 dB and the background noise is 45 dB, then the SNR is +15 decibels. Obviously, the teacher's voice needs to be louder than the background noise for comprehension. How much louder depends on the listener.

The American Speech Language Hearing Association (ASHA) has specified that classroom background noise should not exceed 35 dBA (in an empty room) and reverberation should not exceed .6 seconds.[230] However, numerous studies revealed classrooms that exhibit excessive noise and reverberation.[231] Furthermore, while high levels of background noise remain relatively stable around the classroom, the teacher's voice drops six decibels for every doubling of distance.[232] This decline in the speech signal is reflected in the SNR. According to ASHA, the *normal* hearing child needs the SNR to be at least fifteen decibels for speech intelligibility.[233] In comparison, Bess and Humes (2003) report that adults only need a SNR of +6 decibels to achieve the same level of comprehension, highlighting the differences in hearing ability between adults and children.[234]

While students in close proximity to the teacher may have a SNR of +15 decibels, those seated more than six to eight feet from the teacher likely will not because of the drop in the teacher's voice over distance. **Students not seated in close proximity to the teacher are at a distinct disadvantage.**

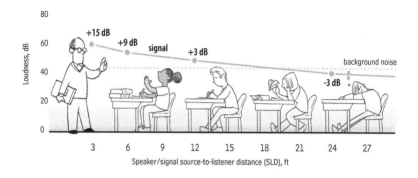

Speaker/signal source-to-listener distance (SLD), ft

A 1990 study by Crandell illustrated the profound effect that teacher-student distance had on speech recognition scores in normal hearing children ages five to seven. Crandell (1990) found that "[m]ean scores for the children…were 82 percent, 55 percent, and 36 percent at six, twelve, and twenty-four feet, respectively."[235] Thus speech recognition and the effectiveness of verbal instruction in the classroom systematically declines as teacher-student distance is increased.

An abundance of research has shown that "a typical classroom provides an inadequate listening environment."[236] Researchers at Ohio State University found that the acoustics of many classrooms are poor enough to make listening and learning difficult for children. Only two of thirty-two classrooms in central Ohio primary schools (public, private, old buildings, new buildings, and across a variety of socioeconomic areas) were found to meet the acoustical standards for background noise and reverberation as set by ASHA.[237] Furthermore, it is not enough to simply hear the teacher; students must be able to detect the teacher's voice, discriminate between similar sounds, identify those sounds, and comprehend the meaning to achieve speech intelligibility and thus to learn.

IMPACT OF HEARING ON LEARNING

When I first discovered that Christopher had difficulty processing the sounds he heard, my greatest concern was that this problem would negatively impact his ability to learn, particularly in the classroom where so much of learning is dependent upon verbal instruction. Unfortunately, my research confirmed this to be true. ASHA researchers have reported that children with a hearing loss are often slower to develop speech and language, can have lower academic achievement, are often socially isolated, and can have a negative self-image.[238] His kindergarten teacher and I had observed all of these effects. A study at Vanderbilt University by Frederick Bess found that "37 percent of students with slight hearing loss had failed at least one grade, as compared to a 3 percent failure rate for hearing students."[239] Looked at from another angle, this means that students who have trouble hearing are ten times more likely to fail than their peers without that difficulty.

Hearing is the foundation for learning. Reading has a strong auditory foundation because phonological and phonemic awareness are the building blocks for developing literacy skills, and that awareness is dependent upon being able to hear the individual sounds in the words.[240] But hearing in the classroom can also negatively impact other factors involved in learning. Gallup (1986) reported that "[w]hen students cannot listen effectively in school, they are more likely to have difficulty staying on task, and discipline and cooperation are difficult to maintain."[241]

How then could I use all of this knowledge to help Christopher? At this time, I was well aware that proximity to the teacher's voice was critical. Students seated close to the teacher had an advantage over their classmates seated further away. Other than preferential seating, how could I ensure that Christopher would be able to clearly hear his teacher? Even if he had preferential seating, at some point the teacher was sure to be moving about the classroom and, therefore, not always within close proximity.

I had read about personal hearing assistive devices (also referred to as FM amplification systems) that students with hearing or processing impairments could use to combat these problems and help to ensure speech intelligibility. When I met with Dr. Seipp, I asked him if he would recommend that Christopher use a hearing assistive device in school. Dr. Seipp explained that there are pros and cons for these types of devices. The pros are, yes, it would ensure that he could hear his teacher's voice because an assistive device requires that the teacher wear a wireless microphone, which then picks up on his or her voice (regardless of proximity to the student) and transmits that voice directly into an earpiece that the student wears much like a hearing aid. The cons are twofold. First, this device does *not* help the student wearing the earpiece to hear his classmates any better during something like a read-aloud, and more importantly, it may carry a certain stigma because it would be noticeable that the device was being used just for the hearing-impaired student.

Christopher was already showing embarrassment and exhibiting anxiety in social situations. He sometimes was withdrawn around other children. For that reason, Dr. Seipp did not recommend this for him at this time. As I continued to educate myself, I still kept thinking, *How can I ensure that Christopher will be able to hear and understand his teacher if he isn't in close proximity to the teacher?* That question would soon be answered.

Christopher avoided large groups and loud environments, August 2004

Step 4

FIND THE BEST SOLUTION

- A good idea might make your problem less burdensome or even solve it.
- A better idea will solve your problem without creating another problem for someone else.
- The best idea will solve your problem and other problems too. Find the best solution! This is one that will gain the most attention and ultimately the most support.
  - Learn everything that you can before you begin to share information.
  - Confirm the credibility of your sources—if using a research study, when and where was it published, is it peer-reviewed, and who were the participants?

FEBRUARY 21, 2005

In the midst of the usual school night's chaos with three young children, my mother phoned and said, "Turn on the TV to CBS right now!"

What I was about to watch—just three minutes—changed the next four years of my life and probably the lives of thousands of students throughout the United States.

It was just a few weeks after I had learned from Christopher's audiologist that he had an Auditory Processing Deficit. CBS aired a segment on their nightly news entitled "Schools Get Wired for Sound." The CBS segment introduced a technology that was similar to the hearing assistive device used by students with hearing impairments but had one key difference: *every* student in the class would benefit from its use.

The segment was filmed at Foothills Elementary School in Riverton, Utah, where the classrooms were wired with a state-of-the-art infrared technology. The idea was simple—the teacher (Ms. Hebertson) wore a small wireless microphone around her neck, and the classroom had four ceiling speakers installed throughout the room. When she spoke, her voice was amplified by about 8 to 10 decibels and transmitted to those speakers, which evenly distributed the teacher's voice throughout the entire room. Therefore, regardless of where any student was seated in the classroom or physical proximity to the teacher, every student had an equal opportunity to hear what she was saying—in a clear, soothing voice.[242]

During the interview, Ms. Hebertson went on to say that she never had to raise her voice, and she felt like the students were better behaved, more likely to ask questions, and more likely to participate. The superintendent of the Jordan district, Barry Newbold, said the one downside was, "I can't get it in classrooms fast enough!" He was having the equipment installed in every school within his district.[243]

Why was this equipment necessary? "Even kids with normal hearing can miss as much as a third of what their teachers say. And remember those troublemakers in the back row? It seems they just may not have been hearing…ditto some kids labeled with ADHD and other learning disabilities. Some wired schools report test scores are up across the board…Ohio has mandated it for every school in the state," said CBS's Bill Whitaker.[244]

As soon as the segment ended, I felt euphoric—this could be a solution. But then I immediately thought, "This is too good to be true." So that night after the kids were put to bed, my research shifted from hearing problems to this technology, and my skepticism turned into advocacy.

While the use of infrared equipment was new, the use of teacher microphones and speakers was not exactly a new concept. According to ASHA, sound-field amplification technology has been used in classrooms since the inception of the Mainstream Amplification Resource Room Study (MARRS) Project in 1978.[245] MARRS was intended to be a three-year study on fourth- through sixth-grade students with minimal hearing loss, a coexisting learning deficit, and normal learning potential, conducted in the Wabash and Ohio Valley schools in southern Illinois.[246]

Approximately half of the students remained in regular classrooms, and the other half were taught in rooms where teachers used sound-field FM amplification systems consisting of wireless microphones and two speakers. "[T]he greatest improvement was documented for the group instructed in amplified classrooms. Not only did these students show significant gains in academic achievement, but they also were noted to achieve in reading and language arts at a faster rate, to a higher level, and at one-tenth the cost of students taken from regular classes and provided instruction in a resource-room setting."[247] Perhaps the most significant result of the study was that **ALL students, not just those with a hearing impairment, showed an increase in academic performance when taught in the room with the teacher microphones.**

It is important to note that the MARRS project was funded by the US Department of Education as part of the National Diffusion Network. The project achieved national validation status in 1981 and was recertified in 1992.[248] Thus, the US Department of Education knew as early as 1980 how beneficial wireless microphones and speakers in classrooms could be for *every* student in the classroom. Since this initial study, several other studies have validated the benefits of this technology for all students. Ray (1990) and Sarff, Ray, and Bagwell (1981) found that "the most cost-effective and acceptable technology for facilitating learning in a typical school classroom is the use of a sound field FM system."[249]

A 2000 study of 166 first-grade students in Broward County, Florida, measured the impact that a favorable SNR had on clearly hearing phonetics. The results showed significantly greater literacy gains for students taught in rooms that used a sound-field FM system—particularly for bilingual and special education students.[250] Flexer et al. (2002) conducted a study to determine if sound-field amplification along with phonological and phonemic awareness training would reduce the number of at-risk readers. The results yielded that the training to promote early literacy was more effective when teacher microphones and speakers were used.[251]

A 2003, two-year study by Paul J. McCarty, EdD and Steven J. Gertel of high-need fifth-grade students showed an improved average of 12 percent in reading, 14 percent in math, 17 percent in language, and 20 percent in science and social studies, with an overall test battery increase of 14 percent for those students taught in the sound-field amplification rooms.[252]

The accolades went on and on, showing improvements in speech recognition abilities, behavior, attention, literacy, and academic achievement when students were taught in a classroom with teacher microphones and speakers. I easily read twenty articles that evening discussing the benefits to ALL students when incorporating this technology in the classroom but especially benefits to the at-risk student population: students who were learning English as a second language, students with ADHD or other attention deficits, students with learning disabilities, and obviously, students with any type of hearing or auditory processing impairment. How could our school superintendents and politicians ignore these overwhelming benefits that could help bridge the gap for so many struggling students?

Late that night, Craig stopped in to see me before going to bed and asked, "Well, is it really too good to be true?" My answer was, "Nope. It's actually even better." How could anyone resist an idea that's cost-effective and improves academic achievement?

Step 5

START THE CONVERSATION AT THE MOST BASIC LEVEL

- Build ground support before moving to higher levels. Gain the support of your peers first and recruit them to join forces with you. It is much harder for people to ignore a group than it is to ignore one person.
- Start where change is the easiest to implement and where you will directly see the benefits. This could be in one classroom, with one particular group of students, **or** it could be throughout an entire school where you teach or where your children attend.
- **People whom you should include in the conversation:** teachers who would be impacted by the change, the principal of the school you are targeting, resource teachers such as the ESL or special education instructor, the School Improvement Team, the school PTA.
- If what you are advocating involves a change to a school facility or will eventually need the approval of the Board of Education, begin to reach out to a board member in charge of your region.

- Continue to research and learn more. Talk to people, schools, or districts that have either tried your idea or have studied it. Don't be afraid to question what is currently or not currently being done, and why.

February 23, 2005, 8:37 a.m.:

Dear Claudia,

My name is Suzanne, and I am a mom of three children in Baltimore, Maryland. My six-year-old son was recently diagnosed with an auditory processing disorder. Upon researching this disorder, I have come to realize how many children suffer from auditory problems and suffer through school, often misdiagnosed with other attention deficit issues or learning disorders. I read the article on the internet that was recently featured on CBS news concerning wiring schools for sound.

I would love to initiate this process in the Maryland schools. Can you give me any advice about where to begin? I feel like this could really help not only my son, but all children. Thank you.

Claudia Anderson is the founder of Audio Enhancement, a Salt Lake City company that created and manufactured the sound equipment used at Foothills Elementary. I first heard her name and learned about her on the CBS segment, "Wired for Sound." Claudia originally designed the equipment back in 1978 to help her two hard-of-hearing sons while they were in elementary school. Without knowing anything else, I immediately connected to this mother's determination to help her children; and from what I had researched, the product of that determination could greatly help Christopher and many other students. I looked up the company contact information on the internet and sent this email—just two days after viewing the CBS segment, and I did get a response from Audio Enhancement on March 1. But my enthusiasm for the idea didn't end with that email.

On February 24, I emailed Dr. Nancy Grasmick, State Superintendent of Maryland Public Schools (1991–2011), sharing the information that I had learned from the CBS segment and my research. As I put it, "I have stumbled upon an idea that could greatly help ALL children in the Maryland Schools." I asked that Dr. Grasmick view the television segment through a link that I provided and that she seriously consider it. "I would do anything to help in this endeavor."

It wasn't simply an idea or the three-minute video that propelled me to take on this mission; it was the *abundance* of research that I continued to discover and learn about every single day, which supported the *necessity* of this technology in our schools. Dr. Grasmick's response arrived in the form of a letter on March 16. She thanked me for the information and said, "At this time, an FM amplification system may be used in local school systems to address a student's auditory needs on an individual basis." I appreciated that someone at her level took the time to personally respond to me.

Dr. Grasmick's response was a wake-up call to me. I needed to channel my efforts toward a goal that was more specific and realistic; start smaller. My target became Stoneleigh Elementary—an older school building in a nearby neighborhood. I had attended Stoneleigh as a child. My daughter, Katie, was currently attending Stoneleigh as a third-grader, and Christopher would be starting Stoneleigh in September as a first-grade student. I emailed the parent chair of Stoneleigh's School Improvement Team (SIT) and requested to be put on the agenda for the next meeting to be held on April 7. My intention was to introduce the idea and share the benefits, hoping that the SIT would consider installing the sound systems in at least some of Stoneleigh's classrooms.

My business background influenced the idea to create a PowerPoint that would be broken into three main parts: the problems with auditory learning in the classrooms (immature auditory capabilities and hearing problems prevalent among the student populations), the solution—a classroom sound amplification system (including the CBS video demonstrating how it worked), and research justifying the expense (supporting increases in academic achievement and reduced costs associated with a reduction in special education referrals and less teacher absenteeism related to vocal fatigue).

I had already begun my investigation and uncovered a lot of research supporting improved academic performance for all students; however, I had some questions on one of the research studies conducted by Dr. Paul McCarty. Audio Enhancement had included Dr. McCarty's research on its website, so I called Audio Enhancement to ask them more specific questions about the study. They redirected me to Dr. McCarty himself and gave me his personal phone number.

Dr. Paul McCarty was a consultant to schools, educational planners, architects, and government agencies for high-performance school design, research, and educational improvement. He was an adjunct professor at Brigham Young with faculty responsibilities for advanced research instruction, learning environment design, instructional technology, life span, child adolescent development, and student achievement. He was also a former teacher and a current Utah public school administrator and principal.

The thought of calling someone whom I didn't know, let alone a university professor of his caliber, was far outside of my comfort zone. But I wanted to ensure that any information I shared was reliable and credible. I couldn't confidently include any data in my presentation unless I was fully prepared to answer *all* questions related to it, and the only way that I could do that—was to call Dr. McCarty.

I nervously phoned the number, almost hoping that he wouldn't pick up. But he did.

Me: "Hello, is this Dr. Paul McCarty?"

Him: *"Yes."*

Me: "Hi. I'm just a mom from Baltimore, Maryland. I have some questions for you about a research study that you did on classroom amplification equipment."

Looking back now, I realize how insecure I was, identifying myself as "just a mom." However, this "mom" was on a mission, and he must have detected the seriousness of my intent because Dr. McCarty took the time not only to answer my questions, but to share with me more information about the technology and the proven benefits of using it. He even went so far as to explain how he had become such a strong advocate.

You see, Dr. McCarty had been a principal in a Utah elementary school when one of his teachers came to him with the news that she would be needing to retire from her teaching profession. It was for medical reasons. Over the years, her vocal chords had suffered damage from straining her voice all day to teach and from attempting to project her voice across the classroom. Determined not to lose one of his best teachers, Dr. McCarty sought out a solution and ended up discovering the classroom sound systems. After installing the equipment in her classroom, he saw for himself the additional benefits to the students, and before long, he had many more teachers requesting the same equipment in their classrooms.

I thanked him for his kindness and generosity and promised to get back to him with the outcome of the presentation—fully expecting that to be the end of our communication. Before we ended our conversation, he gave me one suggestion. He suggested that I use the terminology "classroom sound enhancement system" as opposed to the commonly used term "classroom amplification system." "Amplification" implies just making something louder, causing people to confuse the microphones with a loud Public Address (P.A.) system. "Enhancement" describes how a teacher's voice actually becomes more effective with a higher quality because the teacher no longer has to yell across the room. The teacher is able to speak in a conversational, calming tone to the students as if she or he is standing right next to each student. From that point on, I referred to the technology as a sound enhancement system.

On April 7, 2005, Craig and I arrived at Stoneleigh with just his laptop and my PowerPoint to give my first presentation to the School Improvement Team. As we were walking from the car into the school, I said, "You know, I remember having difficulty hearing my teachers when I was a student here. No one believed me. My parents finally took me to an audiologist who said that my hearing was fine."

We walked into the school library and gave a thirty-minute presentation to a very engaged group of parents and the principal, Dr.

Roach. I was so nervous that I was trying not to let the audience see that my legs and arms were trembling as I spoke. In fact, I was so focused on just finishing that as soon as I ended with the last slide, I sat down, and Craig had to remind me to stand up and ask if there were any questions.

The SIT unanimously agreed to pursue the project under my direction with the suggestion that I give the same presentation at the next school PTA meeting on May 5. It was essential to get the school's PTA to support the idea. The very next day, I wrote another letter to Dr. Grasmick inviting her to attend the upcoming Stoneleigh PTA meeting. This time, I sent her a copy of the PowerPoint and nineteen research studies supporting it.

I was excited at Stoneleigh's response but completely naïve to the arduous process of making any change in a public school facility. Stoneleigh's PTA president gave me a dose of reality. In an email exchange, she said, "I'm not saying this can't be done, but be prepared for a long journey." She also explained that SIT has little authority and absolutely no budget. It is an advisory body of parents and faculty that works to address issues around curriculum, discipline approaches, staffing models, etc.

The PTA only has authority over its own budget and activities; even within that, PTA must respect school policies and the Baltimore County Public Schools (BCPS) policies and needs to secure buy-in from the school administration for its programs *before* they can happen. She went on to explain that BCPS is a bureaucracy. It has to use approved vendors after putting work contracts out for bid and ultimately would be responsible for any maintenance. So, in essence, there is a long process to go through before any equipment could be approved, purchased, or installed in one of the public schools. I had absolutely no idea of the extensive journey that I was just beginning.

Just before the upcoming PTA presentation, I was given the name of someone in the Stoneleigh community who was a respected lawyer and member of the BCPS Board of Education. His name was John Hayden. It was suggested that I should invite Mr. Hayden to attend the Stoneleigh PTA presentation.

I phoned Mr. Hayden on April 28 and gave him a summary of the technology, reasons for it, and the proven benefits of using it. He seemed enthusiastic and offered to share my PowerPoint with the other school board members. He also encouraged me to speak at the upcoming capital budget hearing in May to make a case for including the purchase of this equipment in the district's proposed budget.

On May 3, just two days before the Stoneleigh PTA presentation, Dr. Grasmick sent a letter to me regretfully declining my invitation. However, Dr. Grasmick apparently read the material that I had provided her and told me that the Maryland State Department of Education (MSDE) was currently in the process of developing *Classroom Acoustic Guidelines* based upon the American National Standards Institute's (ANSI) recently adopted *Acoustical Performance Criteria, Design Requirements, and Guidelines for Schools*. These guidelines would be *voluntary* for new construction and renovation projects.

The purpose of issuing the guidelines was to raise awareness of the importance of acoustics in schools and to provide guidance to design teams for major capital projects.[253] Dr. Grasmick stated, "MSDE recognizes a place for Sound Field Amplification Systems in retrofitting existing buildings where partial acoustic modifications have been unsuccessful. However, we do not support widespread use of these systems in new construction. The first and best approach is to design new schools to meet the standard."[254]

Dr. Grasmick concluded her letter by saying that she forwarded my materials to Ms. Barbara Bice, chief of the Business Services School Facilities Branch (of the MSDE), for her information and consideration. "I wish you success with your project at Stoneleigh Elementary School."[255] Even at that time, my vision and commitment extended far beyond this one school.

Some parts of Dr. Grasmick's letter were encouraging. The MSDE was taking notice of the importance that hearing plays in learning and how acoustics impact learning. Clearly, they realized that acoustics are poor in the older school buildings (which are the majority of the school buildings throughout the country), and they were making some effort to improve how new school buildings were being acoustically constructed. But those recommendations were all voluntary, and I had learned through research and discussions with acoustical engineers that the only way to ensure that all students in a class had a SNR of +15 decibels was to use the wireless microphones and surround-sound speakers because acoustics cannot prevent the teacher's voice from dropping over distance.

On May 5, 2005, Craig and I once again returned to Stoneleigh for a presentation to Stoneleigh's PTA. This time the audience included John Hayden, a direct connection to Dr. Joe Hairston, superintendent of BCPS. I had already learned that Stoneleigh wouldn't be able to make any changes to its facility without the support of the Board of Education. We would need to get BCPS Board of Education to propose money for the technology in the next fiscal year budget, get the budget approved by the county executive, get BCPS Facilities to approve specs and get bids from potential vendors, get BCPS Board of Education to approve a vendor for purchase, and get BCPS Facilities to work on the installation. **Many** hands would be involved in passing the baton along for approval, and at any point it could be dropped and come to an end. I was just beginning to get a glimpse of the interwoven web of bureaucracy.

Implementing this idea became my responsibility, though it wasn't yet entirely clear to me how incredibly time-consuming and frustrating the process would be. I needed to gather support from the parents, teachers, and ultimately the Board of Education by doing what I had just started: educating them on the importance of a clear, audible teacher's voice to students, who for a variety of reasons were missing up to a third of verbal instruction, thus jeopardizing their academic achievement. Craig and I had developed a slogan, "*Every child deserves a front-row seat.*"

After the meeting, I was ready for battle but I felt the need to observe the operation and benefits of this equipment for myself. After researching if any schools in my area had a version of it (even if it operated off of FM waves instead of the new infrared technology), I located an elementary school about thirty minutes north of me, named Sparks Elementary, which had the technology in at least some of its classrooms. I arranged to meet with its principal.

I came prepared with all kinds of questions: What type of system was it? Who manufactured the equipment? How often is it used? What benefits have teachers observed? What maintenance issues have you experienced? Do you have a handheld microphone for the students? Have you had any complaints from teachers or parents? But I quickly realized that I wouldn't be asking any questions because it was very apparent that the principal knew little to nothing about the technology *or* the benefits of using it. In fact, most of the classrooms weren't even using the technology, despite its availability—it was optional.

When I asked why, I learned something very important—**we can't just install this equipment in the schools and expect teachers and principals to use it. They have to understand the reasons why they should be using it.** This principal didn't purchase the equipment. It was purchased by a prior principal (now retired), who had wanted it installed during a renovation a few years ago. That principal and most of the teachers who were working in the renovated school with the sound enhancement equipment were now gone. Essentially, the new principal and the new teachers had *no idea* how the equipment was supposed to be used and, more importantly, **why** it should be used. No one had taught them the "why" behind the "how."

What I thought would be an opportunity for me to learn more about the technology in that school turned out to be an opportunity for the principal to learn more about the technology in her own school. I spent most of an hour explaining to her the research on benefits to the students and teachers. Somewhere along the way in sharing all that I had learned about this topic, I realized that I was no longer fighting just for Stoneleigh. This equipment needed to be installed **and used** in **all** of the Maryland schools, beginning with Baltimore County.

Step 6

EXPAND THE CONVERSATION TO LOCAL "AGENTS OF CHANGE"

- **People whom you should include in the conversation:** those who are influential in **local** educational policies and practices—school board members, superintendent of your local school board, local politicians such as the county/city councilmen and county/city executive, local PTA, and local teachers' union.
  - If you are sharing information with the Board of Education (BOE), make your limited time as valuable as possible. Rally other supporters to speak at the same BOE meeting, but as separate speakers, so that a three-minute speech turns into a total of nine minutes. This will make a greater impact and gain more attention.
  - Always provide handouts of materials in addition to verbally sharing the information.
  - If you can find another district in your state that has imple-

mented an idea or suggestion similar to yours, share that with your district. Try to set up a meeting or correspondence between the two districts.

- ○ Be aware of budget cycles, open budget forums, and budget deadlines.
- • Deliver your message clearly and concisely—make it meaningful to your audience.
- • Get the media to help you spread the message. Publicize with social media, then reach out to local newspapers and television news outlets. Contact their reporters directly and propose a story. This may eventually lead to a national news story.

You would think that if someone has an educational idea, grounded in research done by numerous institutions including the US Department of Education, and this idea was currently being implemented in some districts in the US—that one could just pass that idea up to the Board of Education, or meet directly with the Board of Education to at least get *them* to investigate it. But it doesn't work that way.

2005

My first of what would be many presentations to the BCPS Board of Education was on May 24, 2005. Luckily I was told how the process worked in advance of the meeting. Public speakers (parents, teachers, community members) had to arrive at least thirty minutes before the board meeting begins and sign up to be one of, at most, ten allowed public speakers at the conclusion of the board meeting. Speakers were chosen on a first-come, first-serve basis. If you didn't arrive early, you likely wouldn't get a slot to speak. That was difficult for a parent juggling dinner, recreational activities, and bedtime for three young children. The process would surely deter a single parent.

If you were one of the ten selected for public comment, you had a maximum of three minutes to speak, but you were allowed to leave supplemental materials for the Board to examine at a later time. Knowing this, I decided to make the most out of the three minutes by recruiting some of the Stoneleigh parents, whose support I had already won over. I figured if three of us signed up as separate speakers, three minutes each of coordinated public comments would turn into nine minutes of coverage on the same topic. I also left a lot of information to help substantiate our comments. This strategy apparently got some attention. After the meeting, I was approached by a couple of board members who had some questions and by the Baltimore County PTA president, Michael Franklin. He said, "I think we can make this happen—contact me," and he gave me his business card.

The very next evening (May 25), I went to the Board of Education capital budget hearing at John Hayden's suggestion. The capital budget hearing is a public meeting conducted annually to gather suggestions from the public about what should be considered in preparation for the next fiscal year's (in this case, July 1, 2006, through June 30, 2007) capital budget for Baltimore County Public Schools.

Although I didn't have to sign up in advance, I was still limited to speaking for three minutes. Once again, I brought four other supporters with me to speak. Together, we had a total of fifteen minutes to advocate for funds. Listening to all of the other three-minute speeches gave me some perspective about the number of requests for appropriated funds, but how many of those requests (such as for air conditioning in schools) could justify the expense with research demonstrating a proven return on investment in terms of reduced special education referrals and reduced teacher absenteeism? And perhaps more importantly, how many of those capital expenditures, while nice to have, could result in increased academic achievement, particularly among the at-risk student population? These are the points I reiterated in the first of many budget meetings to which I began attending and speaking.

Meanwhile, Paul McCarty and I continued to communicate on the progression in Baltimore County. He was coming to Baltimore as a presenter for a School Facility Planning seminar at Johns Hopkins on June 3 and 4, so he volunteered to meet with me and any interested members of the Board of Education to aid in my advocacy. To thank him for all of his support, I invited him to dinner at my home. He had asked if it was okay to bring with him a special guest—someone who was attending the presentation with him; of course I said yes. But it was a complete surprise to me when I opened the front door of my home and saw Dr. McCarty with Claudia Anderson, the woman featured on the CBS segment who founded the company Audio Enhancement.

Claudia had been the first person whom I reached out to after learning about the teacher microphones in order to get some guidance on beginning the process to get that technology in Maryland schools. Here she was just three months later, sitting in my living room. Paul shared with me two important studies that provided additional inspiration for my cause.

A study at Cornell University in 2001 and one at London University in 2005 found that if students can't focus on the spoken word of the teacher, they not only lose the desire, but also the physical ability to learn. This is referred to as "learned helplessness," when one just gives up after feeling unable to avoid or control a negative situation. I had seen this behavior in Christopher, and the psychologist who tested him brought it to my attention. The thought of any child needlessly experiencing learned helplessness simply because of the inability to properly hear in the classroom intensified my passion to lobby for the sound enhancement technology. Over the course of the evening, Paul and Claudia provided more information to support my cause, and Claudia planted an idea in my head on how to bring more public attention to the issue—get the problem in front of the media.

Before Claudia left, she gave me a portable sound system to use as a demonstration (one small speaker to plug into the back of a classroom, a teacher microphone on a lanyard, and a student handheld microphone). Unfortunately, when I later offered this to Stoneleigh for use in Christopher's classroom (during a meeting with Stoneleigh school administrators and the BCPS audiologist on September 8, 2005), they refused to use the free equipment. We were told that based on county guidelines, there was no need to put one in his class. "A demonstrable hearing loss is justification for an enhancement system, but an auditory processing problem is not, according to current school system guidelines," school system spokesman Charles Herndon explained.[256]

Stoneleigh wasn't legally obligated to use the technology under an IEP, and since it was property not owned by BCPS, they didn't want to be legally obligated for any loss or damage to the equipment. I couldn't believe their refusal to use something offered for free that would not only help my son, but others in the class—not to mention the hypocrisy of that rejection from the same people who encourage more parental involvement in the schools.

Paul stayed in Baltimore until Monday to meet with John Hayden. John and I had invited other board members and Dr. Hairston (the BCPS superintendent), but they all declined the invitation without any explanation. John seemed further convinced that this technology was an essential educational tool, but had some questions for Paul about how the research studies are conducted. Paul was in the process of helping to collect data for a school district near DC on the effectiveness of teacher voice technology in their classrooms. He offered to do the same for BCPS (at no charge), so that BCPS could pilot the effectiveness of the technology in one of its schools before making a huge investment. John had to run that offer through Dr. Hairston. Unfortunately, Paul never heard back from Dr. Hairston. Even someone with Paul's credentials wasn't able to communicate directly with the BCPS superintendent.

By the end of June, Craig and I had gotten the issue in front of the Board of Education on several occasions, and we were invited to meet with the head of BCPS Physical Facilities. During the course of that meeting, the Facilities personnel shared with me the overwhelming number of BCPS school facilities in poor condition, requiring roof and window replacements and plumbing and HVAC repairs. To be honest, I think the meeting was meant to discourage me from seeing this technology as a necessity. One of the participants in the meeting actually referred to "hearing" in the classroom as a luxury. I decided to formally respond to those concerns at the August Board of Education meeting: "I don't expect you to deprive those schools of what they need. But children *need* to hear in order to have the ability and desire to learn. Hearing is not a luxury, and acoustics need to be a top priority."

At the end of summer 2005, before school was getting ready to start, I did everything I could to put this issue front and center, including again reaching out to the MSDE, a Maryland state delegate (Bill Frank), a Maryland state senator (Jim Brochin), and to several local newspapers and television stations. In most cases, I either didn't get a response or got a polite, "I'll look into it." But by early fall 2005, the *Towson Times* wanted to interview me and ultimately published a sizeable article in their October 12 edition entitled, "Sound Advice, One Mother's Mission to Have Sound Enhancement Systems in Every County Classroom." The article chronicled Christopher's struggles with learning and the research that led me to lobby for the equipment in our county schools. "If you want our children to read better, they need to hear better," I said.[257]

The two-page article included the MSDE's position and budgetary concerns, but included Dr. Grasmick's acknowledgment that my research was very thorough and Dr. McCarty's research and comments to back it up. I had very quickly gained credibility. The timing was perfect. I was already speaking at several BCPS Council Advisory Committee meetings advocating for BCPS to include sound enhancement technology in their next budget. These events are filled with many education stakeholders and the press. Later that fall, Jenny Glick, a reporter from the WMAR television station, called to discuss a possible story, which was ultimately filmed and aired on the evening news, January 9, 2006. This was my first experience with a television interview. I never knew that a three-minute slot on a news program would take over two hours to film.

By the conclusion of 2005, Christopher was settled nicely into first grade at his new school and classroom sound enhancement was beginning to gain significant local attention by the BCPS Board of Education and the surrounding community. This once timid "mom," nervous to make a phone call to a researcher in Utah, now had a strong voice demanding attention for a very **necessary issue** that was an **unnecessary problem** in our schools—an inadequate auditory learning environment.

Step 7

FIND STRENGTH IN NUMBERS

- Build a close-knit team to prevent burnout. Include on your team people with different strengths and perspectives. This will make your team stronger and more effective.
- **Have a conversation with groups outside of your immediate peer group that share a common cause or audience.** These may include other schools or districts, the state PTA, state teachers' unions, and the state Department of Education.
  - Utilize all of your connections. Consider all the teachers and administrators whom you have met at professional development seminars or those you have met at school board meetings and public education events.
  - Consider developing a website to publicize your message. This is the most cost-effective way to disseminate information.
  - If you have a website, request to link your website with the other groups that you have aligned with to increase visibility.
- Know your opposition. Don't be blindsided by a question you

can't answer or a position you can't defend. Build your argument with facts and examples, not emotion.

- Find common ground, even with your opponents.
- Follow up on every "no" with a "why."

2006

One of my New Year's resolutions was to get the BCPS Board of Education to realize the need for sound enhancement technology in all of its schools and to make sure that this "educational tool" was included in next year's budget. Craig and I realized that we could only do so much by ourselves; we needed help. I phoned Whitney Meagher, Program Coordinator for Health and Welfare of the National PTA. Whitney suggested that I start with the Maryland PTA and the local PTA because there is strength in numbers and it would be easier to mobilize.

I immediately emailed Ms. Mary Jo Neil, president of the Maryland PTA, and brought her up to speed on the issue. As with every other step I tried to take, this would require patience, waiting, repeating information, and calculated steps beginning at the ground level with the Baltimore County PTA. I would have to gain support at each level before I could move up to the next higher level in the PTA hierarchy, and each time, I was essentially starting over with educating them on the topic and then waiting.

On March 9, 2006, John Hayden called me with the news I had been waiting to hear for so long. **The BCPS Board of Education proposed a FY2007 budget that included $400,000 to install and test sound enhancement systems.** This would enable approximately 267 classrooms to become sound enhanced. I could hear the excitement in his voice. John had become a strong supporter for the cause, not only funneling information to the other board members, but giving me guidance in terms of what audiences to target, events to speak at, and questions that I should address for the skeptics. The proposed budget was a significant victory, especially given the fact that I had only first addressed the Board of Education on May 24, 2005, about ten months ago.

Now, I was no longer the one seeking out the media; they were seeking out me. WMAR ran an update on their original news story, which aired on March 9. Part of their segment included showing sound enhancement systems being used at Sparks Elementary where one of its teachers praised the technology as beneficial to all students. This was the same elementary school that I had visited about a year ago, where I had explained to the principal the advantages of using the technology that was *already* in her school—not being widely used—at that time. In essence, I had two victories to celebrate.

ASHA published an article online entitled, "Sound Field Systems on the Rise in Schools." The article started with Baltimore County's proposal of the $400,000 and stated that at least three new schools in the county had principals who decided not to wait for the money from the school board; they went ahead and allocated a portion of the new school construction funds toward putting the equipment in their classrooms.[258] Excitement was growing.

Liz Kay, an education reporter for *The Baltimore Sun* (which averages close to 200,000 circulated copies daily), approached me after I spoke at a Board of Education meeting, something that I was now doing on a regular basis. She subsequently wrote an article entitled, "Volume Rises in Debate on Classroom Acoustics," which was published on the cover of their March 13 edition. The article cited the benefits of helping the children to hear as well as easing the strain on teachers' voices. I was quoted as saying, "It's the only way to be able to have the children in the back row hear the same as children in the front row."[259]

Pamela Mason, Director of Audiology Professional Practices at ASHA, backed me up: "Seventy percent of the time spent in a classroom is spent listening."[260] She went on to say that while sound enhancement systems were first developed for the hearing-impaired students, they also benefit those with normal hearing.[261] But the two-page article reflected the counterargument shared by the MSDE and other agencies who recommended trying to minimize background noise first before installing the equipment. Lois L. Thibault, coordinator of research at the US Access Board, claimed that in a poor acoustical environment, raising the volume of the teacher's voice would create a "cocktail party" effect where everyone is forced to speak louder.[262]

I had encountered this argument many times before and would continue to debate this theory. I was a supporter of using some acoustic materials in new school construction, such as ceiling tiles. However, I believed that a sound enhancement system was a better financial investment, and some sound absorbing materials, like carpet and tennis balls on the bottom of chairs, had bacterial concerns.

I learned not to be afraid of opposition. Debate is healthy and encourages you to work out the problems and to strengthen your position. This article really got the attention and support from many more throughout Maryland including the Baltimore County PTA. My next goal was to join forces with them. On April 6, I gave a thirty-minute presentation to the Baltimore County PTA Council's Board of Directors. They agreed; my issue should also be their issue, but it would involve the process of writing a resolution and getting that passed by the council. Once again, many more little steps to achieve a bigger one.

Just when I thought we were making progress, a significant setback occurred. The budget proposed by the Board of Education in March proceeds to the county executive's office for review before the final budget is adopted by the county council in June. In June, I was informed by the County Auditor that the Baltimore county executive ended up reducing the money allocated for classroom sound enhancement in the proposed budget from $400,000 to just $50,000. That's an 87.5 percent reduction, meaning that only about 33 classrooms could become sound enhanced for the school year ending in 2007. I saw it as 5,850 students who just had an opportunity to improve their learning experience taken away from them. This prompted me to send an email to the county executive on July 3: "It is hard to imagine such a significant reduction in a PROVEN educational resource, given the current County budget surplus."

The auditor had told me that the county executive wanted to pilot the technology in one school. This was very frustrating because Dr. McCarty had offered a free research-based pilot study for BCPS back in June 2005. His offer was ignored. I wrote the county executive, "Baltimore County is wasting valuable time and putting its students at risk by allowing them to continue learning in an acoustically deprived environment. We simply do not need to reinvent the wheel." I also requested from the county executive an explanation for the reduction in the budget, but as usual, I never received one.

Sometimes when you get knocked down really hard, it motivates you to stand back up. That's what happened to me following the budget "slash." Craig and I had discussed an idea. We strongly believed sound enhancement to be an important educational issue that affected every student in every classroom—not just in Maryland. We felt like this issue needed to be publicized and advocated nationally, and in order to do that, we needed an organization behind our name that could generate funds to help us fight this battle.

I decided to form a non-profit organization, which became known as The Institute for Enhanced Classroom Hearing (commonly referred to as ECH). The purpose of ECH would be to educate the public—parents, teachers, policymakers, Boards of Education, and politicians—about the important auditory learning considerations for all students in a typical classroom and to advocate for the integration of sound enhancement systems in classrooms to accommodate those needs. It was extremely important that a non-profit organization advocate for the equipment as opposed to those currently marketing the technology—the companies themselves who sold the equipment. Those companies, such as Audio Enhancement, may genuinely have good intentions, but unfortunately, their motives are quickly dismissed by skeptics as being *only* profit-driven. Clearly, this is why "just a mom from Baltimore" had gained so much public attention. I never had a personal financial incentive.

Even though it seemed like a simple idea to just form a non-profit, it was an extremely difficult personal decision to go through with it. The process involves first incorporating your entity, which is very easy, and then you file with the IRS for tax-exempt, 501(c)(3) organization status. ECH was legally incorporated on July 25. The paperwork for the tax-exempt status was daunting. The IRS application is extensive and requires many supplementary forms and information. Luckily, I had the advantage of being a CPA, so I could prepare the application myself.

Secondly, the application fee is expensive, $750—that was a lot of money for my family. I had already sacrificed a significant amount of time to promote this cause and had therefore made it impossible to pick up a second income. We had incurred a lot of additional expenses in our educational testing and treatment for Christopher. There were several reasons why writing this check wasn't a great idea, and so after it was signed, I stared at it for at least twenty minutes before sealing it and the application in an envelope. It was a difficult decision, but I felt compelled that this was the right thing to do. Hopefully, the non-profit status would open opportunities for funding through grants aimed at improving education. I believed that the non-profit could take our mission beyond Maryland in a way that I couldn't by myself. On September 29, 2006, ECH officially became a non-profit organization.

By fall 2006, the PTA president whom I had just formed an alliance with had ended his term. The Baltimore County PTA (BCPTA) Council had already voted to make classroom sound enhancement systems a top priority for the next academic year, but now I had the same problem as when Stoneleigh's principal retired: I would have to start over—educating the incoming people to a new position. The incoming BCPTA president was Susan Katz.

Susan quickly got on board with the issue and immediately set a campaign into motion. I was asked to draft a resolution regarding auditory learning and the classroom sound enhancement systems, which the BCPTA Council would vote on to ratify at their upcoming October 26 meeting. "A PTA resolution expresses the position or belief of National PTA, the state PTA and its local units. It interprets the PTA mission and justifies action as members undertake programs and projects."[263]

Unfortunately, the Budget Area Advisory Meetings that are held in the five areas of Baltimore County to solicit public input were all scheduled before that BCPTA General Council meeting. The unfortunate timing meant that the BCPTA would not officially be allowed to endorse the sound systems when voicing their budget requests. I once again would be advocating alone throughout the month of October. The goal was to get the BCPTA to ratify the resolution so that they could officially sponsor the resolution that would then be brought forth to the National PTA by summer 2007.

Ultimately, the BCPTA did ratify the Auditory Resolution on October 26, 2006. BCPTA is an umbrella organization servicing 159 local PTA units. This meant that officially I now had the support of 42,000 PTA members. Work was officially underway to move this issue forward to the National PTA in conjunction with the Maryland PTA.

Craig and Suzanne at BCPTA Workshop & General Council meeting, October 6, 2006, photo courtesy of Veronica Henry

That fall and early winter was extremely busy getting the non-profit up and running and traveling throughout Maryland to advocate for the classroom sound systems. I immediately started applying for grants (such as ones funded by the Carnegie Corporation, The William and Flora Hewlett Foundation, IBM, the Milken Family Foundation, the Panasonic Foundation, The Prudential Foundation, and others), but always ran into the same problems.

Each foundation distributing the grants had certain prerequisites, two of which made it very difficult to get past. The first was they would only consider organizations that had been in existence for at least two years, some longer. Secondly, they wanted the organization to have other funding sources already in place so that the programs would continue to run/exist without the use of their funds. No one wanted to be the first! Many others had additional qualifiers, such as they wanted the non-profit to be giving something tangible to the public, not an educational "service" as ECH had established as its mission.

ECH was also in the process of creating a Board of Directors. When I created the organization, I wanted the board to consist of audiologists, researchers, and educators. Dr. Paul McCarty immediately joined the board, and he suggested a colleague named Dr. Micheal Teixido. Michael was an otolaryngologist with a special interest in medical and surgical conditions that affect hearing and balance. He has an active neurotologic practice. He is the director of the Delaware Otologic Medicine and Surgery Fellowship, director of the Balance and Mobility center of ChristianaCare, and co-director of the Pediatric Cochlear Implant and Auditory Rehabilitation Program of the Dupont Hospital for Children.

He teaches residents in otolaryngology regularly at Thomas Jefferson,

University of Pennsylvania, and Philadelphia College of Osteopathic Medicine, and in collaboration with the Delaware Biotechnical Institute he has created unique 3D materials for teaching anatomy, surgery, and pathophysiology. Paul introduced me to Michael when they were both in Baltimore. I explained the mission of ECH and gave him a copy of our business plan, and he subsequently agreed to join the Board of Directors. Now I had two very strong members, hopefully with some fundraising connections.

By the end of October, I learned that the Board of Education had decided to use the $50,000 for sound enhancement at Stoneleigh Elementary. The systems were to be installed over a long weekend in November. It was another "win." After all, helping Christopher adjust to Stoneleigh was part of what led me to learn about hearing needs of children in the classroom. But the abundance of research that showed the universal benefits of sound enhancement technology to all students and teachers wasn't going to stop me now that Stoneleigh was the recipient of the BCPS money. I couldn't help but think that possibly Dr. Hairston selected Stoneleigh thinking that this would end my lobbying to the Board of Education. If that's what he thought, he was absolutely wrong.

Since February 2005 when I first saw the CBS segment, I had gotten systems installed in every classroom in Stoneleigh school, got the BCPS Board of Education to *propose* spending $400,000 to improve auditory learning, got approximately nine other schools in Maryland interested in getting the systems, gained lots of press on the issue, created a non-profit organization, and passed a resolution with the BCPTA, gaining the support of 42,000 members. There were plenty of highs and lows, but the overall trend was upward. I was hopeful that 2007 would bring more national exposure to the issue, increased local support, and a financially stronger non-profit organization.

Step 8

BROADEN THE CONVERSATION BEYOND THE LOCAL BOUNDARIES

- **People whom you should include in the conversation:** contacts outside of your region such as people whom you have met through social media or your website, attendees at conferences and events you have addressed, members of national organizations that you are affiliated with, politicians that represent your state or have a particular interest in your goal.
- Adapt your message for each recipient. Use easy-to-understand terminology and descriptions.
    - Develop talking points that can be easily and quickly shared.
    - Give examples that are relatable to your audience.
    - Follow up on unreturned phone calls and emails. Balance patience with persistence.
- Move up the ladder with your message. Use your contacts at the district or state level to help you get your message to a national level.

- Expand your network. Create surrogates to help spread your message outside of your locality.

2007

In spring of 2007, I decided to visit an audiologist—not for ECH; for me. Over the course of the last year, I had attended a lot of board meetings, budget meetings, and conferences. Many times people would approach me after the meetings to ask questions or make comments. I realized that I had difficulty understanding them amid the other conversations that were going on around me. That, combined with all of the knowledge that I now had about hearing impairments, led me to question my own hearing ability. I had always had problems hearing in school and had even raised the issue to my parents as far back as elementary school; but those concerns had been dismissed by an audiologist after a quick examination.

Unfortunately, his diagnosis didn't cure the problem. My symptoms became more noticeable as I attended middle and high school, which are more reliant on verbal instruction. Frequently, I noticed when studying my lecture notes that parts of sentences didn't make sense. I often had a word written down that just didn't fit within the context of the sentence. I couldn't help but wonder, had something been missed?

I made an appointment with Dr. Seipp, the same audiologist who had tested Christopher, and I shared with him my observations and concerns before he conducted a battery of tests. Sure enough, I learned that I have a unilateral hearing loss (only in my right ear). There are certain frequencies that my right ear just doesn't detect, and this impairs about 40 percent of my overall speech intelligibility. Dr. Seipp explained to me that it's likely congenital, meaning that I was born with this problem. Hearing tests have improved significantly since I was a child. It's likely that the hearing exam administered thirty years ago just wasn't sophisticated enough to discover the problem; but if it had, I probably would have used the personal FM assistive device that I once questioned if Christopher should use. Unfortunately, I went my whole childhood without identifying the problem.

After this appointment, I felt numb. Is this why, back then, I was always so tired from school and felt like I had to work harder than the other students? Is this why, today, I am so driven to improve hearing conditions in the classroom? I'll never really know. But it certainly begs the question: How many other students are sitting in classrooms unaware of their inability to hear? Informing the public was my number-one priority, and a website was the most efficient way to disseminate that information.

Dr. Teixido (Michael) helped to pay for some professional assistance in establishing a stronger website for ECH than the basic one that Craig and I had first created in 2005. Fortunately, Craig's profession is in information technology. Craig was able to work with the consultant to help load information onto the website and to manage it going forward. This was a huge cost-savings to ECH.

I wanted the website to clearly outline the problems with auditory learning as well as the sound enhancement solution, to have a forum where people could post questions or share their experiences with using the sound systems, and to have a resource section for articles in print and media. It basically followed the format of my presentations, which seemed to be resonating with people from all backgrounds. Paul and Michael were experts in their respective fields. They each had an immense technical knowledge of designing school facilities, acoustics, and hearing issues.

My strength was being able to take some of this very technical information and translate it into simple terms that everyday parents, teachers, and school board members could understand. I had learned early on that the "hearing" process and related problems aren't as noticeable as those associated with the other senses. So I would often start off speeches with analogies that people could relate to. For example, "I didn't realize how bad my eyesight was until I put on a pair of glasses, and then all of a sudden I saw what I had been missing. Children don't realize that they misheard a word or that they missed hearing it all together. But that missed information translates into incorrect speech and grammar, poor literacy, and not achieving their full academic potential."

After getting their attention and making it relatable to the audience, I could then get into the facts and the details. If I was giving a full thirty- or forty-five-minute presentation, I could have people "experience" for themselves some of the more complex details that were important but could get overlooked. For example, I used the slide below to demonstrate the concept of cognitive closure:

I cdnuolt blveiee taht I cluod aulaclty uesdnatnrd waht I was rdanieg The phaonmneal pweor of the hmuan mnid Aoccdrnig to rscheearch taem at Cmabrigde Uinervtisy, it deosn't mttaer in waht oredr the ltteers in a wrod are, the olny iprmoatnt tihng is taht the frist and lsat ltteer be in the rghit pclae. The rset can be a taotl mses and you can sitll raed it wouthit a porbelm. Tihs is bcuseae the huamn mnid deos not raed ervey lteter by istlef, but the wrod as a wlohe. Such a cdonition is arppoiately cllaed Typoglycemia.

Amzanig eh? Yaeh and yuo awlyas thought slpeling was ipmorantt.[264]

Everyone was able to look at the scrambled letters and still read the passage—but it emphasized that children would struggle to achieve the same level of comprehension because they don't have the same language database to make sense of the words.

Sometimes in the middle of my speech, I would turn my back to the audience and continue talking to demonstrate how when a teacher is talking while writing on the chalkboard, their voice drops immediately by 10 decibels. This kind of "theatrics" also worked to dispel the "loud teacher's voice" theory. Many teachers believe they can talk over the noise levels in their rooms, but actually a loud voice only powers the vowels (the lower frequencies), not the consonants (the higher frequencies); yet most of the intelligibility in our speech comes from the consonants. I could demonstrate this by asking an audience member to try to yell the long /e/ sound and then try to project the *sound* that the letter /p/ makes. This again really helped my "listeners" to understand some of the more complicated reasons behind the necessity for sound enhancement equipment.

Many times, audience members would come up to me afterward and say, "This makes so much sense." "I never realized this before." "Now I understand." One of those people was a principal at an elementary school in the southeastern region of Baltimore County. He approached me after a board meeting and shared the following experience. One of his teachers was using a speaker and wireless microphone to assist a hearing-impaired student.

Unlike a personal FM assistive device, which directs the teacher's voice directly into the hearing impaired student's ears, this speaker sat on the desk of the hearing impaired student. What the teacher noticed was that all of the students surrounding the desk of the hearing impaired student started doing academically better. Their grades were all improving. The teacher had shared this observation with the principal at the school. He was in attendance at the board meeting, heard my three-minute speech, and connected the teacher's observation with the information that I shared. That principal now wanted to get these sound systems in more classrooms.

I was able to connect the dots on many different in-depth issues such as certain populations of students being more at risk and how children's speech perception and discrimination of sounds in an acoustically poor classroom can be easily overlooked by their teacher or mistaken as being inattentive.

During speaking engagements, I would frequently share personal observations from when I was volunteering in my children's classrooms. For example, I was once volunteering in Christopher's second-grade classroom where the teacher had just finished giving a science lesson from the front of the room. A little girl who sat in the back row next to a heating radiator raised her hand and said, "Did you say 'wetter' or 'weather'?" The teacher's response was, "You need to pay better attention."

This was so upsetting to me because I did not see an inattentive student. What I saw was a young girl who sat easily twenty feet away from the teacher's voice, surrounded by another twenty-three students making noises with pencils tapping and feet shuffling, and she was next to the radiator. At that location, the background noise likely exceeded the volume of the teacher's voice—meaning that her immature auditory processing skills prevented her from distinguishing between similar-sounding words. The teacher's abrupt response embarrassed the girl, and how likely would that little girl be to ever to ask her teacher to repeat any information again?

Those were the kinds of observations and analogies that I was able to communicate effectively—that all people could relate to. I wanted the website to communicate those same experiences and put the research data and technical specifications in easily understandable terms. The website became a comprehensive, credible, reliable source of information. I know this because I received emails from people from various careers, all over the United States, and outside of the US from places like Britain and Australia, praising our information. Audiologists, speech and language pathologists, and even a researcher in Australia reached out to say that they were learning information from our site. Even better than praise was that parents and teachers from all over were using the information on the website to advocate for sound enhancement systems in their schools and districts.

One such person was Katie (Golinveaux) Halberg. Katie was a teacher at Garin Elementary in Brentwood, California. She called me in February 2007 to ask some questions. She had discovered our website when she was writing a thesis for her master's degree in education. After doing the research, Katie became a firm believer in the need for this technology in the classrooms. She presented information from our website to the faculty at her school and used it to apply for a grant from the Clorox Service Company Community Foundation so that her school could purchase some sound systems for their classrooms. In May 2007, Garin Elementary was awarded an $11,000 grant from Clorox based on that information. Katie and I became partners in a mission and good friends.

That gave me an idea. What about recruiting people like Katie to be regional support experts to aid website visitors more directly in their local area? In light of ECH's lack of funds, it was more feasible for me to send our information and PowerPoints to surrogates who could locally present rather than for me to travel myself. I had done this unofficially with some parents and teachers in Florida and Connecticut, but wanted to officially expand on the idea. Katie agreed to take on this responsibility, and she continued to give presentations and funnel information to other parts of California, resulting in many other California classrooms getting the equipment.

Eventually, a special education teacher at a high school in Oklahoma would also connect with ECH. Jeanne Pease, a teacher of deaf students and one with a hearing loss herself, had her master's degree in curriculum development and was accepted to be one of twenty Special Education Master Teachers for the State of Oklahoma in 2008. She was under contract with the State Department to present ten workshops across Oklahoma. Jeanne chose the topic of minimal hearing loss for her presentations because she noticed that many teachers do not understand the ramifications of even a minimal hearing loss. As she was researching information, Jeanne came across the ECH website and "fell in love with it!" It prompted her to work with her district's educational audiologist to do a pilot study in an elementary school, and then to submit a grant proposal in an effort to get systems into a high school. Jeanne joined ECH as another regional support expert at the end of 2007.

The non-profit organization was successfully reaching many people around the country as a credible source of information on children's hearing needs in a classroom and provided information and suggestions for advocating to schools and districts. But we still didn't have sufficient funds. Fortunately, Craig handled all of the technology issues at night after his full-time job, along with caring for and transporting our children to and from baseball, field hockey, gymnastics, guitar, and other miscellaneous events while I was off giving presentations at night and sometimes on the weekend. I never received any compensation for my time or work. Between the two of us, we were donating all of our spare time and financial resources to pursue ECH's mission. But we desperately needed funds in order to be able to travel for out-of-state conventions and presentations.

In 2006 and early 2007, there were primarily four companies that manufactured and sold the wireless microphones and speakers: Audio Enhancement, FrontRow, Lightspeed, and Phonic Ear. All four knew my name, likely through *The Baltimore Sun* article and the ECH website. Some of them traveled to meet me, and others offered to fly me to their headquarters to meet with them. Representatives from each of those companies personally reached out to me at various times offering to help me and my cause. Some offered donations and others offered to sponsor my presentations at national education conferences. This presented a moral dilemma.

ECH's mission was to sell a concept, not a product. People were clearly listening to my message because I did not represent the interest of any particular company. ECH's non-profit mission was to educate the public about the auditory issues, limitations, and needs specific to children in a classroom setting. As such, part of our mission included advocating sound enhancement as a means to compensate for those issues and increase academic potential, but we did *not* promote a particular brand. We could not be seen **or perceived** as a revenue source for the sound amplification/enhancement industry. Therefore, I rejected all of their offers, but I did accept donations of their portable equipment to display or demonstrate at workshops. It was really difficult to turn that financial help away when we so desperately needed it.

Despite insufficient funds, ECH was leading the way to educate the public and to advocate for the technology. In the spring of 2007, BCPS proposed another $500,000 for sound enhancement equipment in their FY2008 budget. In the past two years, the Board of Education had proposed a total of $900,000—that's not an insignificant amount of money even for a large school system.

Christopher & Mom, May 2007

Secondly, a leading national education technology journal with a readership of about 100,000 people, known as *T.H.E.*, published an article called "Sound Solutions" by Neal Starkman.[265] Part of the article highlighted ECH and my advocacy with the subtitle, "Can You Hear Her Now?" *T.H.E.* described my personal journey and quoted my comment, "When research overwhelmingly supports an educational need that is financially justified and reasonable, we as a society owe it to the children to supply them with that resource. Every child deserves a chance to hear the teacher. Every teacher is important enough to be heard."[266] This perspective resonated with teachers.

A third event was something that I had been working toward for the past two years. On June 28, 2007, I traveled to St. Louis, Missouri, to present a resolution on Classroom Auditory Learning at the 111th Annual National PTA Convention and Exhibition. Over the two days that I was there with my Baltimore County PTA partners, together we talked with hundreds of PTA members and delegates, explaining how critical this resolution was. On June 28, as author of the resolution, I had to address thousands of PTA members from around the United States before the official vote and be prepared for any challenges or questions from the delegates. Yes, that once-timid "mom" who spoke to fewer than twenty people in Stoneleigh's library back in April 2005 was two years later speaking to a crowd of several thousand at a large convention center in Missouri.

During a lag in the convention, I was touring a large room next door for exhibitors, companies and people that pay to have a booth and advertise their product or service to the convention attendees. As I was walking around, a woman working as an exhibitor stopped me. She said, "You're the woman who spoke about the hearing issues in our schools."

I reluctantly said yes because I had learned that not everyone is a supporter. She went on to say, "It all makes sense to me now. My son struggles in school. I kept asking the teachers to put my son in the front of the classroom, and they said it didn't matter where he was seated. You're right. It matters, and now I know why. Thank you."

I knew exactly how she felt without knowing any more details—without even knowing her name or her child's name. It was a connection that I had made so many times before but mostly through emails, not in person. She was the reason that I was here. She was the reason that

I brought this issue to the attention of the National PTA. I needed their help in getting the word out so parents and teachers understood that every child needed to have the ability to hear their teacher as if they were all seated in the front row.

After presenting the resolution and answering their questions, a vote was taken. The National PTA ratified the resolution sponsored by the Maryland PTA. This meant that the resolution was now integrated into the National PTA's legislative platform, thus enabling advocacy for integrating sound enhancement in classrooms at the national level. ECH had just gained the support of nearly six million PTA members around the United States. I felt like a huge burden had been lifted from my shoulders, because surely the National PTA would be the voice for all children.

Following the convention, Jeff Anderson, CEO of Audio Enhancement, invited me out to Utah in August. Paul was going to meet me there. Even though ECH included all sound enhancement vendors on its website and never influenced interested buyers in one over the other, I had a personal fondness for Jeff and the Anderson family at Audio Enhancement. Everyone who worked for the company seemed to genuinely care about children and their ability to hear; after all, the company was founded because Claudia (Jeff's mother) was trying to help her two profoundly hearing-impaired sons. Those sons also worked for Audio Enhancement.

I also respected this company because their products were superior. The sound quality was amazing, and all the reviews from existing clients confirmed that the products required little to no service. This was extremely important because I didn't want teachers to get equipment in their rooms that was unreliable and then have one more burden or interruption to instruction. Faulty equipment would sabotage my cause.

There were several reasons for this trip. Jeff and Paul introduced me to US Representative Chris Cannon from the state of Utah and Utah State Senator Howard Stephenson. According to Paul, Senator Stephenson was very influential with US Senator Orrin Hatch. Senator Hatch was working closely with Ted Kennedy on the No Child Left Behind Reform Legislation. Behind the scenes, work was being done to have the sound enhancement systems become part of that legislation. Unfortunately, it ultimately did not occur. While visiting Audio Enhancement, I also met with Dell and Panasonic representatives.

Audio Enhancement was in the process of developing an agreement with Panasonic. Panasonic would now be selling Audio Enhancement's equipment with the Panasonic label attached. The trip allowed me to share my thoughts with those I met, learn what was potentially on the horizon in regard to legislation, meet with Paul—something that distance made it difficult to do—and once again, bring up Audio Enhancement's offer to help out ECH. Again, I struggled with that moral dilemma over accepting funds.

During the first part of my flight home, a passenger seated next to me asked what I had been doing in Utah. I didn't really know how to respond. I explained that I had formed a non-profit organization, how it came about, and what its purpose was, along with our recent success at the national PTA convention. The passenger was probably in her late fifties, and she looked at me and said, "You're living the dream."

I looked at her kind of puzzled. I didn't really feel like I was living a dream—sometimes it felt more like a nightmare—and then she explained. She told me that I had a passion for something—something that would improve the lives of others—*and* I was acting on it. She said, "That's the dream. Most people don't ever discover something they are really passionate about, and most of those that do rarely act on it."

I still think about that conversation, many years later. There's no doubt that I was passionate about the cause I was advocating, and maybe that is "a dream." But unfortunately, that same passion created a lot of frustration and disappointment, especially when it seemed like we were on the cusp of a major breakthrough or reform—which ultimately fell short of expectations. One of my greatest disappointments occurred a few months after the National PTA (NPTA) ratified the resolution.

The National PTA is the largest volunteer child advocacy association in the country, consisting today of approximately four million members[267] and, according to their 2019 annual report, holds approximately $18 million in net assets.[268] Back in 2007, the membership was even greater—about five and a half million.[269] It is undoubtedly a prestigious organization, which is why I was incredibly honored to receive the National PTA's Life Achievement Award in May 2007, an award given only to a person who daily lives out his or her commitment to children.

When I joined forces with the local, Baltimore County PTA (BCPTA) and the Maryland PTA (MDPTA), there was a clear plan to create a relationship and to harness the National PTA's power, to achieve the goal of changing the auditory experience of children nationwide. Together, we followed that plan and thought we had accomplished the goal—the national resolution was approved. According to the National PTA's statement on the Approved Convention Resolutions page of its website, "The power of a resolution is to enable PTA members, leaders, and public policy and program teams to join with others to build partnerships, form coalitions, increase awareness, develop programs and lobby policy makers."[270] Therefore, when the resolution was ratified, it was my understanding, and the understanding of the BCPTA, that this large powerful child advocacy organization would be obligated to carry out the plan of action as specified in the "Resolves" and that they would partner with ECH to do this.

At the convention, several national members affirmed my belief in a dual-purpose relationship and told me what to expect for immediate next steps. Those next steps included getting publicity out about the passage of the resolution and educating the PTA leaders and members through workshops at upcoming state-level PTA conventions and at the next annual national PTA convention in 2008. Unfortunately, these things didn't happen. Why? I don't know.

The NPTA would not coordinate the state workshops and even declined my proposal to present a workshop at their upcoming national 2008 (and eventually their 2009) annual convention. What could have been an opportunity to immediately educate all of the state leadership and many local constituents, was regrettably delayed until April 2008 (ten months later) when *Our Children*, the PTA's national magazine, published a three-page article that I authored, entitled, "Can Your Children Hear Their Teachers?" It made the front cover, but no doubt was less effectual than a workshop. It did, however, catch the attention of at least one PTA leader and mother in Florida. She became a powerful ally, lobbying for and eventually getting sound enhancement systems in her child's school and throughout the district.

The war wasn't over, but slowly—we were winning many small battles.

CLASSROOM AUDITORY LEARNING ISSUES

Whereas, Children spend a significant portion of their school day engaged in auditory learning, which relies on their brains' effectively receiving and processing incoming auditory signals from teachers and peers;

Whereas, Children do not have the ability to process auditory information as adults do, and their auditory neurological network is not fully developed until approximately age 15;

Whereas, Poor acoustical conditions in classrooms can interfere with students' development of spoken language, reading, and writing skills and academic performance;

Whereas, A significant portion of the United States' student population has a permanent or temporary hearing problem that impairs their ability to learn and is exacerbated by poor acoustical conditions in classrooms;

Whereas, An increasing percentage of the United States' student population has additional auditory needs that put them at greater risk for learning problems and may contribute to increasing the achievement gap; and

Whereas, The integration of classroom sound enhancement technology provides greater acoustic accessibility to every student in the classroom, benefits teachers and students, and provides significant cost savings for school districts; therefore be it

Resolved, That National PTA and its constituent organizations provide information to educate their members, educators, school administrators, public health officials, and the public at large about the hearing needs and limitations of all children in a classroom setting; and be it further

Resolved, That National PTA and its constituent organizations increase every child's chance for academic success by encouraging school systems to integrate sound enhancement technology in each classroom to compensate for poor acoustics, students' immature auditory abilities, and other hearing-related problems.

Adopted: by the June 2007 convention delegates VI.4

Step 9

BE RESILIENT

Adapt the Plan as Necessary

- Modify your plan **before** you abandon it.
- Tap into all potential resources to help accomplish your goals. Reach out to all those whom you have helped along the way and/ or those who will also benefit from your success. This may be a person, group, or entity.
- Know when to move on. Some battles just aren't worth fighting, and you don't need to win every battle in order to win the war.

LATE 2007-2008

After the National PTA ratified the resolution, I continued to be very active in lobbying for the technology in Maryland schools, still speaking at many local meetings and speaking in other parts of Maryland that were more proactive than Baltimore County. As of October 2007, Baltimore County had eleven schools now using sound enhancement systems to varying degrees. These schools had obtained the equipment using various funding sources—new construction, principals' discretionary funds, or BCPS funds. The overall feedback was favorable. Administrators categorized the experience with sound enhancement as positive and described it as an effective tool for keeping students engaged. One school principal reported that student use of microphones leads to increased participation and prevents students from having to routinely repeat, "What did you say?" Yet we still couldn't get the county executive on board even after repeated invitations to presentations and workshops from me and from the PTA. He seemed to make no attempt to educate himself on the issue or to have a conversation about it.

Other parts of Maryland were also getting on board with the technology with support from the BCPTA and the Maryland PTA. We had been informed by the MSDE that at least five districts in Maryland were planning to use sound enhancement routinely as part of new construction, contrary to the MSDE's position on the technology two years ago. Some pilot projects were underway. Patuxent Publishing local newspapers ran another article by Mike Fila, "Helping Kids Hear in Class Is Goal of PTA."

By spring 2008, some progress on a national front was being made. The Maryland PTA, determined to make something of the national resolution, had found another way to reach the state PTA presidents. The MDPTA president, Debbie Ritchie, addressed the sound enhancement topic at the National PTA's Council of States and State Presidents' meeting. A member of the NPTA resolutions committee and parliamentarian for the MDPTA was planning to discuss my call for action at the national convention in June, and the National PTA finally sent an e-newsletter to all of the state presidents instructing, "Raise Awareness about the Inability of Students to Hear in the Classroom."

At the state and national level, we were making significant progress, but Baltimore County was slipping backward—primarily due to one politician. Back in November 2007, a vote had come before the BCPS Board of Education to approve a vendor for the sound enhancement technology equipment as selected by the Facilities group. Four vendors had submitted bids during a pre-bid meeting in October. BCPS Facilities had selected Dell for a new school and LightSpeed for all others.

The board voted five to four in favor of approving the contract, but at least seven votes are necessary to approve it; hence, a vendor wasn't officially selected. Several board members declined to vote on a vendor because the county executive had taken away the entire proposed $500,000 from the final budget; without the funds, some members thought it useless to approve a vendor. However, that decision had unintended consequences. Since the Board of Education had never officially approved a vendor, this was now making it **impossible** for any BCPS schools to get any equipment, even if they used their own funds to do so.

I found this out only because an elementary school principal shared the information with me out of concern for himself and other interested principals. He had previously purchased equipment for eight classrooms and loved it. In May 2008, he wanted to purchase more systems using his own funds and contacted BCPS Facilities. He was then told that since the BCPS Board officially didn't select a vendor, ALL Baltimore County schools were prevented from purchasing any systems even with their own funds.

Basically, the bureaucracy was preventing those who are most directly involved with education from making decisions that they feel is in the best interest of their students. Even more disturbing was that apparently at least three other principals wanted the equipment in their schools after visiting other schools that already had it. But unfortunately, due to politics, everyone was afraid to speak out. Essentially, one politician had undone all of the progress in Baltimore County over the past two years. Everyone who was *educated* on the issue seemed to believe in it: the PTA, the Board of Education, and local school principals.

The county executive, purely a politician—who **chose** to remain uninformed, who chose to never meet with me, who chose to never respond to me, and who chose to never attend an information workshop at the request of the BCPTA—eliminated the entire proposed allocation of $500,000, which ultimately caused some board members not to approve a vendor. Now the county executive had taken away the choice of the principals in Baltimore County to get this technology in their schools. It was time to focus my energy strictly on a national level. I had done all that I could with Baltimore County.

In the past, Paul and I had applied as a workshop presenter for several large annual education-related conferences like the ASCD (Association for Supervision and Curriculum Development), NASSP (National Association of Secondary School Principals), and others. This spring, we decided to apply to one more—to the National School Boards Association's (NSBA) 2009 annual convention. The proposal that we submitted the previous year to the NSBA had been rejected as were many other prior proposal submissions. The selection criteria for these national conventions is rigid, and the NSBA convention is arguably the most influential in regard to education practices and policy. Paul and I decided to ask John Hayden to present with us because our chances for selection would be greater if we had a school board member as part of the presenter team. John agreed, though his term on the school board would be ending in June of 2008, prior to the conference.

On August 26, 2008, I was notified that we had been selected to present a workshop entitled, "Case for Improving Student Achievement with Teacher Voice Enhancement Technology" at the April 2009 NSBA Annual Convention in San Diego, California. This was our chance to educate school board members from around the country. We accepted. I had estimated the costs of the NSBA presentation and a three-day stay to total about $8,000 for all three presenters, which included a required registration fee of $850 for each of us. ECH was in desperate need of sponsors. Conference registration would open on September 15 and close on December 30. That didn't leave a lot of time to secure funding, and I personally wasn't in a position to front the money myself—like I had for other ECH-related expenses. The economy was just beginning a significant downturn, and Craig was seriously concerned about the longevity of his employer.

Audio Enhancement had recently partnered with Panasonic. Paul learned that Panasonic had offered to sponsor our trip and cover all of our expenses. They had also expressed interest in partnering with ECH in a research capacity. Paul was a board member of ECH, but he also conducted research on educational facilities through Brigham Young. Panasonic wanted to pay ECH for additional research on the effects of using sound enhanced classrooms for learning. ECH would then reimburse Paul for his time and expenses involved in the studies. The research would be available for all to see and use, not just Panasonic or its partners. While the idea to collaborate with a well-known company was very enticing and would certainly ease my financial concerns for the non-profit, I had many concerns from a tax perspective and in regard to ECH's image. How independent would ECH appear if our research was completely paid for by a company that sells the equipment?

Research into potential conflicts with the IRS's non-profit status uncovered issues with having only one sponsor for the trip. This could ultimately lead to the interpretation that ECH was a private foundation of that sponsor. A one-time occurrence would likely be fine, but if this occurred again, it could jeopardize the tax status of the non-profit. The idea of the research arrangement with Paul presented other concerns. As a non-profit, ECH could not benefit individually any of its officers or directors. With no other options, ECH decided to send out a letter soliciting sponsorship of our 2009 presentations, specifically the 2009 National School Board Association Conference, to all of the leading audio equipment companies: Panasonic, Lightspeed, Front Row, and Logical Choice. At Michael's suggestion, we decided to encourage sponsorship by recognizing sponsors on our website and in the handout materials at different levels based on the contributed amount. These letters were sent out in September 2008.

Over the past two and a half years, I had received several informal offers by companies that sell the microphones and speakers to sponsor professional conferences; but this was a very different time. According to Ben Bernanke, an American economist and former chair of the Federal Reserve, "'September and October of 2008 was the worst financial crisis in global history, including the Great Depression'...Of the 13 'most important financial institutions in the United States, 12 were at risk of failure within a period of a week or two.'"[271] All businesses were hurting and reluctant to make any financial commitment, especially ones that relied on school systems for their sales revenue.

By the end of December, I still had not received any sponsorship money or any commitments to fund the upcoming conference. Paul had been recently named to the school board in his Utah district, so his district would now fully cover his portion of the fees. That was a much-needed relief. I reached out to the NSBA, explaining the financial predicament of our non-profit due to the economy, and they agreed to waive one of the registration fees. That left one remaining fee that still needed to be paid by December 30. I went ahead and paid the fee, but decided that if we didn't have enough funds for the remaining travel fees by early March, I would cancel the registrations and withdraw our names from the list of presenters. At this point, it was difficult to see ECH surviving the recession—a sad reality because we had gained credibility among many established organizations such as ASHA and the Better Hearing Institute. ECH was even cited in many articles and debates in Canada and the UK.

2009

I was determined to find a way for ECH to be financially stable. At the beginning of 2009, I had one more idea to try out. Paul, Michael, and I had always discussed the need for ECH to educate college/university students preparing for a career in education. The purpose was to explain these auditory issues to prospective teachers BEFORE they step foot into a classroom and make incorrect judgments about the students' ability and desire to learn. Part of the education would include use of sound enhancement technology to compensate for hearing issues and poor acoustics to improve academics and to improve instruction.

It was my hope that this pre-service education would create advocates out of these future teachers so that they would initiate getting the equipment in their eventual school or district. I saw this avenue of education as a revenue-producing program, which could really help ECH to be more self-sufficient and less reliant on donations or sponsorships. To help launch this program, I reached out to my alma mater, Gettysburg College, and offered a free seminar if they would give me some feedback in return. Gettysburg accepted my invitation, and I subsequently presented an hour-long seminar to their education professors and education students on January 22, 2009.

The Gettysburg seminar was an absolute success, as evident by survey responses from the professors and the students. Four out of five professors expressed an interest in having this presentation repeated in subsequent semesters. Four out of five would recommend it to a colleague, and four out of five thought it was very relevant to students preparing for a career in education. All of the professors said that the seminar increased their personal knowledge on how children hear differently than adults and/or how sound enhancement technology can increase student performance. The student responses were just as positive. In fact, the professor who coordinated the seminar with me emailed some additional comments that students sent to her following the presentation. Included in those comments was this one:

> "This is definitely a presentation that should be offered to all prospective teachers. It ties in so well with things we talk about, and also addresses practical concerns of classroom management that can, let's admit it, fall by the wayside while immersed in theory. The information, especially the statistics and actual science, presented today is invaluable not only to encourage implementation of these systems but to make current and prospective teachers aware that a request for repetition can have a variety of causes and is not always indicative of not paying attention or ADD/ADHD or another LD."

After receiving the feedback, I was so optimistic about the direction that ECH **could** go. I was convinced that this program was a necessity. The next step was to determine how to get colleges and universities to pay for it? The chair and associate professor of the Education Department at Gettysburg College offered an official endorsement of the program to educate prospective teachers. The difficulty was the timing. The economy was still in a recession with no end in sight, and I had decided that by spring, I would make a personal decision about my future commitment to ECH.

By March 2009, ECH had secured just enough donations to make attendance at the NSBA conference possible. We were rapidly putting together handout materials for each workshop attendee. NSBA requested that we send in advance at least 175 copies. Each booklet that we were compiling was forty pages of articles and research for take-home resources. In the past, ECH avoided paying printing and publication expenses through an agreement that Craig had made with his employer. His employer allowed Craig to copy and print our non-profit materials for free in their office building, provided that we supplied the paper and toner cartridges. Craig then did all of our copying during his free time at night and on weekends. But his company was struggling with the financial crisis and could no longer offer that service to us. Fortunately, John Hayden volunteered his law firm to do the photocopying and the entire DeMallie family, including Katie and Christopher, assembled booklets up until the last possible moment. Despite every obstacle that came our way, we were headed to California to share our message and the research with school board members from around the country. Finally, our voices would be heard!

Step 10

ACCEPT THE OUTCOME

Focus on the Positive

- There inevitably will come a time when you have to make a personal decision about continuing "the conversation" or not. It is easy to see "the end" as a defeat, but instead focus on what you started. You have paved the way for someone else to continue the change.
- **There is no improvement that is too small.** Anything that you have done to improve someone's chances for a better education will ultimately have a profound impact on their life—allowing them the opportunity to have a positive impact on someone else's life. So never minimize the extent of your efforts.

SPRING 2009

On April 4, 2009, John, Paul, and I all boarded a plane to present a workshop entitled, "Case for Improving Student Achievement with Teacher Voice Enhancement Technology," at the 2009 NSBA Annual Convention in San Diego, California. Unfortunately, we were assigned a workshop session on Monday, April 6, from 2 p.m. until 3:15 p.m., one of the worst time slots. By Monday afternoon, many attendees would be leaving to travel home, and to make matters worse, Monday was a gorgeous day in San Diego, meaning that those still in attendance would be tempted to enjoy the beautiful weather outside.

We had no control over the workshop schedule and could only hope that our message would inspire those who attended, to take what knowledge they gained back home, and to then share it with the rest of their school board members. Hopefully our information would then influence their districts to incorporate sound enhancement technology in their classrooms. One of those attendees worked for the US Department of Education and was sent to report back to the Secretary of Education, Arne Duncan.

The success of our presentation would be seen and heard in subsequent months. In West Virginia, a school board member who attended our presentation shared the handout material with his board, resulting in ALL schools and every classroom in the district being outfitted with the equipment. In Connecticut, we influenced all elementary classrooms in an entire district to become sound enhanced and some of the middle and high school classrooms as well. On May 5, US Representative Ben Chandler from Kentucky introduced Classroom Acoustics as part of the School Modernization Bill (H.R. 2187), the 21st Century Green High-Performing Public School Facility Act. Little by little, we were making a difference.

These states were just the ones with people who personally reached out to me after the conference. In addition to those, we know for certain that Maryland, California, Florida, and Oklahoma installed systems in some districts or schools, due to our influence. I can't quantify the number of other schools that either independently or through their district gave their teachers microphones based on information that came directly from the ECH website, the National PTA, a related website like ASHA, through a publication that featured ECH or an article written by one of the ECH board members, or from a related news media article. All I can say is that we made a difference in four and half years, since I first began this mission in one school library.

When I returned home from the conference, my decision was made. As much as I wanted to continue the ECH mission full-time, I needed to now put my family first. In September, Megan would be starting first grade, Christopher would be in fourth grade, and Katie would be in seventh grade. Beginning June (2009), I would start a master's in the Art of Teaching program at Goucher College. It was time to pursue that dream of mine to become a math teacher. ECH had awakened my passion for education and an opportunity for every child to achieve their full potential. Maybe I could make a difference in education more on an individual level, and rather than fighting to get ideas up to the top, I could focus my efforts on implementing my ideas with those at the bottom—the students.

Even while obtaining my master's degree, I continued to run the non-profit organization and advocate for sound enhancement technology. My platform had actually grown because I now was able to speak my message to a whole group of teachers and education professors who were part of the graduate program. I finished my master's degree and earned my teaching certification by May 2011.

SEPTEMBER 2012—WASHINGTON, DC

During the summer of 2012, Craig attended a high school reunion in his hometown of Worcester, Massachusetts. There, he met up with an alum of Worcester Academy, a democratic member of the United States House of Representatives from Massachusetts, named Jim McGovern.

Craig did not know Representative McGovern prior to meeting him at this reunion. A friend introduced them and brought up the work that Craig and I had been doing for our non-profit organization. Representative McGovern was interested in our education reform objectives and said that he would like to learn more about our mission and the research. He gave Craig his contact information and encouraged us to reach out to him once Congress was back in session. We did so and were subsequently invited to visit Washington, DC, to meet with the representative in September 2012.

On the day before our scheduled presentation to Representative McGovern, I sat at my desk and meticulously went through each slide in the PowerPoint. Which ones were the most meaningful to him? What data needed to be updated for more current information? What graphics would grab his attention? I was told by his assistant that I would have approximately forty-five minutes of one-on-one time with the representative. I needed to make the most of every single minute. Right when I was running through the final slides, the phone rang. I stopped to answer. It was the principal of Raven Elementary inviting me to come for an interview the day after my trip to DC. It seemed like all my goals were falling into place, oddly at the same time.

The next morning, Thursday, September 13, 2012, Craig and I boarded the MARC train headed for DC. There are very few life experiences that, when you recall them, you relive them. That day, when Craig and I arrived at Union Station in Washington, DC, is one of those moments for me.

Believe it or not, I had never taken the train to DC before and had only visited the nation's capital twice, even though I had always lived not more than sixty miles from Washington. Walking through Union Station, I was in awe of the marble surround, broad arches, gold embellishments, and glass ceiling. It was stunning. Everyone was bustling around us, most of them dressed in business clothes and carrying briefcases. I could smell the coffee they carried and hear their shoes shuffling on the floor. I felt like one of *them* at that moment—no longer just a stay-at-home mom in sweat clothes or an older-looking exhausted graduate student in college. The atmosphere of DC was invigorating. I felt as if this morning was a beginning to my new future, either taking the non-profit on a new nationwide mission or taking a permanent position as a math teacher. Today's outcome would determine in which direction I would go.

We walked from Union Station toward the US Capitol building. It was slightly less than a mile but it seemed much farther. Craig was walking at a fast pace, but despite the urgency to get there early, I wanted to slow down and absorb it all. As we got closer to the US Capitol, I realized the significance of **us** being there—just two parents who had discovered a problem in our schools and proposed a solution that was grounded in research. We were just two ordinary people with no political connections. All we had was determination and perseverance—a voice that refused to be unheard.

As we arrived outside the Capitol, there was an active police presence, a small group of protestors, and a group of reporters and television cameras. The reporters were interviewing Representative McGovern, the congressman whom we were coming to meet. Our meeting was in a large building directly across from the Capitol, where it appeared most of the representatives have their offices. After we cleared security and entered, I couldn't help but recognize many important names on the office doors that we passed.

Once all of our equipment was set up, Representative McGovern entered the room and introduced himself to me. He was very friendly and approachable, which helped me to relax...just a little. Just like in that little library six and half years ago, I was nervous; but this time I was confident. I started right into a forty-five-minute presentation, talking directly to the representative. Most of the details were in what I said, not words cluttering up the slides. It was well organized, concise, and all research-based. The format of this presentation was similar to many that I had done over the past six years, but the conclusion focused on what our organization should be doing in the future to help get the sound equipment in all schools and to educate the teachers so that they would be more likely to use the equipment. Craig and I desperately hoped that Representative McGovern could help earmark some funds for this type of professional development. As much as I remember our day in DC, I don't remember much about the first forty of those forty-five minutes. It was like I was on auto-pilot.

When I finished, there was a pause, and then Representative McGovern said, "It seems like a no-brainer to me. It all makes sense."

He proceeded to ask some questions, but he got it. He understood our message. Unfortunately, he also told us that earmarks were a thing of the past. In light of the economy there was little-to-no hope of getting any direct funding for our organization. He would, however, recommend that the US Department of Education meet with us.

His assistant would arrange something and be in touch with us soon. Craig and I thanked him for his time, gathered our things, and left.

Craig was disappointed, but I didn't feel defeated; not yet. After all, we were leaving a building where some of the most influential people in our country work. We had just pitched an idea directly to a congressman for forty-five minutes. How many people can say that they've had that opportunity?

Craig and I found a little outdoor café to eat at, and we sat to have some lunch. It was a beautiful day and what would turn out to be probably the last relaxing moment for Craig and me for a very long time. It had gone really well. Even if nothing came of it, we did a very professional job that obviously conveyed the importance of the topic. There wasn't anything more we could have done to prepare for this day. We spent the next hour eating and talking about all of the "what-ifs", revisiting all of our sacrifices and hard work over the past six years, and how everything could change with tomorrow's interview for a teaching job. Just before we left, Craig said, "I think good things are finally coming our way."

The next day was my interview at Raven Elementary, which resulted in a job offer that I accepted. A few weeks later, Craig and I received the awaited invitation from the US Department of Education to meet with them in late October, but by that time, I was overwhelmed with the responsibilities as a brand-new teacher. After some inquiries were made, we learned that the meeting could likely entail an offer to coordinate a research project on the effectiveness of the classroom sound systems on instruction and student achievement. I immediately realized that I could not feasibly manage a research project and be a full-time new teacher. Not to mention, why should the government pay more money to research something that had already been proven effective? This seemed like a waste of resources all the way around, so I sadly declined the invitation.

At that point there was only one part of my life that I could eliminate to free up some extra time...ECH. Despite the inevitability of this decision, it was devastating to let go of something that I was so passionate about and had worked so hard to promote.

Sometimes you have to recognize when it is time to move on and accept what progress you have made, even if it's not to the full extent that you had hoped. A sound system in one classroom would impact at least twenty-five students each year, and a good piece of equipment should have a life of at least ten years. That's a lot of students who were ultimately helped. Who knows how many classrooms across the US ended up with a system as a result of my advocacy? It is easy to focus on what didn't happen, and neglect to consider what did. In 2017, twelve years after I began voicing my concerns and advocating for classroom sound enhancement systems, I was giving a speech at the College of William & Mary, in Virginia. Afterward a college student came up to me and said, "I think you are the reason that my teachers all started wearing microphones when I was in elementary school." I asked where she was from, and she said, "Iowa." You may never know how far your impact can travel.

TEN STEPS TO IMPROVE PUBLIC EDUCATION

- Step 1: Admit There Is a Problem
- Step 2: Identify the Root Cause of the Problem
- Step 3: Do the Research—Educate Yourself
- Step 4: Find the Best Solution
- Step 5: Start the Conversation at the Most Basic Level
- Step 6: Expand the Conversation to Local "Agents of Change"
- Step 7: Find Strength in Numbers
- Step 8: Broaden the Conversation beyond the Local Boundaries
- Step 9: Be Resilient—Adapt the Plan as Necessary
- Step 10: Accept the Outcome—Focus on the Positive

FINAL THOUGHTS

A few years ago, I had a student ask me, "Mrs. DeMallie, why do you love math so much?"

No one had ever asked me that question before, and honestly, I'm not sure that I had ever given it that much thought. After pausing for a moment, I said, "I think because in math, every problem can be solved. There's always an answer."

It's funny how a ten-year-old can make an adult think about their life, passions, and character. My affinity for math aligns with my personality. I am a problem solver—or at least, I try to be. In my heart, I want to make everything right, and admittedly, I am often naïve in believing that it's possible.

Fifteen years ago, my son had a problem, and like any good parent would do, I looked for a solution. I was determined to give him every opportunity to be the very best that he could be. I saw through a mother's eyes how a bright, happy, capable child could become withdrawn, depressed, and discouraged because something was inhibiting his ability to understand what he heard and to then express what he felt. My quest was simply to solve Christopher's problems, but in the process, I opened up a door that revealed a much larger one. Students were learning in classrooms that didn't support their auditory needs, and while some may adequately compensate, many others undoubtedly had their academic potential and their attention and desire to learn inhibited, similar to what I saw in Christopher.

It would have been much easier for me and my family if I could have just closed that door and ignored what I had discovered. But that's just not me. I want to find answers to problems, and in this case, the answer found me. The CBS news segment that revealed teacher microphones and speakers was such a simple, cost-effective solution. I thought, *I just need to share this information with the people who are in charge of our schools because obviously they want to increase academic achievement and close the equity gaps.* But my innocence hadn't yet been exposed to the web of bureaucracy and politics embedded in our public school system that makes it so difficult for ordinary people to make a change.

Did I positively impact our national education system? Yes, to some extent. Each classroom that ultimately became sound enhanced impacts on average at least twenty-five students every year. Multiplying that times the number of classrooms in schools and districts across the US that integrated this technology and the number of years that classrooms have had it reveals at least tens of thousands if not hundreds of thousands of students who benefited from my advocacy. But that change was incomplete, unnecessarily slow, and painful because of barriers that insulate those at the highest levels of the education paradigm from listening to the people who are affected by their decisions.

How many times did politicians, superintendents, and school board members ignore opportunities to hear from the parents, teachers, audiologists, researchers, and speech and language pathologists? Why is the public's input limited to a three-minute speech? How many times did policies and procedures prevent even the principals and parents themselves from purchasing the technology using their own funds? How can an organization as large and powerful as the National PTA ratify a resolution and then do little to nothing in regard to follow-up action? How can we expect education to improve if changes can only be made from the top down?

I can't begin to express the frustration that I felt as a mother and as a person advocating for an improvement grounded in numerous research studies. Time and time again, I was given excuses for the delays in progress such as finances, wanting a pilot study first, and established procedures for getting approvals from the board and facilities, etc. Yet, when those excuses would prohibit something that the higher powers want done, they are waived or ignored. Take, for example, when Dr. Dance was hired as the superintendent for Baltimore County Public Schools. His two years of teaching experience did not meet the minimum three-year requirement, but that was waived. Not to mention the hundreds of millions of dollars that BCPS invested in one-to-one devices for students as young as first grade, despite any research proving that the benefits outweighed the costs.

As much as I learned about how politicians and the Board of Education impact school system decisions, nothing gave me true insight into the problems with education until I became a teacher. For me, becoming a teacher was an intentional, purposeful commitment to education. I had already experienced how difficult it was to make a positive change in education at the national and local level. I believed that as a teacher, I could at least make a difference at the individual level.

My teaching experience at Raven Elementary, what became a high-need school, was eye-opening. I am well versed in the local and national news and aware of problems that threaten society, but no one really understands the impact of those problems until you work with children in this situation on a daily basis. It was often difficult to reconcile my life with that of my students. Every year, I had a class where at least one child had a parent in prison and abuse and/or drugs in the family. Most of my students were entitled to Free and Reduced Meals (FARMS), few of my students lived in a house, and most were being raised by a single parent. Academically, most of the students in the fourth grade were at least one to two grade levels behind. Emotionally, many were prone to anger and lacked self-control. Sadly, Raven represents today's average classroom.

Schools today are no longer just a place for instruction. The teacher now has the additional responsibility for teaching children social skills and helping them with their emotional needs. The teacher now takes on the role of parent, social worker, and psychiatrist along with the expectation to teach a rigorous curriculum often above the ability level of the student. My typical day included arriving an hour early, leaving at least an hour late, grading papers and making lesson plans most nights, and usually spending at least four hours on a weekend preparing for the next week or two. Many professionals spend an equal amount of time or more working in their careers, but how many of those professionals have a master's degree, make less than $55,000 a year, can only use the bathroom once during their workday, have to buy their own supplies, often get cursed at by children, and are talked down to by the parents? It's no wonder that many teachers are leaving the profession and there's a decline in the number of teachers entering the profession.

Can education problems be solved? Well, "solved" is a strong word. The math person in me wants to say yes, but my experience from all angles isn't so sure. However, I do know that **it can be improved** if all people, from the bottom up, start honestly discussing the problems and listening to each other's ideas. Unfortunately, too many current teachers and administrators are afraid to express their opinions for fear of retribution. Even when teacher online surveys are anonymous, most teachers I know are afraid to give an honest answer in fear that the source of the answer will be identifiable.

My hope is that this book will encourage conversation at all levels of the education system, because the more people who speak up, the harder it is not to hear. Many of the radical changes in regard to the curriculum, grading policies, discipline, and technology have been imposed from the top down and ignore the reality of a very diverse student population. What may be a good policy for one school, may not be for another. We can't assume that one size fits all, and it is honestly the teachers and school administrators at the individual schools who can best predict how a new initiative will impact their students. They are the ones who deal with the consequences of new policies, so at least let them have a say in what those policies include and how they are enforced. Treat them like the professionals they are.

Finally, I've shared several student stories throughout this book. Each student impacted me on a personal level. This last story shows how **all of us** can impact each student.

I had a student named Khalan in my fourth-grade class. Khalan was a challenge. He was prone to anger outbursts and frequently eloped from class. His home life was rough. He lived with two younger siblings and his mother, who admitted that she didn't know what to do with him. He never saw his father, who was incarcerated. I was told by another teacher, who taught one of Khalan's siblings, that the mother flaunted on social media her drug use, and that occasionally she entertained boyfriends who allegedly were abusive.

About two months into the school year, I learned that Khalan had been purposely placed in my classroom because I was thought to be a good fit for his behaviors. During the prior school year, Khalan had been moved around among three different classes, in an attempt to find a teacher and classmates who wouldn't exacerbate his problematic behaviors.

Khalan was adjusting to my classroom, and we had come to the understanding that he could leave the room if he felt angry, but he had to stay in the hall where I could see him. There was one morning when Khalan clearly had been upset by either something that happened at home or something that happened on the bus because he arrived visibly upset. He walked out of my room shortly after homeroom, and I was keeping an eye on him to make sure that he didn't run off. I had already tried unsuccessfully to talk to him and calm him down when he arrived. Even though he was allowed to go into the hall, I was concerned because the more time he missed from the classroom, the further he would fall behind. Academically, Khalan was on a second-grade level.

As I was teaching the class, I looked in the hall and saw Mr. Ron, our custodian, kneeling down on the ground and talking to Khalan as he leaned against the lockers. They were talking for about three to five minutes. When they finished, Khalan immediately walked back into the classroom, sat back down at his desk, and began to work. In that one moment, the school custodian had more of an impact on Khalan's education than did I or anyone else.

Here's my point: **Everyone** has the power to make a difference in education…as long as someone's listening. Is anyone listening to me? Can you hear me now?

Will we hear you?

Christopher & Mom, high school graduation 2017

EPILOGUE

My story wouldn't be complete without sharing where Christopher is today.

That little boy, who once struggled to express his thoughts and count to twenty, went on to graduate from high school near the top of his class and now attends the College of William & Mary in Virginia. He will graduate in spring 2021 with a major in economics.

Christopher's story could be one of any child who starts off their educational journey with some sort of disadvantage—but he was lucky. He had a teacher who had the courage to speak up about a problem and a family who had the resources and perseverance to do something about it. Without those two things, the outcome may have been very different.

You, too, have the power to change someone's life—with as much as the simple act of closing this book and opening up a conversation to share what you've learned. Create a "lollipop moment!" Use your voice to write a better ending to another child's story.

Christopher at the College of William & Mary, spring 2018

ACKNOWLEDGMENTS

I would like to thank Scribe Media for giving me a platform to start this conversation using my own voice. There's truly a whole team of people to thank in this regard: Natalie Aboudaoud, my publishing manager, who patiently answered all of my questions; Jane Borden and Hal Clifford, who lent me their editing expertise, which strengthened my book and its objectives; and the entire design team that supported my mission and magically could read my mind to create the perfect graphics!

Special thanks to my son, Christopher, for having the courage to share his early struggles. I am certain that your story will bring comfort and encouragement to other families who are experiencing the same difficulties.

I would also like to thank Paul McCarty for your steadfast belief in me and my purpose for this book, and for allowing me to share our advocacy adventures in detail. You are a true mentor and friend.

Thank you to all the teachers and students whom I have worked with over the years. You are the inspiration for this book. Truly, you prove that "the sum is greater than the value of each of its parts." I hope that I was able to adequately convey the importance of what you taught me.

Thank you to Harris, Wiltshire, and Grannis for your legal expertise.

Finally, thank you to my daughter Katie who encouraged me back in 2017 to tell my story. Your support has never wavered, and your feedback has always been valuable. Thank you for all the time that you took from your busy schedule as a legal assistant and now a student at Georgetown Law to read and reread my ideas, offer your opinions, and double-check my facts. You've always been a great daughter and soon will be a great lawyer!

ABOUT THE AUTHOR

SUZANNE DEMALLIE was a math teacher in the Baltimore County Public School (BCPS) system in Maryland for seven years. She has taught math to students in grades one through eight in Baltimore City and Baltimore County.

Prior to becoming a teacher, she worked to reform education first as a parent and then as the founder and director of a non-profit organization, the Institute of Classroom Hearing (ECH). Suzanne's mission to educate people on children's auditory learning issues and the need for integrating a simple technology in classrooms began in March 2005, when research into her son's learning difficulties uncovered problems and issues that plague ALL young children in an auditory learning environment, jeopardizing their academic potential.

Suzanne authored the Classroom Auditory Learning Issues resolution that was adopted by the National PTA in July 2007, adding the support of an additional six million members. She has written or contributed to articles published in *Our Children* Magazine (2008), *T.H.E. Journal* (2007), *Towson Times*, and *Baltimore Sun*.

She has presented at the National School Boards Association's annual convention; to national, state, and local PTA groups; and to politicians. Suzanne was awarded the National PTA's Life Achievement Award in May 2007. This is the highest honor from the nation's largest child advocacy organization, given to a person who daily lives out his or her commitment to children.

Prior to becoming an educator, Suzanne was a CPA employed with USF&G. She obtained her undergraduate degree from Gettysburg College in 1989 and a master of arts in teaching degree from Goucher College in 2011.

REFERENCES

Acosta, Joie, Matthew Chinman, Patricia Ebener, Patrick S. Malone, Andrea Phillips, and Asa Wilks. "Evaluation of a Whole-School Change Intervention: Findings from a Two-Year Cluster-Randomized Trial of the Restorative Practices Intervention." *Journal of Youth and Adolescence* 48, (2019): 876–90. https://doi.org/10.1007/s10964-019-01013-2.

Akhtar, Allana. "One Third Fewer People Are Training to Become Teachers." *BusinessInsider.com*, December 4, 2019. https://www.businessinsider.com/one-third-fewer-people-are-training-to-become-teachers.

American Immigration Council. "Plyler v Doe Public Education Immigrant Students." October 24, 2016. https://www.americanimmigrationcouncil.org/research/plyler-v-doe-public-education-immigrant-students.

American Speech-Language-Hearing Association. "Acoustics in Educational Settings: Position Statement." 2005. https://www.asha.org/uploadedFiles/elearning/jss/6173/6173Article3.pdf.

American Speech-Language-Hearing Association. "Guidelines for Addressing Acoustics in Educational Settings." 2005. https://www.asha.org/uploadedFiles/elearning/jss/6173/6173Article4.pdf.

American Speech-Language-Hearing Association. "Position Statement and Guidelines for Acoustics in Educational Settings." *ASHA* 37, no. 14 (1995): 15–19.

Augustine, Catherine H, John Engberg, Geoffrey E. Grimm, Emma Lee, Elaine Lin Wang, Karen Christianson, and Andrea A. Joseph. "Can Restorative Practices Improve School Climate and Curb Suspensions." Santa Monica, CA: RAND Corporation, 2018. https://www.rand.org/pubs/research_reports/RR2840.html.

Balingit, Moriah, and Donna St. George. "Is It Becoming Too Hard to Fail? Schools Are Shifting Toward No-Zero Grading Policies." *The Washington Post*, July 5, 2016. https://www.washingtonpost.com/local/education/is-it-becoming-too-hard-to-fail-schools-are-shifting-toward-no-zero-grading-policies/2016/07/05/3c464f5e-3cb0-11e6-80bc-d06711fd2125_story.html.

Baltimore County Public Schools. "Policy 5210." July 1, 2016. https://www.bcps.org/system/policies_
rules/policies/5000Series/POL5210a.pdf.

Baltimore County Public Schools. "About Team BCPS." System. Accessed January 8, 2020. https://
www.bcps.org/system.

Baltimore County Public Schools. "Child Find Services." Accessed February 13, 2020. https://dci.bcps.
org/cms/One.aspx?portalId=9047042&pageId=10680701.

Barshay, Jill. "The Promise of 'Restorative Justice' Starts to Falter Under Rigorous
Research." *Hechinger Report.* May 6, 2009. https://hechingerreport.org/
the-promise-of-restorative-justice-starts-to-falter-under-rigorous-research.

Bell, Douglas, and Barry L. Bogan. "English Language Learners: Problems and Solutions Found in the
Research of General Practitioners of Early Childhood." *The Journal of Balanced Literacy Research
and Instruction* 1, no. 2, article 5 (2013): 18–23. https://digitalcommons.lsu.edu/jblri/vol1/iss2/5.

Berg, Frederick, James C. Blair, and Peggy V. Benson. "Classroom Acoustics: The Problem, Impact, and
Solution." *Language, Speech, & Hearing Services in Schools* 27, no. 1 (January 1996): 16–20.

Bess, Fred H., and Humes, Larry. *Audiology: The Fundamentals.* Philiadelphia: Lippincott Williams &
Wilkins, 2003.

Bialik, Kristen, Alissa Scheller, and Kristi Walker. "6 Facts about English Learners
in US Public Schools." October 25, 2018. https://www.pewresearch.org/
fact-tank/2018/10/25/6-facts-about-english-language-learners-in-u-s-public-schools.

Black, Susan. "If They Can't HEAR It, They Can't LEARN It." *Education Digest* 69, no. 2 (October
2003): 56–61. http://search.ebscohost.com/login.aspx?direct=true&AuthType=ip,shib&db=f5h&AN
=11143715&site=ehost-live&scope=site.

Boswell, Susan. "Sound Field Systems on the Rise in Schools: Improved Test Scores Cited as Benefit."
The ASHA Leader, May 23, 2006. https://teachlogic.com/wp-content/uploads/2018/02/soundfield_
systems_on_the_rise.pdf.

Bowie, Liz. "Baltimore County School Board OK's $205 Million Technology Contract." *The Baltimore
Sun*, March 11, 2014. https://www.baltimoresun.com/education/bs-md-co-technology-schools-
20140311-story.html.

Bowie, Liz. "Baltimore County Schools Scaling Back Ambitious Laptop Program That Has Met
Criticism." *The Baltimore Sun*, May 21, 2019. https://www.baltimoresun.com/education/bs-md-co-
laptop-changes-20190517-story.html.

Bowie, Liz. "Dance's Career Impresses Some, Worries Others." *The Baltimore Sun*, March 28, 2012.
https://www.baltimoresun.com/news/bs-xpm-2012-03-28-bs-md-co-dance-20120328-story.html.

Bowie, Liz. "Four Years in, Baltimore County Schools' $147M Laptop Program Has Produced Little
Change in Student Achievement." *The Baltimore Sun*, December 13, 2018. https://www.baltimoresun.
com/education/bs-md-co-laptop-schools-achievement-20181127-story.html.

Bowie, Liz. "Baltimore County Schools Are Rapidly Adding Students. More Than Half Are Immigrants
or Speak Another Language." *The Baltimore Sun*, February 7, 2019. https://www.baltimoresun.com/
maryland/baltimore-county/bs-md-co-immigrant-enrollment-20190204-story.html.

Bowie, Liz, and Doug Donovan. "Superintendent Dallas Dance Sentenced to Six Months in Jail." *The Baltimore Sun*, April 20, 2018. https://www.baltimoresun.com/politics/bs-md-co-dance-sentencing-20180416-story.html.

Bowie, Liz,, Talia Richman, and Christine Zhang. "Maryland 2019 Test Scores." *The Baltimore Sun*, August 27, 2019. https://www.baltimoresun.com/education/bs-md-maryland-2019-test-scores-20190827-f7bmkyju3vbo3odiiddzbhh5w4-story.html.

Brown University. "Browns Grading System." Accessed September 20, 2020. https://www.brown.edu/about/administration/registrar/course-enrollment/grades#grading

Budiman, Abby, Christine Tamir, Lauren Mora, and Luis Noe-Bustamante. "Facts on US Immigrants, 2018." Pew Research Center. August 20, 2020. https://www.pewresearch.org/hispanic/2020/08/20/facts-on-u-s-immigrants.

Butler, Ruth. "Enhancing and Undermining Intrinsic Motivation: The Effects of Task-Involving and Ego-Involving Evaluation on Interest and Performance." *British Journal of Educational Psychology* 58, no. 1 (February 1988): 1–14. https://bpspsychub.onlinelibrary.wiley.com/doi/epdf/10.1111/j.2044-8279.1988.tb00874.x.

Butler, Ruth and Nisan, Mordecai. "Effects of No Feedback, Task-Related Comments, and Grades on Instrinsic Motivation and Performance." *Journal of Educational Psychology* 78, no. 3 (June 1986): 210–216. https://psycnet.apa.org/doi/10.1037/0022-0663.78.3.210.

CBS. "Schools Get Wired for Sound." Aired February 21, 2005. https://www.cbsnews.com/news/schools-get-wired-for-sound.

Core Standards. "Development Process—Common Core State Standards Initiative." Accessed September 24, 2019. http://www.corestandards.org/about-the-standards/development-process.

Core Standards. "Grade 4 Number & Operations in Base Ten B.5." Accessed August 23, 2020. http://www.corestandards.org/Math/Content/4/NBT/B/5.

County Health Rankings and Roadmaps. "Restorative Justice in the Criminal Justice System." March 24, 2017. https://www.countyhealthrankings.org/take-action-to-improve-health/what-works-for-health/policies/restorative-justice-in-the-criminal-justice-system.

Crandell, Carl. "Effect of Classroom Acoustics on Speech Recognition in Pediatric Populations." F. Berg (Chair) *Listening in Classrooms* workshop. Utah State University, Logan. November, 1990.

Crandell, Carl C, Joseph J Smaldino, and Carol Flexer. *Sound Field Amplification Applications to Speech Perception and Classroom Acoustics*. Second Edition. Canada: Thomson Delmar Learning, 2005.

Cuttler, Garen. "Educators Report Growing Behavioral Issues among Young Students." *Globe Newswire*, February 14, 2019. https://www.globenewswire.com/news-release/2019/02/14/1725406/0/en/Educators-Report-Growing-Behavioral-Issues-Among-Young-Students.html.

Darai, Betea. "Using Sound Field FM Systems to Improve Literacy Scores." *ADVANCE for Speech Language Pathologists and Audiologists* 10, no. 27, (July 2000): 5–13.

Davis, Alicia J. and Heather Pfeifer, "How Has the Baltimore County Public School System Addressed Disproportionate Minority Suspensions." *Schaefer Center for Public Policy, University of Baltimore*, 2014. http://www.ubalt.edu/cpa/centers/schaefer-center/minority_-suspensions_report_revised.pdf.

Desilver, Drew. "Fact Tank." Pew Research. February 15, 2017. https://www.pewresearch.org/fact-tank/2017/02/15/u-s-students-internationally-math-science.

Dobie, Robert and Berlin, Charles I. "Influence of Otitis Media on Hearing and Development." *The Annals of Otology, Rhinology & Laryngology* 88, no. 5, pt. 2, suppl. 60 (September 1979): 45–83. https://doi.org/10.1177%2F00034894790880S505.

Donovan, Doug and Liz Bowie. "Ethics Complaint Filed against Baltimore County School Superintendent Verletta White." *The Baltimore Sun*, November 15, 2017. https://www.baltimoresun.com/maryland/baltimore-county/catonsville/bs-md-ethics-complaint-verletta-white-20171113-story.html.

Eberhard, John P. "Children's Brains Are the Key to Well-Designed Classrooms." *AI Architect*, June 2006, http://info.aia.org/aiarchitect/thisweek06/0623/0623eberhard.htm.

Eden, Max. "Studies and Teachers Nationwide Say School Discipline Reform Is Harming Students' Academic Achievement and Safety." *The 74*, June 10, 2019. https://www.the74million.org/article/eden-studies-and-teachers-nationwide-say-school-discipline-reform-is-harming-students-academic-achievement-and-safety.

Englund, Michelle M., Amy E. Luckner, Gloria J. L. Whaley, and Byron Egeland. "Children's Achievement in Early Elementary School: Longitudinal Effects of Parental Involvement, Expectations, and Quality of Assistance." *Journal of Educational Psychology* 96, no.4 (2004): 723–30.

Fabelo, Tony, Michael D. Thompson, Martha Plotkin, Dottie Carmichael, Miner P. Marchbanks III, and Eric A. Booth. "Breaking Schools' Rules: A Statewide Study of How School Discipline Relates to Students' Success and Juvenile Justice Involvement." Council of State Governments Justice Center. July 2011. https://csgjusticecenter.org/wp-content/uploads/2020/01/Breaking_Schools_Rules_Report_Final.pdf.

Fast ForWord. "What Is Fast ForWord?" Accessed February 13, 2020. https://www.fastforwordhome.com/what-is-fast-forword.

Flexer, Carol, Biley, Kate Kemp, Hinkley, Alyssa, Harkema, Cheryl, and Holcomb, John. "Using Sound-field Systems to Teach Phonemic Awareness to Pre-Schoolers." *The Hearning Journal* 55, no. 3 (March 2002): 40–41.

Gallup, Alec M. "The 18th Annual Gallup Poll of the Public's Attitudes towards the Public Schools." *Phi Delta Kappan* 68, no. 1 (September 1986): 43–59.

Garland, Sarah. "The Man Behind Common Core Math." NPREd. December 29, 2014. https://www.npr.org/sections/ed/2014/12/29/371918272/the-man-behind-common-core-math.

Georgetown University. "Civil Rights Act 1964, 1968." Accessed December 5, 2019. https://guides.ll.georgetown.edu/c.php?g=592919&p=4172702.

Golod, Amy. "Common Core: Myths and Facts." *US News & World Report*, March 4, 2014. https://www.usnews.com/news/special-reports/a-guide-to-common-core/articles/2014/03/04/common-core-myths-and-facts.

Gustin, Georgina. "PTA Says All Parent-Teacher Groups Not Created Equal." *Deseret News*, July 1, 2007. https://www.deseret.com/2007/7/1/20027547/pta-says-all-parent-teacher-groups-not-created-equal.

Harris, Jennifer, Mohammed T. Al-Bataineh, and Adel Al-Bataineh. "One to One Technology and Its Effect on Student Academic Achievement and Motivation." *Contemporary Educational Technology* 7, no. 4 (2016): 368–81. https://files.eric.ed.gov/fulltext/EJ1117604.pdf.

Harvard University Archives—Harvard University. "Annual Report of the President of Harvard University to the Overseers on the State of the University for the Academic Year 1830–31." Accessed August 29, 2020. https://iiif.lib.harvard.edu/manifests/view/drs:427074494$4i.

Hearing Health Foundation. "Auditory Processing Deficit Demographics." Accessed February 5, 2020. https://hearinghealthfoundation.org/apd-demographics.

Ingraham, Loni. "Soundadvice." *Towson Times*, October 12, 2005.

Johnson, C.E. 2000. "Children's Phoneme Identification in Reverberation and Noise." *Journal of Speech, Language and Hearing Research* 43, no. 1 (February 2000): 144–57. https://pubs.asha.org/doi/pdf/10.1044/jslhr.4301.144.

Kay, Liz. "Volume Rises in Debate on Classroom Acoustics." *The Baltimore Sun*, March 13, 2006.

KIDS COUNT Data Center a Project of the Annie E. Casey Foundation. "Children Who Live in Two-Parent Families, by Race Ethnicity in the United States." Accessed October 23, 2019. https://datacenter.kidscount.org/data/tables/8053-children-who-live-in-two-parent-families-by-race-ethnicity.

Knecht, Heather A., Peggy B. Nelson, Gail M. Whitelaw, and Lawrence L. Feth. "Background Noise Levels and Reverberation Times in Unoccupied Classrooms: Predictions and Measurements." *American Journal of Audiology* 11, (2002): 65–71.

Knight, David S., Elena Izquierdo, and David E. DeMatthews. "Implementation, Cost, and Funding of Bilingual Education in Texas: Lessons for Local and State Policymakers." El Paso: Center for Education Research and Policy Studies, College of Education at University of Texas (El Paso). February 2017. https://scholarworks.utep.edu/cgi/viewcontent.cgi?article=1001&context=cerps_pb.

Kohut, Andrew. "From the Archives: In '60s, Americans Gave Thumbs-Up to Immigration Law That Changed the Nation." Fact Tank—Pew Research. October 25, 2018. https://www.pewresearch.org/fact-tank/2019/09/20/in-1965-majority-of-americans-favored-immigration-and-nationality-act-2.

Locke, Charley. "Computerized Common Core Testing Poses Challenge for Schools." EdSurge. July 9, 2014. https://www.edsurge.com/news/2014-07-09-computerized-common-core-testing-poses-challenge-for-schools.

Marken, Stephanie. "Say Teachers Unprepared Handle Discipline." Gallup. May 1, 2019. https://news.gallup.com/poll/249185/say-teachers-unprepared-handle-discipline.aspx.

Mary Boswell McComas. "Baltimore County Schools Are Looking to Hire More ESOL Teachers." Interview by Tim Tooten. WBAL TV, January 16, 2019. https://www.wbaltv.com/article/baltimore-county-schools-are-looking-to-hire-more-esol-teachers/25924224.

Maryland State Department of Education. "2019 Demographics for 'Raven.'" Accessed August 29, 2020. https://reportcard.msde.maryland.gov/graphs/#/demographics/enrollment.

Maryland State Department of Education. "School Discipline and Academic Success: Related Parts of Maryland's Education Reform." July 2012. http://www.marylandpublicschools.org/stateboard/Documents/StudentDiscipline/SchoolDisciplineandAcademicSuccessReport0712.pdf.

Maryland State Department of Education. "Report Cards." June 2019. https://reportcard.msde.maryland.gov/graphs/#/reportcards/reportcardschool.

McKeon, Denise. "Research Talking Points on English Language Learners." National Education Association. June, 2005. http://www.nea.org/home/13598.htm.

Metzner, Janet. "***** Elementary Named a National Blue Ribbon School." *Patch*, September 7, 2012.

Minero, Emelina. 2018. "Do No-Zero Policies Help or Hurt Students?" Edutopia. July 3, 2018. https://www.edutopia.org/article/do-no-zero-policies-help-or-hurt-students.

Montoya Avila, Angelica. "Trends in Maryland Public Schools: English Language Learner Enrollment." Maryland Equity Project. University of Maryland, College of Education. March 2017. https://education.umd.edu/research/centers/mep/research/k-12-education/trends-maryland-public-schools-english-language-learner.

National Center for Education Statistics. "Fast Facts: English Language Learners." Accessed December 3, 2019. https://nces.ed.gov/fastfacts/display.asp?id=96.

National Center for Education Statistics. "Highlights of US PISA 2018 Results Web Report." Accessed April 12, 2020. https://nces.ed.gov/surveys/pisa/pisa2018/index.asp#/math/intlcompare.

National PTA. "PTA Reports and Financials." Accessed February 4, 2020. https://www.pta.org/home/About-National-Parent-Teacher-Association/PTA-Reports-Financials.

National PTA. "PTA Reports-Financials." Accessed August 22, 2020. https://online.fliphtml5.com/dtoi/qjpy/#p=14.

National PTA. "Approved Convention Resolutions." Accessed February 3, 2020. https://www.pta.org/home/advocacy/ptas-positions/Individual-PTA-Resolutions/Approved-Convention-Resolutions.

Niskar, Amanda S., Stephanie M. Kieszak, and Alice Holmes. "Prevalence of Hearing Loss among Children 6 to 19 Years of Age." *Journal of American Medical Association* 279, no. 14 (1998): 1071–75. https://jamanetwork.com/journals/jama/fullarticle/187415.

Organisation for Economic Co-Operation and Development. "PISA 2018 Country Note USA." Accessed August 24, 2020. https://www.oecd.org/pisa/publications/PISA2018_CN_USA.pdf.

Palmer, Catherine V. "Hearing and Listening in a Typical Classroom." *Language, Speech & Hearing Services in Schools* 28, (1997): 213–18.

Papst, Chris. "Project Baltimore." *Project Baltimore*. June 11, 2018. https://foxbaltimore.com/news/project-baltimore/baltimore-county-teachers-culture-of-leniency-leading-to-violence.

Paul, Catherine A. "Elementary and Secondary Education Act of 1965." Virginia Commonwealth University Social Welfare History Project. 2016. https://socialwelfare.library.vcu.edu/programs/education/elementary-and-secondary-education-act-of-1965.

Pennsylvania PTA. "Issues/Action." Accessed January 31, 2020. https://www.papta.org/Page/309.

Ramu, Kayleswari. "Maryland's Role in Bridging Language Disparities: Accommodating New Waves of ELL Students." *University of Maryland Law Journal of Race, Religion, Gender and Class* 17, no. 2 (2017): 394–413. https://digitalcommons.law.umaryland.edu/cgi/viewcontent.cgi?article=1291&context=rrgc.

Ray, Helen. "Beginning and Validation of Sound Field FM in Classrooms," F. Berg (Chair) *Listening in Classrooms* workshop. Utah State University, Logan. November, 1990.

Reeves, Douglas B. 2008. "Teaching Students to Think." *Educational Leadership* 65, no. 5 (February 2008): 85–87. http://www.ascd.org/publications/educational-leadership/feb08/vol65/num05/Effective-Grading-Practices.aspx.

Richmond, Talia. "Computer Based Tests Are Another Challenge for Low Income Students Teachers Say." *The Washington Post.* April 30, 2018. https://www.washingtonpost.com/local/education/computer-based-tests-are-another-challenge-for-low-income-students-teachers-say/2018/04/30/add5d118-43fb-11e8-8569-26fda6b404c7_story.html.

Sanchez, Claudio. "English Language Learners: How Your State Is Doing." NPR. February 23, 2017. https://www.npr.org/sections/ed/2017/02/23/512451228/5-million-english-language-learners-a-vast-pool-of-talent-at-risk.

Sarff, Lewis S., Ray, Helen, and Bagwell, C. "Why Not Amplification in Every Classroom?" *Hearing Aid Journal* 34, no. 10 (1981): 11, 44, 47–48, 52.

Schinske, Jeffrey, and Kimberly Tanner. "Teaching More by Grading Less (or Differently)." *CBE Life Sciences Education* 13, no. 2 (Summer 2014): 159–66. https://www.ncbi.nlm.nih.gov/pmc/articles/PMC4041495.

Schleicher, Andreas. "PISA 2018 Insights and Interpretations." OECD. 2019. https://www.oecd.org/pisa/PISA%202018%20Insights%20and%20Interpretations%20FINAL%20PDF.pdf.

Schott Foundation for Public Education. "Restorative Practices Fostering Healthy Relationships & Promoting Positive Disipline in Schools." March 2014. http://schottfoundation.org/resources/restorative-practices-toolkit.

Schwartz, Katrina. "How Teachers Are Changing Grading Practices with an Eye on Equity." KQED. Accessed February 10, 2019. https://www.kqed.org/mindshift/52813/how%20teachers%20are%20changing%20grading%20practices%20with%20an%20eye%20on%20equity.

Song, Samuel Y., and Susan M. Swearer. "The Cart before the Horse: The Challenge and Promise of Restorative Justice Consultation in Schools." *Journal of Educational and Psychological Consultation* 26, no. 4 (November 2016): 313–24. https://doi.org/10.1080/10474412.2016.1246972.

Starkman, Neal. "Sound Solutions." *T.H.E. Journal.* Article dated June 1, 2007. Accessed April 18, 2008. http://www.thejournal.com/articles/20758.

Stewner-Manzanares, Gloria. "The Bilingual Education Act: Twenty Years Later." *The National Clearinghouse for Bilingual Education*, no. 6 (Fall 1988). https://ncela.ed.gov/files/rcd/BE021037/Fall88_6.pdf.

Stoltzfus, Kate. "The No Grades Movement." *Education Week*, January 10, 2018. https://www.edweek.org/ew/articles/2018/01/10/no-students-dont-need-grades.html.

Sugarman, Julie, and Courtney Geary. "Fact Sheet 2018 English Learners in Maryland." Migration Policy Institute. August 2018. https://www.migrationpolicy.org/sites/default/files/publications/EL-factsheet2018-Maryland_Final.pdf.

United States Courts. "Access Education Rule of Law." Accessed December 8, 2019. https://www.uscourts.gov/educational-resources/educational-activities/access-education-rule-law.

US Department of Education. "Academic Performance and Outcomes for English Learners." Accessed December 10, 2019. https://www2.ed.gov/datastory/el-outcomes/index.html.

US Department of Education. "Programs, Race to the Top Fact Sheet." December 29, 2009. https://www2.ed.gov/programs/racetothetop/factsheet.html.

US Department of Education. "Results from the 2019 Mathematics and Reading Assessments." Nation's Report Card. 2019. https://www.nationsreportcard.gov/mathematics/supportive_files/2019_infographic.pdf.

US Department of Education. "Secretary Duncan, Attorney General Holder Announce Effort to Respond to School-to-Prison Pipeline by Supporting Good Discipline Practices." Press Release. July 21, 2011. https://www.ed.gov/news/press-releases/secretary-duncan-attorney-general-holder-announce-effort-respond-school-prison-pipeline-supporting-good-discipline-practices.

US Department of Education. "Supportive School Discipline Initiative." School Discipline Policy. Summer 2011. https://www2.ed.gov/policy/gen/guid/school-discipline/appendix-3-overview.pdf.

US Department of Education Office for Civil Rights. "Civil Rights Data Collection Data Snapshot: School Discipline." March 2014. https://ocrdata.ed.gov/Downloads/CRDC-School-Discipline-Snapshot.pdf.

US Department of Education Office for Civil Rights. "Fact Sheet—Ensuring English Learner Students Can Participate Meaningfully and Equally in Educational Programs." January 2015. https://www2.ed.gov/about/offices/list/ocr/docs/dcl-factsheet-el-students-201501.pdf

US Department of Education Office of Educational Technology. "Reimagining the Role of Technology in Education." January 31, 2017. https://tech.ed.gov/files/2017/01/NETP17.pdf.

University of Cambridge. "People." Accessed August 26, 2020. http://www.mrc-cbu.cam.ac.uk/people/matt.davis/cmabridge.

Wells, Carrie. "Baltimore County School System Modifies New Grading Policy." *The Baltimore Sun*, November 3, 2016. https://www.baltimoresun.com/education/bs-md-co-grading-policy-change-20161103-story.html.

Worstall, Tim. "Ben Bernanke: The 2008 Financial Crisis Was Worse Than The Great Depression." *Forbes.com*. August 27, 2014. https://www.forbes.com/sites/timworstall/2014/08/27/ben-bernanke-the-2008-financial-crisis-was-worse-than-the-great-depression/#69204d347684.

NOTES

1 "About Team BCPS," System, Baltimore County Public Schools, accessed January 8, 2020, https://www.bcps.org/system.

2 Liz Bowie, "Dance's Career Impresses Some, Worries Others," *The Baltimore Sun*, March 28, 2012, https://www.baltimoresun.com/news/bs-xpm-2012-03-28-bs-md-co-dance-20120328-story.html.

3 Bowie, "Dance's Career Impresses Some, Worries Others."

4 Bowie, "Dance's Career Impresses Some, Worries Others."

5 Janet Metzner, "***** Elementary Named a National Blue Ribbon School," *Patch*, September 7, 2012.

6 Metzner, "***** Elementary Named a National Blue Ribbon School."

7 Liz Bowie and Doug Donovan, "Former Superintendent Dallas Dance Sentenced to Six Months in Jail," *The Baltimore Sun*, April 20, 2018, https://www.baltimoresun.com/politics/bs-md-co-dance-sentencing-20180416-story.html.

8 Bowie and Donovan, "Former Superintendent Dallas Dance Sentenced to Six Months in Jail."

9 Bowie and Donovan, "Former Superintendent Dallas Dance Sentenced to Six Months in Jail."

10 Doug Donovan and Liz Bowie, "Ethics Complaint Filed against Baltimore County School Superintendent Verletta White," *The Baltimore Sun*, November 15, 2017, https://www.baltimoresun.com/maryland/baltimore-county/catonsville/bs-md-ethics-complaint-verletta-white-20171113-story.html.

11 "Report Cards," Maryland State Department of Education, June 2019, https://reportcard.msde.maryland.gov/graphs/#/reportcards/reportcardschool.

12 "Results from the 2019 Mathematics and Reading Assessments," Nation's Report Card, US Department of Education, 2019, https://www.nationsreportcard.gov/mathematics/supportive_files/2019_infographic.pdf.

13 US Department of Education, "Results from the 2019 Mathematics and Reading Assessments."

14 Max Eden, "Eden: Studies and Teachers Nationwide Say School Discipline Reform Is Harming Students' Academic Achievement and Safety," *The 74*, June 10, 2019, https://www.the74million.org/article/eden-studies-and-teachers-nationwide-say-school-discipline-reform-is-harming-students-academic-achievement-and-safety.

15 Allana Akhtar, "One Third Fewer People Are Training to Become Teachers," *BusinessInsider.com*, December 4, 2019, https://www.businessinsider.com/one-third-fewer-people-are-training-to-become-teachers.

16 "Development Process—Common Core State Standards Initiative," Core Standards, accessed September 24, 2019, http://www.corestandards.org/about-the-standards/development-process.

17 Sarah Garland, "The Man behind Common Core Math," NPREd, December 29, 2014, https://www.npr.org/sections/ed/2014/12/29/371918272/the-man-behind-common-core-math.

18 Garland, "The Man behind Common Core Math."

19 "Development Process—Common Core State Standards Initiative."

20 Garland, "The Man behind Common Core Math."

21 Garland, "The Man behind Common Core Math."

22 Garland, "The Man behind Common Core Math."

23 "Development Process—Common Core State Standards Initiative."

24 "Programs, Race to the Top Fact Sheet," US Department of Education, December 29, 2009, https://www2.ed.gov/programs/racetothetop/factsheet.html.

25 "Programs, Race to the Top Fact Sheet."

26 Amy Golod, "Common Core: Myths and Facts," *US News and World Report*, March 4, 2014, https://www.usnews.com/news/special-reports/a-guide-to-common-core/articles/2014/03/04/common-core-myths-and-facts.

27 Garland, "The Man behind Common Core Math."

28 Drew Desilver, "Fact Tank," Pew Research, February, 15, 2017, https://www.pewresearch.org/fact-tank/2017/02/15/u-s-students-internationally-math-science.

29 "PISA 2018 Country Note USA," Organisation for Economic Co-Operation and Development, accessed August 24, 2020, https://www.oecd.org/pisa/publications/PISA2018_CN_USA.pdf.

30 "Highlights of US PISA 2018 Results Web Report," National Center for Education Statistics, accessed April 12, 2020, https://nces.ed.gov/surveys/pisa/pisa2018/index.asp#/math/intlcompare.

31 "Highlights of US PISA 2018 Results Web Report."

32 "PISA 2018 Country Note USA."

33 "Grade 4 Number & Operations in Base Ten B.5," Core Standards, accessed August 23, 2020, http://www.corestandards.org/Math/Content/4/NBT/B/5.

34 Andreas Schleicher, "PISA 2018 Insights and Interpretations," OECD, 2019, https://www.oecd.org/pisa/PISA%202018%20Insights%20and%20Interpretations%20FINAL%20PDF.pdf.

35 "Results from the 2019 Mathematics and Reading Assessments."

36 Charley Locke, "Computerized Common Core Testing Poses Challenge for Schools," EdSurge, July 9, 2014, https://www.edsurge.com/news/2014-07-09-computerized-common-core-testing-poses-challenge-for-schools.

37 Locke, "Computerized Common Core Testing Poses Challenge for Schools."

38 Locke, "Computerized Common Core Testing Poses Challenge for Schools."

39 Locke, "Computerized Common Core Testing Poses Challenge for Schools."

40 Talia Richmond, "Computer Based Tests Are Another Challenge for Low Income Students Teachers Say," *The Washington Post*, April 30, 2018, https://www.washingtonpost.com/local/education/computer-based-tests-are-another-challenge-for-low-income-students-teachers-say/2018/04/30/add5d118-43fb-11e8-8569-26fda6b404c7_story.html.

41 Richmond, "Computer Based Tests Are Another Challenge for Low Income Students Teachers Say."

42 Jennifer Harris, Mohammed T. Al-Bataineh, and Adel Al-Baltaineh, "One to One Technology and Its Effect on Student Academic Achievement and Motivation," *Contemporary Educational Technology* 7, no. 4 (2016): 368, https://files.eric.ed.gov/fulltext/EJ1117604.pdf.

43 "Reimagining the Role of Technology in Education," US Department of Education Office of Educational Technology, January 31, 2017, https://tech.ed.gov/files/2017/01/NETP17.pdf.

44 "Reimagining the Role of Technology in Education."

45 Liz Bowie, "Baltimore County School Board OKs $205 Million Technology Contract," *The Baltimore Sun*, March 11, 2014, https://www.baltimoresun.com/education/bs-md-co-technology-schools-20140311-story.html.

46 Bowie, "Baltimore County School Board OKs $205 Million Technology Contract."

47 Bowie, "Baltimore County School Board OKs $205 Million Technology Contract."

48 Liz Bowie, "Four Years In, Baltimore County Schools' $147M Laptop Program Has Produced Little Change in Student Achievement," *The Baltimore Sun*, December 13, 2018, https://www.baltimoresun.com/education/bs-md-co-laptop-schools-achievement-20181127-story.html.

49 Liz Bowie, "Baltimore County Schools Scaling Back Ambitious Laptop Program That Has Met Criticism," *The Baltimore Sun*, May 21, 2019, https://www.baltimoresun.com/education/bs-md-co-laptop-changes-20190517-story.html.

50 Bowie, "Baltimore County Schools Scaling Back Ambitious Laptop Program That Has Met Criticism."

51 Bowie, "Baltimore County Schools Scaling Back Ambitious Laptop Program That Has Met Criticism."

52 Jeffrey Schinske and Kimberly Tanner, "Teaching More by Grading Less (or Differently)," *CBE Life Sciences Education* 13, no. 2 (Summer 2014): 159, https://www.ncbi.nlm.nih.gov/pmc/articles/PMC4041495.

53 Schinske and Tanner, "Teaching More by Grading Less (or Differently)," 159–60.

54 Harvard University, "Annual Report of the President of Harvard University to the Overseers on the State of the University for the Academic Year 1830-1831," Harvard University Archives—Harvard University, accessed August 29, 2020, https://nrs.harvard.edu/urn-3:HUL.ARCH:30047961?n=4.

55 Schinske and Tanner, "Teaching More by Grading Less (or Differently)," 160.

56 Schinske and Tanner, "Teaching More by Grading Less (or Differently)," 160.

57 Schinske and Tanner, "Teaching More by Grading Less (or Differently)," 160.

58 "Browns Grading System," Brown University, accessed September 20, 2020, https://www.brown.edu/about/administration/registrar/course-enrollment/grades#grading.

59 Douglas B. Reeves, "Teaching Students to Think," *Educational Leadership* 65, no. 5 (February 2008): 85–86, http://www.ascd.org/publications/educational-leadership/feb08/vol65/num05/Effective-Grading-Practices.aspx.

60 Ruth Butler and Mordecai Nisan, "Effects of No Feedback, Task-Related Comments, and Grades on Intrinsic Motivation and Performance," *Journal of Educational Psychology* 78, no. 3 (June 1986): 210, https://psycnet.apa.org/doi/10.1037/0022-0663.78.3.210.

61 Schinske and Tanner, "Teaching More by Grading Less (or Differently)," 161.

62 Ruth Butler, "Enhancing and Undermining Intrisic Motivation: The Effects of Task-Involving and Ego-Involving Evaluation on Interest and Performance," *British Journal of Educational Psychology* 58, no. 1 (February 1988): 12–13, https://bpspsychub.onlinelibrary.wiley.com/doi/epdf/10.1111/j.2044-8279.1988.tb00874.x.

63 Butler and Nisan, "Effects of No Feedback," 210.

64 Kate Stoltzfus, "The No Grades Movement," *Education Week*, January 10, 2018, 14, https://www.edweek.org/ew/articles/2018/01/10/no-students-dont-need-grades.html.

65 Moriah Balingit and Donna St. George, "Is It Becoming Too Hard to Fail? Schools Are Shifting toward No-Zero Grading Policies," *The Washington Post*, July 5, 2016, https://www.washingtonpost.com/local/education/is-it-becoming-too-hard-to-fail-schools-are-shifting-toward-no-zero-grading-policies/2016/07/05/3c464f5e-3cb0-11e6-80bc-d06711fd2125_story.html.

66   Emelina Minero, "Do No-Zero Policies Help or Hurt Students," Edutopia, July 3, 2018, https://www.edutopia.org/article/do-no-zero-policies-help-or-hurt-students.

67   Minero, "Do No-Zero Policies Help or Hurt Students?"

68   Minero, "Do No-Zero Policies Help or Hurt Students?"

69   Balingit and St. George, "Is It Becoming Too Hard to Fail? Schools Are Shifting toward No-Zero Grading Policies."

70   Balingit and St. George, "Is It Becoming Too Hard to Fail? Schools Are Shifting toward No-Zero Grading Policies."

71   "Policy 5210," Baltimore County Public Schools, July 1, 2016, https://www.bcps.org/system/policies_rules/policies/5000Series/POL5210a.pdf.

72   Carrie Wells, "Baltimore County School System Modifies New Grading Policy," *The Baltimore Sun*, November 3, 2016, https://www.baltimoresun.com/education/bs-md-co-grading-policy-change-20161103-story.html.

73   Wells, "Baltimore County School System Modifies New Grading Policy."

74   Balingit and St. George, "Is It Becoming Too Hard to Fail? Schools Are Shifting toward No-Zero Grading Policies."

75   Balingit and St. George, "Is It Becoming Too Hard to Fail? Schools Are Shifting toward No-Zero Grading Policies."

76   Katrina Schwartz, "How Teachers Are Changing Grading Practices with an Eye on Equity," KQED, accessed February 10, 2019, https://www.kqed.org/mindshift/52813/how%20teachers%20are%20changing%20grading%20practices%20with%20an%20eye%20on%20equity.

77   Schwartz, "How Teachers Are Changing Grading Practices with an Eye on Equity."

78   Schinske and Tanner, "Teaching More by Grading Less (or Differently)," 163-65.

79   Schwartz, "How Teachers Are Changing Grading Practices with an Eye on Equity."

80   Abby Budiman, Christine Tamir, Lauren Mora, and Luis Noe-Bustamante, "Facts on US Immigrants, 2018," Pew Research Center, August 20, 2020, https://www.pewresearch.org/hispanic/2020/08/20/facts-on-u-s-immigrants.

81   Budiman, Tamir, Mora, and Noe-Bustamante, "Facts on US Immigrants, 2018."

82   Andrew Kohut, "From the Archives: In '60s, Americans Gave Thumbs-Up to Immigration Law That Changed the Nation," Fact Tank—Pew Research, September 20, 2019, https://www.pewresearch.org/fact-tank/2019/09/20/in-1965-majority-of-americans-favored-immigration-and-nationality-act-2.

83   Kristen Bialik, Alissa Scheller, and Kristi Walker, "6 Facts about English Learners in US Public Schools," Fact Tank—Pew Research, October 25, 2018, https://www.pewresearch.org/fact-tank/2018/10/25/6-facts-about-english-language-learners-in-u-s-public-schools.

84 Bialik, Scheller, and Walker, "6 Facts about English Learners in US Public Schools."

85 Denise McKeon, "Research Talking Points on English Language Learners," National Education Association, June 2005, http://www.nea.org/home/13598.htm.

86 "Civil Rights Act 1964, 1968," Georgetown University, accessed December 5, 2019, https://guides. ll.georgetown.edu/civilrights.

87 Catherine A. Paul, "Elementary and Secondary Education Act of 1965," Virginia Commonwealth University Social Welfare History Project, 2016, https://socialwelfare.library.vcu.edu/programs/ education/elementary-and-secondary-education-act-of-1965.

88 Paul, "Elementary and Secondary Education Act of 1965."

89 Kayleswari Ramu, "Maryland's Role in Bridging Language Disparities: Accommodating New Waves of ELL Students," *University of Maryland Law Journal of Race, Religion, Gender and Class*, 17, no. 2 (2017): 401–2, https://digitalcommons.law.umaryland.edu/cgi/viewcontent. cgi?article=1291&context=rrgc.

90 Ramu, "Maryland's Role in Bridging Language Disparities: Accommodating New Waves of ELL Students," 402.

91 Gloria Stewner-Manzanares, "The Bilingual Education Act: Twenty Years Later," *The National Clearinghouse for Bilingual Education*, no. 6 (Fall 1988): 1, https://ncela.ed.gov/files/rcd/BE021037/ Fall88_6.pdf.

92 Ramu, "Maryland's Role in Bridging Language Disparities: Accommodating New Waves of ELL Students," 396–97.

93 Stewner-Manzanares, "The Bilingual Education Act: Twenty Years Later," 3.

94 Ramu, "Maryland's Role in Bridging Language Disparities: Accommodating New Waves of ELL Students," 396–95.

95 Bialik, Scheller, and Walker, "6 Facts about English Learners in US Public Schools."

96 "Public Education for Immigrant Students: Understanding Plyler v. Doe," American Immigration Council, October 24, 2016, https://www.americanimmigrationcouncil.org/research/ plyler-v-doe-public-education-immigrant-students.

97 "Access to Education—Rule of Law," United States Courts, accessed December 8, 2019, https:// www.uscourts.gov/educational-resources/educational-activities/access-education-rule-law.

98 "Access to Education—Rule of Law."

99 "Fast Facts: English Language Learners," National Center for Education Statistics, accessed December 3, 2019, https://nces.ed.gov/fastfacts/display.asp?id=96.

100 "Fast Facts: English Language Learners."

101 "Fast Facts: English Language Learners."

102 "Fast Facts: English Language Learners."

103 Claudio Sanchez, "English Language Learners: How Your State Is Doing," NPR, February 23, 2017, https://www.npr.org/sections/ed/2017/02/23/512451228/5-million-english-language-learners-a-vast-pool-of-talent-at-risk.

104 "Fact Sheet—Ensuring English Learner Students Can Participate Meaningfully and Equally in Educational Programs," US Department of Education Office for Civil Rights, January 2015, 1, https://www2.ed.gov/about/offices/list/ocr/docs/dcl-factsheet-el-students-201501.pdf.

105 "Fact Sheet—Ensuring English Learner Students Can Participate Meaningfully and Equally in Educational Programs," 3.

106 "Fact Sheet—Ensuring English Learner Students Can Participate Meaningfully and Equally in Educational Programs," 1.

107 "Fact Sheet—Ensuring English Learner Students Can Participate Meaningfully and Equally in Educational Programs," 1.

108 Sanchez, "English Language Learners: How Your State Is Doing."

109 Douglas Bell and Barry L. Bogan, "English Language Learners: Problems and Solutions Found in the Research of General Practitioners of Early Childhood," *The Journal of Balanced Literacy Research and Instruction* 1, no. 2, article 5 (2013): 19, https://digitalcommons.lsu.edu/jblri/vol1/iss2/5.

110 Sanchez, "English Language Learners: How Your State Is Doing."

111 Bell and Bogan, "English Language Learners: Problems and Solutions Found in the Research of General Practitioners of Early Childhood," 19.

112 "Fact Sheet—Ensuring English Learner Students Can Participate Meaningfully and Equally in Educational Programs," 2.

113 Bell and Bogan, "English Language Learners: Problems and Solutions Found in the Research of General Practitioners of Early Childhood," 19.

114 Bell and Bogan, "English Language Learners: Problems and Solutions Found in the Research of General Practitioners of Early Childhood," 19.

115 Sanchez, "English Language Learners: How Your State Is Doing."

116 "Academic Performance and Outcomes for English Learners," US Department of Education, accessed December 10, 2019, https://www2.ed.gov/datastory/el-outcomes/index.html.

117 McKeon, "Research Talking Points on English Language Learners."

118 Sanchez, "English Language Learners: How Your State Is Doing."

119 David S. Knight, Elena Izquierdo, and David E. DeMatthews, "Policy Brief #2—Implementation, Cost, and Funding of Bilingual Education in Texas: Lessons for Local and State Policymakers," *Center for Education Research and Policy Studies*, February 2017, 7, https://scholarworks.utep.edu/cgi/viewcontent.cgi?article=1001&context=cerps_pb.

120 Knight, Izquierdo, and DeMatthews, "Policy Brief #2—Implementation, Cost, and Funding of Bilingual Education in Texas: Lessons for Local and State Policymakers," 7.

121 "Fact Sheet—Ensuring English Learner Students Can Participate Meaningfully and Equally in Educational Programs," 2.

122 Sanchez, "English Language Learners: How Your State Is Doing."

123 McKeon, "Research Talking Points on English Language Learners."

124 McKeon, "Research Talking Points on English Language Learners."

125 Bell and Bogan, "English Language Learners: Problems and Solutions Found in the Research of General Practitioners of Early Childhood," 18-19.

126 Bell and Bogan, "English Language Learners: Problems and Solutions Found in the Research of General Practitioners of Early Childhood," 21.

127 "Fact Sheet—Ensuring English Learner Students Can Participate Meaningfully and Equally in Educational Programs," 3.

128 "Academic Performance and Outcomes for English Language Learners."

129 "Academic Performance and Outcomes for English Language Learners."

130 "Academic Performance and Outcomes for English Language Learners."

131 Angelica Montoya Avila, "Trends in Maryland Public Schools: English Language Learner Enrollment," Maryland Equity Project, The University of Maryland, March 2017, https://education.umd.edu/research/centers/mep/research/k-12-education/trends-maryland-public-schools-english-language-learner.

132 Montoya Avila, "Trends in Maryland Public Schools: English Language Learner Enrollment."

133 Julie Sugarman and Courtney Geary, "Fact Sheet 2018 English Learners in Maryland," Migration Policy Institute, August 2018, 3, https://www.migrationpolicy.org/sites/default/files/publications/EL-factsheet2018-Maryland_Final.pdf.

134 Sugarman and Geary, "Fact Sheet 2018 English Learners in Maryland," 7.

135 Sugarman and Geary, "Fact Sheet 2018 English Learners in Maryland," 7.

136 Sugarman and Geary, "Fact Sheet 2018 English Learners in Maryland," 7.

137 Sugarman and Geary, "Fact Sheet 2018 English Learners in Maryland," 4.

138 Sugarman and Geary, "Fact Sheet 2018 English Learners in Maryland," 8.

139 Sugarman and Geary, "Fact Sheet 2018 English Learners in Maryland," 6.

140 Montoya Avila, "Trends in Maryland Public Schools: English Language Learner Enrollment," 3.

141 Montoya Avila, "Trends in Maryland Public Schools: English Language Learner Enrollment," 3.

142 Mary Boswell McComas, "Baltimore County Schools are Looking to Hire More ESOL Teachers," interview by Tim Tooten, WBAL TV, January 16, 2019, https://www.wbaltv.com/article/baltimore-county-schools-are-looking-to-hire-more-esol-teachers/25924224.

143 Liz Bowie, "Baltimore County Schools Are Rapidly Adding Students. More Than Half Are Immigrants or Speak Another Language," *The Baltimore Sun*, February 7, 2019, https://www.baltimoresun.com/maryland/baltimore-county/bs-md-co-immigrant-enrollment-20190204-story.html.

144 Bowie, "Baltimore County Schools Are Rapidly Adding Students. More Than Half Are Immigrants or Speak Another Language."

145 "2019 Demographics for 'Raven'," Maryland State Department of Education, accessed August 29, 2020, https://reportcard.msde.maryland.gov/graphs/#/demographics/enrollment.

146 Bowie, "Baltimore County Schools Are Rapidly Adding Students. More Than Half Are Immigrants or Speak Another Language."

147 Garen Cuttler, "Educators Report Growing Behavioral Issues among Young Students," *Globe Newswire*, February 14, 2019, https://globenewswire.com/news-release/2019/02/14/1725406/0/en/Educators-Report-Growing-Behavioral-Issues-Among-Young-Students.html.

148 Cuttler, "Educators Report Growing Behavioral Issues among Young Students."

149 Cuttler, "Educators Report Growing Behavioral Issues among Young Students."

150 Cuttler, "Educators Report Growing Behavioral Issues among Young Students."

151 Tony Fabelo et al., "Breaking Schools' Rules: A Statewide Study of How School Discipline Relates to Students' Success and Juvenile Justice Involvement," Council of State Governments Justice Center, July 19, 2011, https://csgjusticecenter.org/wp-content/uploads/2020/01/Breaking_Schools_Rules_Report_Final.pdf.

152 Fabelo et al., "Breaking Schools' Rules: A Statewide Study of How School Discipline Relates to Students' Success and Juvenile Justice Involvement," ix.

153 Fabelo et al., "Breaking Schools' Rules: A Statewide Study of How School Discipline Relates to Students' Success and Juvenile Justice Involvement," 54–55.

154 Fabelo et al., "Breaking Schools' Rules: A Statewide Study of How School Discipline Relates to Students' Success and Juvenile Justice Involvement," x.

155 Fabelo et al., "Breaking Schools' Rules: A Statewide Study of How School Discipline Relates to Students' Success and Juvenile Justice Involvement," 47.

156 Fabelo et al., "Breaking Schools' Rules: A Statewide Study of How School Discipline Relates to Students' Success and Juvenile Justice Involvement," 66.

157 "Secretary Duncan, Attorney General Holder Announce Effort to Respond to School-to-Prison Pipeline by Supporting Good Discipline Practices," Press Release, US Department of Education, July 21, 2011, https://www.ed.gov/news/press-releases/secretary-duncan-attorney-general-holder-announce-effort-respond-school-prison-pipeline-supporting-good-discipline-practices.

158 "Supportive School Discipline Initiative," School Discipline Policy, US Department of Education, Summer 2011, https://www2.ed.gov/policy/gen/guid/school-discipline/appendix-3-overview.pdf.

159 "Supportive School Discipline Initiative."

160 Alicia J. Davis and Heather Pfeifer, "How Has the Baltimore County Public School System Addressed Disproportionate Minority Suspensions," *Schaefer Center for Public Policy University of Baltimore*, 2014, 4, https://www.ubalt.edu/cpa/centers/schaefer-center/minority_-suspensions_report_revised.pdf.

161 Davis and Pfeifer, "How Has the Baltimore County Public School System Addressed Disproportionate Minority Suspensions," 6–7.

162 "School Discipline and Academic Success: Related Parts of Maryland's Education Reform," Maryland State Department of Education, July 2012, http://www.marylandpublicschools.org/stateboard/Documents/StudentDiscipline/SchoolDisciplineandAcademicSuccessReport0712.pdf.

163 "Rethinking School Discipline," Speeches, US Department of Education, January 8, 2014, https://www.ed.gov/news/speeches/rethinking-school-discipline.

164 "Rethinking School Discipline."

165 "Rethinking School Discipline."

166 "Rethinking School Discipline."

167 "Rethinking School Discipline."

168 "Rethinking School Discipline."

169 "Civil Rights Data Collection Data Snapshot: School Discipline," US Department of Education Office for Civil Right, March 2014, https://ocrdata.ed.gov/Downloads/CRDC-School-Discipline-Snapshot.pdf.

170 Davis and Pfeifer, "How Has the Baltimore County Public School System Addressed Disproportionate Minority Suspensions," 7.

171 Davis and Pfeifer, "How Has the Baltimore County Public School System Addressed Disproportionate Minority Suspensions," 22.

172 Davis and Pfeifer, "How Has the Baltimore County Public School System Addressed Disproportionate Minority Suspensions," 22.

173 "Restorative Practices: Fostering Healthy Relationships & Promoting Positive Discipline in Schools," Schott Foundation for Public Education, March 2014, http://schottfoundation.org/resources/restorative-practices-toolkit.

174 "Restorative Practices: Fostering Healthy Relationships & Promoting Positive Discipline in Schools," 2.

175 "Restorative Justice in the Criminal Justice System," County Health Rankings and Roadmaps, March 24, 2017, https://www.countyhealthrankings.org/take-action-to-improve-health/what-works-for-health/strategies/restorative-justice-in-the-criminal-justice-system.

176 Samuel Y. Song and Susan M. Swearer, "The Cart before the Horse: The Challenge and Promise of Restorative Justice Consultation in Schools," *Journal of Educational and Psychological Consultation* 26, no. 4 (November 2016): 313, https://doi.org/10.1080/10474412.2016.1246972.

177 Song and Swearer, "The Cart before the Horse: The Challenge and Promise of Restorative Justice Consultation in Schools," 313.

178 Song and Swearer, "The Cart before the Horse: The Challenge and Promise of Restorative Justice Consultation in Schools," 319-321.

179 "Restorative Practices: Fostering Healthy Relationships & Promoting Positive Discipline in Schools," 3.

180 "Restorative Practices: Fostering Healthy Relationships & Promoting Positive Discipline in Schools," 4.

181 "Restorative Practices: Fostering Healthy Relationships & Promoting Positive Discipline in Schools," 4.

182 Song and Swearer, "The Cart before the Horse: The Challenge and Promise of Restorative Justice Consultation in Schools," 314–15.

183 Song and Swearer, "The Cart before the Horse: The Challenge and Promise of Restorative Justice Consultation in Schools," 318.

184 Song and Swearer, "The Cart before the Horse: The Challenge and Promise of Restorative Justice Consultation in Schools," 318.

185 Catherine H. Augustine et al., "Can Restorative Practices Improve School Climate and Curb Suspensions? An Evaluation of the Impact of Restorative Practices in a Mid-Sized Urban School District," RAND Corporation, 2018, https://www.rand.org/pubs/research_reports/RR2840.html.

186 Jill Barshay, "The Promise of 'Restorative Justice' Starts to Falter Under Rigorous Research," *Hechinger Report*, May 6, 2019, https://hechingerreport.org/the-promise-of-restorative-justice-starts-to-falter-under-rigorous-research.

187 Barshay, "The Promise of 'Restorative Justice' Starts to Falter Under Rigorous Research."

188 Barshay, "The Promise of 'Restorative Justice' Starts to Falter Under Rigorous Research."

189 Augustine et al., "Can Restorative Practices Improve School Climate and Curb Suspensions? An Evaluation of the Impact of Restorative Practices in a Mid-Sized Urban School District," xv.

190 Barshay, "The Promise of 'Restorative Justice' Starts to Falter Under Rigorous Research."

191 Acosta et al., "Evaluation of a Whole-School Change Intervention: Findings from a Two-Year Cluster-Randomized Trial of the Restorative Practices Intervention," *Journal of Youth and Adolescence* 48 (2019): 881, https://doi.org/10.1007/s10964-019-01013-2.

192 Barshay, "The Promise of 'Restorative Justice' Starts to Falter Under Rigorous Research."

193 Song and Swearer, "The Cart before the Horse: The Challenge and Promise of Restorative Justice Consultation in Schools," 321.

194 Cuttler, "Educators Report Growing Behavioral Issues among Young Students."

195 "Rethinking School Discipline."

196 Chris Papst, "Baltimore County Teachers: Culture of Leniency Leading to Violence," *Project Baltimore*, June 11, 2018, https://foxbaltimore.com/news/project-baltimore/baltimore-county-teachers-culture-of-leniency-leading-to-violence.

197 Max Eden, "Studies and Teachers Nationwide Say School Discipline Reform Is Harming Students' Academic Achievement and Safety," *The 74*, June 10, 2019, https://www.the74million.org/article/eden-studies-and-teachers-nationwide-say-school-discipline-reform-is-harming-students-academic-achievement-and-safety.

198 Cuttler, "Educators Report Growing Behavioral Issues among Young Students."

199 Eden, "Studies and Teachers Nationwide Say School Discipline Reform Is Harming Students' Academic Achievement and Safety."

200 Eden, "Studies and Teachers Nationwide Say School Discipline Reform Is Harming Students' Academic Achievement and Safety."

201 Liz Bowie, Talia Richman, and Christine Zhang, "Maryland 2019 Test Scores," *The Baltimore Sun*, August 27, 2019, https://www.baltimoresun.com/education/bs-md-maryland-2019-test-scores-20190827-f7bmkyju3vbo3odiiddzbhh5w4-story.html.

202 Bowie, Richman, Zhang, "Maryland 2019 Test Scores."

203 Bowie, Richman, Zhang, "Maryland 2019 Test Scores."

204 Stephanie Marken, "Say Teachers Unprepared Handle Discipline," News, Gallup, May 1, 2019, https://news.gallup.com/poll/249185/say-teachers-unprepared-handle-discipline.aspx.

205 "Supportive School Discipline Initiative."

206 "Rethinking School Discipline."

207 Michelle M. Englund et al., "Children's Achievement in Early Elementary School: Longitudinal Effects of Parental Involvement, Expectations, and Quality of Assistance," *Journal of Educational Psychology* 96, no. 4 (2004): 723.

208 "Children Who Live in Two-Parent Families, by Race Ethnicity in the United States," KIDS COUNT Data Center a Project of the Annie E. Casey Foundation, accessed October 23, 2019, https://datacenter.kidscount.org/data/tables/8053-children-who-live-in-two-parent-families-by-race-ethnicity.

209 "Children Who Live in Two-Parent Families, by Race Ethnicity in the United States."

210 Marken, "Say Teachers Unprepared Handle Discipline."

211 Carl C. Crandell, Joseph J. Smaldino, and Carol Flexer, *Sound Field Amplification Applications to Speech Perception and Classroom Acoustics*, second edition (Canada: Thomson Delmar Learning, 2005), 98–99.

212 "Child Find Services," Baltimore County Public Schools, accessed February 13, 2020, https://dci.bcps.org/cms/One.aspx?portalId=9047042&pageId=10680701.

213 Claire A.B. Freeland, Psychoeducational Evaluation report to author, January 4, 2005.

214 Freeland, report.

215 Freeland, report.

216 Freeland, report.

217 Stephen W. Seipp, Audiologic Report to author, January 5, 2005.

218 Seipp, report.

219 "What Is Fast ForWord?," Fast ForWord, accessed February 13, 2020, https://www.fastforwordhome.com/what-is-fast-forword.

220 Crandell, Smaldino, and Flexer, *Sound Field Amplification Applications to Speech Perception and Classroom Acoustics*, 6.

221 Amanda S. Niskar, Stephanie M. Kieszak, and Alice Holmes, "Prevalence of Hearing Loss among Children 6 to 19 Years of Age," *Journal of American Medical Association* 279, no. 14 (1998): 1072, https://jamanetwork.com/journals/jama/fullarticle/187415.

222 Niskar, Kieszak, and Holmes, "Prevalence of Hearing Loss among Children 6 to 19 Years of Age," 1073.

223 Crandell, Smaldino, and Flexer, *Sound Field Amplification Applications to Speech Perception and Classroom Acoustics*, 66.

224 Robert Dobie and Charles I. Berlin, "Influence on Otitis Media on Hearing and Development," *The Annals of Otology, Rhinology & Laryngology* 88, no. 5, pt. 2, suppl. 60 (September 1979): 48, https://doi.org/10.1177%2F00034894790880S505.

225 Crandell, Smaldino, and Flexer, *Sound Field Amplification Applications to Speech Perception and Classroom Acoustics*, 66.

226 "Auditory Processing Deficit Demographics," Hearing Health Foundation, accessed February 5, 2020, https://hearinghealthfoundation.org/apd-demographics.

227 C. E. Johnson, "Children's Phoneme Identification in Reverberation and Noise," *Journal of Speech, Language and Hearing Research* 43, no. 1 (February 2000): 156, https://pubs.asha.org/doi/pdf/10.1044/jslhr.4301.144.

228 Crandell, Smaldino, and Flexer, *Sound Field Amplification Applications to Speech Perception and Classroom Acoustics*, 6.

229 J. P. Eberhard, "Children's Brains Are the Key to Well-Designed Classrooms," *AI Architect*, June 2006, http://info.aia.org/aiarchitect/thisweek06/0623/0623eberhard.htm.

230 "Acoustics in Educational Settings: Position Statement," American Speech-Language-Hearing Association, 2005, https://www.asha.org/uploadedFiles/elearning/jss/6173/6173Article3.pdf.

231 American Speech-Language-Hearing Association, "Position Statement and Guidelines for Acoustics in Educational Settings," *ASHA* 37, no. 14 (1995): 15.

232 Crandell, Smaldino, and Flexer, *Sound Field Amplification Applications to Speech Perception and Classroom Acoustics*, 27.

233 American Speech-Language-Hearing Association, "Acoustics in Educational Settings: Position Statement."

234 Fred H. Bess and Larry Humes, *Audiology: The Fundamentals* (Philidelphia: Lippincott Williams & Wilkins, 2003).

235 Carl Crandell, "Effect of Classroom Acoustics on Speech Recognition in Pediatric Populations," in F. Berg (Chair), *Listening in Classrooms* workshop conducted at Utah State University, Logan, (November 1990).

236 Catherine V. Palmer, "Hearing and Listening in a Typical Classroom," *Language, Speech & Hearing Services in Schools* 28, (1997).

237 Heather A. Knecht, Peggy B. Nelson, Gail M. Whitelaw, and Lawrence L. Feth, "Background Noise Levels and Reverberation Times in Unoccupied Classrooms: Predictions and Measurements," *American Journal of Audiology* 11 (2002).

238 Susan Black, "If They Can't HEAR It, They Can't LEARN It," *Education Digest* 69, no. 2 (October 2003).

239 Black, "If They Can't HEAR It, They Can't LEARN It," 58.

240 Crandell, Smaldino, and Flexer, *Sound Field Amplification Applications to Speech Perception and Classroom Acoustics*, 4–5.

241 Alec M. Gallup, "The 18th Annual Gallup Poll of the Public's Attitudes towards the Public Schools," *Phi Delta Kappan* 68, no. 1 (September 1986): 43–59.

242 "Schools Get Wired for Sound," CBS, aired February 21, 2005, https://www.cbsnews.com/news/schools-get-wired-for-sound.

243 "Schools Get Wired for Sound."

244 "Schools Get Wired for Sound."

245 "Guidelines for Addressing Acoustics in Educational Settings," American Speech-Language-Hearing Association, 2005, 6, https://www.asha.org/uploadedFiles/elearning/jss/6173/6173Article4.pdf.

246 Crandell, Smaldino, and Flexer, *Sound Field Amplification Applications to Speech Perception and Classroom Acoustics*, 76.

247 Crandell, Smaldino, and Flexer, *Sound Field Amplification Applications to Speech Perception and Classroom Acoustics*, 79.

248 Crandell, Smaldino, and Flexer, *Sound Field Amplification Applications to Speech Perception and Classroom Acoustics*, 79.

249 Helen Ray, "Beginning and Validation of Sound Field FM in Classrooms," in F. Berg (Chair), *Listening in Classrooms* workshop conducted at Utah State University, Logan, November 1990. Lewis S. Sarff, Helen Ray, and C. Bagwell, "Why Not Amplification in Every Classroom?" *Hearing Aid Journal* 34, no. 10 (1981): 11, 44, 47–48, 52.

250 Beata Darai, "Using Sound Field FM Systems to Improve Literacy Scores," ADVANCE for Speech Language Pathologists and Audiologists 10, no. 27 (July 2000): 5.

251 Carol Flexer, et. al., "Using Sound-field Systems to Teach Phonemic Awareness to Pre-Schoolers," *The Hearning Journal* 55, no. 3 (March 2002): 40–41.

252 Crandell, Smaldino, and Flexer, *Sound Field Amplification Applications to Speech Perception and Classroom Acoustics*, 83.

253 Dr. Nancy S. Grasmick, letter to author, May 3, 2005.

254 Dr. Nancy S. Grasmick, letter to author, May 3, 2005.

255 Dr. Nancy S. Grasmick, letter to author, May 3, 2005.

256 Loni Ingraham, "Soundadvice," *Towson Times*, October 12, 2005, 23.

257 Ingraham, "Soundadvice," 1.

258 Susan Boswell, "Sound Field Systems on the Rise in Schools: Improved Test Scores Cited as Benefit," *The ASHA Leader*, May 23, 2006 32–33, https://teachlogic.com/wp-content/uploads/2018/02/soundfield_systems_on_the_rise.pdf.

259 Liz Kay, "Volume Rises in Debate on Classroom Acoustics," *The Baltimore Sun*, March 13, 2006, 4A.

260 Kay, "Volume Rises in Debate on Classroom Acoustics," 1A.

261 Kay, "Volume Rises in Debate on Classroom Acoustics," 4A.

262 Kay, "Volume Rises in Debate on Classroom Acoustics," 4A.

263 "Issues/Action," Pennsylvania PTA, accessed January 31, 2020, https://www.papta.org/Page/309.

264 "People," University of Cambridge, accessed August 26, 2020, http://www.mrc-cbu.cam.ac.uk/people/matt.davis/cmabridge.

265 Neil Starkman, "Sound Solutions," *T.H.E. Journal* article dated June 1, 2007, accessed April 18, 2008, http://www.thejournal.com/articles/20758.

266 Starkman, "Sound Solutions."

267 "PTA Reports and Financials," National PTA, accessed February 4, 2020, https://www.pta.org/home/About-National-Parent-Teacher-Association/PTA-Reports-Financials.

268 "PTA-Reports-Financials," National PTA, accessed August 22, 2020, http://online.fliphtml5.com/dtoi/qjpy/#p=14.

269 Georgina Gustin, "PTA Says All Parent-Teacher Groups Not Created Equal," *Deseret News*, July 1, 2007, https://www.deseret.com/2007/7/1/20027547/pta-says-all-parent-teacher-groups-not-created-equal.

270 "Approved Convention Resolutions," National PTA, accessed February 3, 2020, https://www.pta.org/home/advocacy/ptas-positions/Individual-PTA-Resolutions/Approved-Convention-Resolutions.

271 Tim Worstall, "Ben Bernanke: The 2008 Financial Crisis Was Worse Than The Great Depression," *Forbes.com*, August 27, 2014, https://www.forbes.com/sites/timworstall/2014/08/27/ben-bernanke-the-2008-financial-crisis-was-worse-than-the-great-depression/#69204d347684.

CPSIA information can be obtained
at www.ICGtesting.com
Printed in the USA
FSHW022048230121
77856FS

9 781544 517957